PRAISE FOR EMOTIONAL SOBRIETY

"In *Emotional Sobriety*, Dr. Tian Dayton explains in helpful detail how our hearts, minds, and spirits are wounded and what is needed to recover. She describes neuroscience in lay terms so clinicians, recovering people, and families are able to understand how and why our inner selves struggle to find balance and peace. Her understanding of the connections between mind, body, heart, and spirit are what have been needed in the recovery field for a long time. We now have scientific evidence as to why 'recovery' works. This is a masterful piece of work.

"When I wrote *Another Chance* and introduced the roles within the addicted family system, we were in the beginning stages of truly understanding the devastating effect that addiction and other serious forms of dysfunction had on the entire family system. What we were looking at was emotional imbalance that led to both personal and familial imbalance. Today, neuroscience is 'proving' that the mind/body treatment approaches we have been taking for the last three decades are indeed evidence based."

—Sharon Wegscheider-Cruse, M.A.,
author of *Another Chance*, Founder of Onsite Workshops

"Bill W., cofounder of Alcoholics Anonymous in 1935, took eighteen years to realize the importance of our emotions for a total and balanced recovery. In the article 'The Next Frontier: Emotional Sobriety' he wrote that once he addressed this aspect of his life, he was 'given a quiet place in bright sunshine.' He had no scientific basis for this. As the founding medical director at the Betty Ford Center, I taught that our emotions are our 'sixth sense' and must be given great credence in our decisions. I had no basis for this. Cellular memory studies and the field of psycho-neuro-immunology are providing the basis for many of our metaphors regarding the heart and our emotions. Dr. Dayton has proven once again that she can interpret, apply, and lovingly teach new knowledge to us in an understandable way. These are attributes of the great teacher she is.

—Joseph R. Cruse, M.D., Addictionologist and Founding Medical Director, Betty Ford Center and Onsite Workshops, Inc.

W9-BMN-344

"*Emotional Sobriety* will be a valued resource for all who want to have a better understanding of the trauma of addiction, relationships, related stress, the effect on families, and the biology that binds these together. It provides insight into the importance of balance in our lives and strategies for healing. A lack of emotional sobriety can lead to self-medication and addiction, a problem that not infrequently destroys the health and well-being of affected youth. Dr. Dayton describes how the skills of emotional regulation are both built and undermined and offers practical suggestions for getting back on track to a healthy lifestyle supported by healthy relationships."

—Hoover Adger, Jr., M.D., M.P.H., M.B.A.,
Professor of Pediatrics, Director, Adolescent Medicine;
Faculty Leader; Florence Sabin College;
Johns Hopkins Medical Institutions

"When primary caregivers consistently allow a child to be over-stimulated or grossly understimulated, as can be the case in homes where relationship trauma is present, the child may not learn how to develop an affective range. Instead of being able to regulate emotions, these individuals may bounce from one emotional extreme to another.

"In *Emotional Sobriety*, Dr. Dayton outlines the neurobiology and neuropsychology of this emotional imbalance and with compassion and beautiful clarity outlines the steps one can chose to achieve resilience and healthy self-soothing. *Emotional Sobriety* is a beautiful creation from a very beautiful person."

—C.C. Nuckles, Ph.D.

"Emotional sobriety, recovery from relationship trauma, and resilience are what we try to teach our clients each and every day in our Codependency Program at Caron, where Dr. Dayton serves as Director of Program Development & Staff Training. As Bill W. said, it is the next 'frontier.' We all need to learn how to live with 'greater maturity and balance.' In this book, Tian Dayton shows us how."

—Doug Tieman, President & CEO, Caron Treatment Centers
in Wernersville, PA, with facilities and offices in Boca Raton, FL;
Philadelphia, PA; New York, NY; and Bermuda.

"The right book at the right time—the addiction recovery community is hungry for understanding and healing the chronic rifts and sores of family trauma. Tian Dayton's latest book, which integrates neurological research, clinical insights, the arts, and practical exercises, affirms and uplifts whole-family life-long recovery."

—Todd Whitmer, Vice President,
Alumni & Development,
Father Martin's Ashley

"Tian Dayton has written a book that not only helps people identify personal patterns of behavior and emotions, and understand their roots, but gives people the tools to begin to deal with life today, in a balanced way. Her straightforward, caring style translates easily to the reader's daily lives including examples that will ring true for many and make sense of memories and behaviors that may have confused people while growing up. Tian helps individuals unlock the mysteries of their past and enables them to understand connections to their current behaviors. It provides the necessary tools to take action toward recovery and wellness."

—Kieth Arnold, Executive Director, Sierra Tucson

"We are an agency committed to creating a safe and just society. TASC (Treatment Alternatives for Safe Communities) facilitates access to treatment for drug-involved offenders and guides them on the path to recovery. We see thousands of women and men whose adverse childhood experiences have later manifested themselves in substance abuse disorders and entry into the justice system. *Emotional Sobriety* gives hope that the generational trauma of addiction can be healed, and it offers tools to help individuals and families renew themselves in mind, body, and spirit. This book is a must-read for those who want to understand more about emotional development and resilience building."

—Peter Palanca, Vice President, TASC, Inc. of Illinois
(Treatment Alternatives for Safe Communities)

"The beauty of Tian Dayton's work is that she has continued to grow and evolve. *Emotional Sobriety* is a necessary step if we're going to get beyond our addiction to drama and our story. Recovery is a pathway to freedom and Tian is a guiding light on that pathway."

—Lee McCormick, Founder and President of the Ranch recovery center in Tennessee and director of Spirit Recovery Inc. program creator for Alta Mira Recovery Centers, author *Spirit Recovery Meditation Journal*

Emotional
Sobriety

Emotional Sobriety

From Relationship Trauma to Resilience and Balance

Tian Dayton, Ph.D.

Health Communications, Inc.
Deerfield Beach, Florida

www.hcibooks.com

Library of Congress Cataloging-in-Publication Data

Dayton, Tian.
    Emotional sobriety : from relationship trauma to resilience and
balance / Tian Dayton.
        p. cm.
    Includes index.
    ISBN-13: 978-0-7573-0609-9 (trade paper)
    ISBN-10: 0-7573-0609-8 (trade paper)
    1. Emotions.   I. Title.
    BF531.D34 2007
    152.4—dc22
                                                        2007037726

Publisher: Health Communications, Inc.
            3201 S.W. 15th Street
            Deerfield Beach, FL 33442-8190

Cover design by Larissa Hise Henoch
Inside book design and formatting by Dawn Von Strolley Grove

To Mom with love and appreciation
Afta lipon

Contents

We either make ourselves miserable,
or we make ourselves strong.
The amount of work is the same.

—*Carlos Castaneda*

$\mathcal{A}$cknowledgments

$\mathcal{T}$here are so many people who have contributed to the pages of this book and who have supported me on this journey. For starters I want to thank all those who are and have been in my client and training groups at the New York Psychodrama Training Institute at Caron, New York. As you have walked the road to emotional sobriety, you have all produced the content of this book.

The clinician groups that I have worked with throughout the United States at conferences, trainings, and treatment centers have constantly challenged me to refine experiential approaches to healing that meet their pressing and very practical needs. They have shown me over and over again that there is a need for a book like this.

I want to acknowledge the tireless work of many organizations and professionals with whom I have consulted and who work daily to put the kind of information that is in this book into the lives of others, including the National Association for Children of Alcoholics (NACOA), Caron, Onsite, Sierra Tucson, Freedom Institute, Hazelden, Betty Ford, The Ranch, Alina Lodge, Father Martin Ashley, and SAMHSA, to name a few. They have continued to bring me to new levels of awareness about how lives can really change when we are intentional and methodical about that change. These institutions make such a valuable contribution to our society.

Next, thank you to my publisher, Health Communications, Inc., which has been so supportive of publishing books designed to help people heal. To Gary Seidler, thank you for being such a friend to psychodrama by producing "The Process" and keeping psychodrama a part of the community of U.S. Journal Conferences, and to Peter Vegso and Gary Seidler for publishing this and so many other books because you believe they could make a contribution. I want to thank my editors at HCI for their kind, intelligent, and helpful support. Michele Matrisciani and Andrea Gold have been wonderful, fun, and inspiring to work with. Their guidance has been sensitive and professional during each step of the process, and I am most grateful.

Also many thanks to Julie Cummings, Larry Arius, Esq., and Matt Klauer, who were generous enough to read material and offer much valued insight and advice. I thank you for your time and your helpful input; your point of view was most welcome.

And to Brandt, Marina, and Alex, for all of the reasons you already know. You are the ones with whom I have taken this journey step-by-step. You are the motivation and the light on my path, and at times, you are the path itself. No one could ask for better, finer, or more pleasant companions.

. . . when Icarus fell
it was spring
a farmer was ploughing
his field . . .
the whole pageantry
of the year was
awake tingling
near the edge of the sea
concerned with itself . . .
sweating in the sun
that melted the wings' wax.
insignificantly . . .
off the coast . . .
there was a splash . . .
quite unnoticed . . .
this was . . .
Icarus drowning

—*William Carlos Williams*

Introduction

*F*or the past twenty-five years, I have been traveling throughout the country speaking and doing workshops for people in recovery from family dysfunction and the psychological and emotional trauma that follows in its wake, as well as for therapists who are working tirelessly with clients who have been affected by addiction, abuse, and relationship trauma. Most of our wounds, when we speak of relationship trauma, are wounds of the heart, mind, and spirit. They are held in the muscle tissue of the body and are imprinted on our neurological systems. We're literally wired to experience *love,* warmth, and a sense of well-being through closeness and to *fear* abandonment. We have evolved this *biology of love and fear* because our very survival depends on our ability to form lasting and durable attachments, to maintain nourishing and sustaining relationships. That's why the emotions associated with these "survival" relationships are so intense. We literally would not survive without them.

Love is both the cruelty and the cure. When our hearts are wounded through disappointment or loss, love restores us to comfort and balance. Fear triggers us into self-protective responses like fight (anger, rage), flight (taking off, dissociating), or freeze (shutting down, withdrawing), while love and caring soothes us and brings us back to a state of equilibrium. We are in a constant state of healing small and large insults to our sense of self, our sense of relationship, and our sense of personal and worldly order.

Perhaps we suffer from not being loved enough or in the right way, or losing the attention and reliability upon which we

depend, or our orderly and familiar world has ruptured somehow. These wounds, unfortunately, don't necessarily disappear
on their own, particularly if they occurred before our own age
of reason; that is, during early childhood. Just as "there's nothing that succeeds like success," as unfair as it seems, pain all
too often begets more pain. In any case, if we can't seem to live
comfortably in adult relationships, we may be re-creating
familiar patterns that carry the echoes of hidden pain from the
past. What we need to do in understanding these emotional
traumas is to be willing to feel our sore spots long enough to
attach words to them, develop emotional literacy, and process
them with our thinking minds. We also need to identify the
problematic patterns that we're repeating—even, at times,
against our better judgment—and work through the pain and
confusion that are driving them so we can learn new and more
successful patterns of relating. We need to mine our own issues
for information about ourselves, life, and relationships, and
become what we might call "adept livers," studiers of life,
people who learn and grow from adversity and turn it into
strength. We have nothing less than a medicine chest inside of
us that is designed to regulate body rhythms, moods, and emotional health—if we can learn to use it.

Countless times I have found myself wanting to be able to
say, just read this, it will guide you through, help you understand what happened to you, what happened to your family,
what happened to your nervous system, and it will lay out a
simple plan to turn these affects around. So many times, when
speaking to therapists who are struggling to help clients understand, in the short time they have with them, the strange, intergenerational pathway of emotional pain or recovery from
addiction and the tenacious and destructive patterns that surround it, I have wanted to put together a simple overview.
That's why I wrote this book, so that anyone who wants to
understand the mind/body impact of what I refer to as "rela-

tionship trauma" in whatever form they have experienced it—emotional, psychological, or physical—will be able to do so. And anyone who wants to turn their life around will have a sense of what actions they will need to take in order to do that. This book will not in and of itself heal you, but it tells you what steps you need to take in order to heal yourself.

I am introducing the idea of relationship trauma in this book because that is primarily what I work with: psychological or emotional trauma that has occurred in the context of a relationship. Whether the trauma is from abuse, neglect, or addiction, our bodies and minds react to being frightened, hurt, or overwhelmed with more intense emotion than we can process and integrate, which interferes with the development of our emotional sobriety.

HOW EXPERIENCE BECOMES BIOLOGY AND BIOLOGY BECOMES EXPERIENCE

Neuroscience is now lending scientific authority to what has intuitively guided treatment approaches for many of us in the addictions field for decades. We have understood and recognized how emotional trauma changes not only the mind and heart of a person, but the body as well; how living with chronic emotional pain affects what we now know to be our limbic system; how when the limbic system is impacted, our ability to regulate our emotions is undermined; and why we can't "just get over it" when we have been impacted by the repeated mobilization of our own fear/stress response.

The ability to self-regulate, to bring ourselves into balance, is key to emotional sobriety. But when our limbic system has become deregulated through chronic stress or crisis, when our emotional switch gets stuck at "on," our emotional rheostat loses some of its capacity to regulate itself. When we have a hard time regulating ourselves, our moods, relationships, life and emotional balance are affected.

Research in neuroscience is at a place where it can now truly be helpful. Through advances in technology we can actually get a picture of how the brain works. Science can now illuminate why approaches like psychodrama, 12-step programs, group therapy, journaling, bodywork, yoga, exercise, and massage work; why one-to-one therapy can help us learn a new style of attachment; why changing the way we live and the nature of our relationships can change the way we think and feel, and vice versa; and why quick fixes don't work but why a new design for living does.

The essence of emotional sobriety is good self-regulation. It means that we have mastered those mind/body skills that allow us to balance our moods, nervous systems, appetites, sexual drive, and sleep, and that we've developed the ability to experience our inner worlds without running from them so that we can come to understand what makes us tick. Emotional sobriety also means that we have learned how to tolerate our intense emotions without acting out in dysfunctional ways, clamping down and foreclosing on our feeling world, or self-medicating. Self-medicating and compulsive behaviors reflect a lack of good self-regulation.

WE CAN FEEL BEFORE WE CAN THINK ABOUT WHAT WE'RE FEELING

Emotions predate reason. Our emotional wiring, that is, our limbic system, is in place from birth but our thinking wiring isn't in place until we're around twelve, and even then, we're only beginning to learn how to use it. Because of this discrepancy in development, young children cannot use their thinking to make sense of and to regulate their emotional responses to life.

We learn the skills of self-regulating, initially, through being in the presence of an adequate "external regulator," say, a mother or a father. We depend on them not only to actually calm us down when we're upset but to show us how to do that through their own behavior. When we get out of balance, they woo us back into a state of balance. They hold us, physically and emotionally, until we restore our own calm, until our nervous system settles. Gradually we absorb the ability to do that for ourselves. We internalize their regulation and make it our own. Through a successful attachment, we gradually build these skills into our own self system and make them portable.

When our skills of self-regulation are well learned during childhood, they feel as if they come naturally, as if we always had them. When they are not well learned, we may reach to sources outside of ourselves to provide the sense of calm and good feeling that we cannot achieve on our own, or to re-create that sense of calm that we remember having as a small child. Some of our society's common self-medicators are drugs, alcohol, food, sex, work, and money. Part of recovery from relationship trauma is to find and adopt healthy sources of self-regulation—healthy "external regulators"—so that we can let go of unhealthy ones.

Good emotional sobriety reflects a well-balanced limbic system. The limbic system is the mind/body system that governs our mood, emotional tone, appetite, and sleep cycles, to name just a few of its wide-ranging functions. Repeated painful experiences—over which we have no sense of control and from which we feel we cannot escape—can, over time, deregulate our limbic systems. When this happens, our capacity to self-regulate may be undermined. We may find ourselves depressed, anxious, or irritable, unable to regulate our moods, emotions, appetites, and behaviors. Here's where we're at risk for wanting to self-medicate in order to restore inner calm. We may reach for a substance or behavior, a way to feel better fast. Issues with excessive self-medication—such as with an overreliance on food, alcohol, or drugs, or compulsive approaches to activities like sex, work, or spending—in order to regulate our moods reflect a lack of ability to comfortably self-regulate.

IT'S NATURAL TO WANT TO HAVE MORE PLEASURE AND LESS PAIN

We're wired by nature to be pleasure seekers and to avoid pain. This is why we self-medicate; we don't want to feel the pain we're in and we do want to feel pleasure. Our neurological wiring coalesces around this principle. Once we accept and understand that this is at the base of our human and even animal nature, we can make intelligent choices about just how to meet these very fundamental needs and drives—how to actively create enough healthy pleasure in our lives so that we feel satisfied and how to manage pain and stress in ways that don't make us want to eradicate it through self-medicating because we can't handle it. Both pain and pleasure are natural. Our limbic system governs these feelings of pleasure and pain. That's why maintaining a balanced limbic system is so central and important; if our limbic system is balanced we tend to feel more pleasure and less pain. Obviously this reduces our urge to self-medicate. Part of emotional sobriety lies in learning how to live with and manage a certain amount of stress, ambivalence, fear, anxiety, and disappointment, and how to temper those emotions and feelings with love, acceptance, productivity, and community.

Emotional Sobriety is for people who are trying to live a balanced life or attempting to understand what relationship trauma is all about.

You need not have lived with addiction. Any relationship pain that you have experienced and are still hanging on to may mean that you find yourself within the pages of this book. I came to it through my father's addiction, my parent's divorce, and the pain that followed in its wake, but these are only some forms of relationship trauma. Neglect, divorce, physical or emotional abuse, living with mental illness, or prolonged separations are some others. The reason that it's worth the time and effort to work through wounds from the past is simply so they do not interfere with our living comfortably in the present; so we don't unconsciously repeat emotional, psychological, and behavioral patterns that get us nowhere, patterns that are driven by unresolved emotional issues having their origins in times gone by; so we can get on with life.

The best way to read this particular book is front to back. It is written to guide the reader through a step-by-step understanding of how emotions and thoughts affect our mind, body, and behavior and how to work through issues into greater emotional maturity and balance. After you have this basic understanding, skipping around is fine. You can zero in on the chapters that draw you or that you feel you want to learn about in more depth. The material is sometimes dense, but I have tried to make it as accessible and as engaging as possible through easy-to-grab examples, case studies, my own history, and up-to-date, inspiring research. I have also developed a website to go with the book that you can access through tiandayton.com. The site provides further information on emotional sobriety, journaling exercises, and actual guided relaxations that you can download onto a CD and use at home.

MY STORY

I am an adult child of an alcoholic (ACOA) who fell in love with another ACOA at age twenty-three. Until 1980 we had no idea that growing up with addiction as children could drive and define the way we lived in relationships as adults. We thought what happened in the past stayed neatly fenced within the past.

But, as it turns out, nothing could be further from the truth. In fact, it is precisely those early experiences that lay down the neural template from which we operate for the rest of our lives.

Falling in love with my husband was easy. It hardly took six seconds. Living happily ever after was one of the most challenging things I've ever done, and one of the best things I have ever done. Intimacy, with its accompanying feelings of vulnerability and dependence, brought up every insecurity, unresolved wound, and frantic hope I had stored in me. All chickens came home to roost.

My husband and I grew up in the 1950s, when feelings were things you felt every three months or so and talked about rarely. Occasionally you had a good cry or a "heart-to-heart," but most of the time we lived on a steady diet of thought and duty. It wasn't that thought and duty weren't great, but this formula works only if nothing goes terribly wrong. If, for example, someone needs to untangle the effects of relationship trauma or addiction, well, there was really no emotional language to cover that sort of thing. People who saw (shhhhh) a psychiatrist were considered to be (shhhhh) . . . well . . . a little off or crazy. People who didn't fit the mold were patronizingly described as "different."

When my husband and I married, we were two idealistic and wounded people looking for a life. Many of the decisions we made about our life together were based on our overpowering need to feel okay again. We arrived in each other's arms, tired people at twenty-three and twenty-four. We had each watched our parents' marriages fall apart, our beloved parents disappear slowly and excruciatingly into alcoholism, and our once-happy families collapse from within. Brandt's family was high-profile in many ways. Disintegrating in public can be somewhat unbearable, especially if your family has previously been the envy of everyone. My family was high-profile in the Greek American community, having made it, attaining the

American dream. My mother had remarried to my stepfather, also from a high-profile Minneapolis family, also dogged by a legacy of familial addiction. Luckily Mom and Walt were recovery-minded and out of denial (mostly). But none of us really knew what to do about the surrounding relationship trauma that we were all experiencing. There wasn't a name for it, much less a language with which to address it. Both of our families are filled to the brim with wonderful, smart, good- hearted, fun, and accomplished people. There is really nothing missing on those levels; in fact, there is abundance everywhere you look. We are incredibly blessed. But even blessed and intelligent families lose it when their emotional problems overwhelm them. For our families it appeared to be alcoholism that led to relationship trauma . . . or was unhealed relationship trauma the prequel that led to using alcohol to self-medicate emotional pain?

My journey as an ACOA started with Vern Johnson's book, *I'll Quit Tomorrow*. My husband and I were in New York City staying at his mother's beautiful Fifth Avenue apartment with our daughter Marina, who was just a few months old. I realized that, though I thought I'd escaped addiction, I had landed squarely in another alcoholic family system. This was nothing I didn't know from the outset. I had simply ignored it. Actually, it had made me comfortable. My husband and I understood each other. Anyway, the night I figured out that it was surrounding us, even though we had supposedly escaped (that is, we didn't drink), I took Marina, got on a bus to Honesdale, Pennsylvania, where we were living at the time, drove home through a snowstorm, and went to bed. The next day I opened a book that had been on our bookshelf unread for a few months, probably given to me by my mother, a longtime proponent of recovery, or Wheelock Whitney, a family friend and founder of the Johnson Institute.

There was no such term as an ACOA in 1977. Nor was

codependency out there in the general public. But every word of that book spoke to me. It described the insidious denial that is part of the disease of addiction; the rewriting of reality to make it not what it is, but something less threatening; the twists and turns in thinking that characterize the alcoholic and the family members surrounding the alcoholic. I read it twice in a day and a half. Anyone who has ever taken care of a baby knows how hard this might be. I read during Marina's nap time, at night when I was exhausted and wanted to be asleep, during stolen moments when Marina was content looking around for five or ten minutes. After reading it, I knew I had a serious problem. I don't drink, so that wasn't it. But everything else that characterized addiction—"stinkin' thinking"; the kind of thinking that is loaded down with circular rationalizations, distortions, and denial of reality that made you feel either you're crazy or everyone else is; repeating the same dysfunctional relationship patterns over and over and over again—I had it all. The only thing I didn't have was the alcohol part. But all of the rest was in me, absorbed a day at a time through living in a world where people were denying the reality that was all around us, denying it with the best of intentions, because that was what people in the 1950s were supposed to do with problems. Put on a happy face. Buck up.

In our family, we didn't have an emotional language in place for handling the losses and the incumbent pain and confusion we were experiencing. So we did what anyone does who visits a country where they can't communicate. We scanned each other's faces for information and a sense of what was going on. We spoke in short phrases. We used sign language. We developed antennae for reading people without words, and when the frustration built and we had no words to give civilized voice to what was going on inside of us, we burst open like hot water pipes or we turned off the water at its source. We disappeared.

It was becoming increasingly obvious to me that both my

husband and I had a problem. Even though the terms "ACOA" and "codependent" did not exist, the term "co-addict" did. I figured I was at least one of those, and probably he was, too. The intimacy and intensity of marriage and parenthood were triggering our unresolved family pain. After reading a list of the Twelve Steps in Vern Johnson's book, I reckoned I would just start with the first step and see what I could do. I was powerless not over alcohol, exactly, but powerless over the effects that living with addiction had had on my heart and mind. My husband was powerless too, as far as I could see.

When the term "ACOA" surfaced in Janet Woititz's book *Adult Children of Alcoholics,* I knew just what she was talking about. At the first ACOA conference, I was on my way. I had a mission: to enter this journey called recovery and see if I could figure out what had happened and how to, as we called it then, break the chain—how to make sure that I passed as little unresolved pain on to my children as possible. But it was hard going; we were learning as we went. Today I have a much clearer picture of what recovery is all about, and I can put science behind what used to feel like trial and error.

Brandt and I more or less followed our noses into the kinds of activities that seemed to help us address our rather pressing personal needs. We spent five years in a spiritual community where we studied Eastern philosophy, yoga, and meditation. This was remarkably healing for our bodies as well as our minds and brought us back into balance in many ways. It also deepened our personal spirituality in ways that have benefited us profoundly. But I was always haunted by my growing awareness that though we all sat assiduously in meditation, did intense yoga practices, and ate as carefully as you could possibly eat, we could not outrun our pasts. Though we were daily working to cleanse and refine our personalities, the unresolved residue of pain that many of us came into a spiritual community looking to heal, whether consciously or not, still blocked our ability to achieve true inner peace. It was only too obvious. So our next discovery was ACOA recovery. We did every program for codependency that we could find. We found therapists, psychodrama groups, and 12-step programs and made them part of our lives. We vigorously addressed the unhealed pain that each of us carried from our pasts. For a while this made our lives feel rocky. We didn't know who we were, who each other was, or who we might become. But we were carried by the excitement and promise of growth and our commitment to our children and to each other. Luckily we made it through to the other side together, though it wasn't easy.

Still another important part of my healing has been to reconnect with the unique gifts and strengths of my childhood. I didn't have far to look. I owe so much to my family of origin—my extended Greek family of grandparents, uncles, aunts, and cousins—and to my Greek church. The way Greek people raise children—the way I was raised—is as neurologically sound as it gets. It's resilience building in situ. We cuddle, kiss, and cajole children into being. The Greek way in which my family operated is to be family centered and to let everyone speak up, as long as they show respect for elders. Kids in Greek families are very highly valued, dragged everywhere their parents go, and treated like little people from the beginning. We talk constantly and about everything; silence is definitely not golden for the average Greek. The bonds of family are strong, which always gave me a wonderful sense of place. It also made having those bonds tested, tugged at, and torn very shocking and painful. But the philosophical and spiritual underpinnings of our culture, along with the sense of relatedness that surrounded me, helped me to cope effectively. There was always a safety net of extended family and church community to turn to. I was never without resources.

Greeks have a fundamental respect and feeling of celebration about life. All Greeks think they are Plato or Aristotle. We have a powerful sense of the meaning behind life—behind everything, for that matter—and we read hidden meaning into just about anything that happens. Greeks tend to be spiritual; our religion is laced into our culture. With this kind of foundation, coping well came naturally. Relationship trauma blocked me from being able to access, feel, and revel in these gifts. Recovery gave them back to me.

Clearly the idea of seeking balance in life is not a new one. The ancient Greeks grappled with these and other basic themes through myth, philosophy, and theater. The Eastern philosophies talk about the middle path. Seeking stability and balance has been a goal of any society that aimed for an ideal of healthy or enlightened living. We are fortunate enough in America to have the education, leisure, and security so we can contemplate the questions that have been preoccupying mankind through the ages. Emotional sobriety is a modern look at an ancient problem.

In the story of Icarus we see this struggle for finding the middle road take shape. The famous labyrinth from Greek legends was built by Daedalus for King Minos. However, once he finished it, Daedalus fell out of favor with the king and was shut up in a tower with his beloved son, Icarus. Trapped and desperate, he hatched a plan for them to escape. The sea was closely watched by the king's soldiers, so Daedalus imagined that if they were ever to return home, they would have to make wings and escape by air. He laced the feathers together with thread and rope and held them in place with wax. When the wings were finished, Daedalus hitched them onto Icarus's and his own back, and they stood poised on a cliff ready to take their flight to freedom. Being a mature adult Daedalus was worried about how his adolescent son would handle the heady gift of flight. Still, he had no choice but to let him fly on his own strength, or forever remain a prisoner. Daedalus tried in a single sentence to teach his son what can take a lifetime to learn.

"'Icarus, my son,' said Daedalus, 'I charge you to keep at a moderate height, for if you fly too low the damp will clog your wings, and if too high the heat will melt them. Keep near me and you will be safe.' While he gave him these instructions and fitted the wings to his shoulders, the face of the father was wet with tears, and his hands trembled. He kissed the boy. . . . Then rising on his wings, he flew off, encouraging Icarus to follow, and looked back from his own flight to see how his son managed his wings. As they flew the ploughman stopped his work to gaze, and the shepherd leaned on his staff and watched them, astonished at the sight, and thinking they were gods who could thus cleave the air" (Bulfinch 2000).

Icarus and his father soared away from their prison tower. But Icarus couldn't contain his excitement even though it could mean his own demise. Heady with the sudden gift of flight he began to soar higher and higher toward the heavens, ignoring the ever-increasing heat from the sun beating down on him. Horrifyingly, the wax on his wings began to melt, and his feathers started to sag. Icarus fluttered madly trying to get them to work again, but they would no longer hold his weight. As they became heavier and heavier he sank uncontrollably toward the sea. His feathers became soggy with constant spatter and mist rising from the sea. And though he tried to cry out, his voice was not strong enough to carry on the wind. His father called his name, "Icarus, Icarus, where are you?" But at last he saw the feathers bobbing up and down on the water, floating on the waves. Icarus drowned.

Icarus's flight symbolizes living in the extremes. The art in life is perhaps to learn both to spread our wings and to chart a sane and healthy course. Without the risk of flight, we go nowhere, but without an understanding of middle ground, we ignore our own shadow. Soaring from grandiose highs to depressive lows doesn't allow us to integrate some of both, to find middle ground where we can be all of who we are, where we can be whole people with many parts, many sides, both dark and light—from where we can remain in flight.

Like Icarus, we need to learn to fly in the middle range. The challenge of emotional sobriety is to learn to seek and respect moderation and to value the experience of being poised in flight from where we can see clearly in all directions, from where we can steer a fruitful path and respond to the elements without being unnecessarily overtaken by them. Icarus's journey illustrates the dangers of bouncing from one extreme to the other and the benefits of living in balance, what Aeschylus must have meant when he said, "everything in moderation." This is emotional sobriety.

What Is Emotional Sobriety?

Curiously the subject of emotions was studied very little until the past couple of decades. Previously we were worshippers of the mind. We lived as if our emotions were incidental little things that leaked out over sentimental songs or bubbled forward during evocative occasions like beach walks, graduations, or weddings. We imagined our thoughts ruled the day and emotions followed neatly in line.

But recent research in neuroscience suggests just the opposite. Emotions, it turns out, impact our thinking more than our thinking impacts our emotions. The emotional part of our brain actually sends more inputs to the thinking part of our brain than the opposite (Damasio 1999). In other words, when our emotions are out of control, so is our thinking, and when we can't bring our feeling and thinking into some sort of balance, our life and our relationships feel out of balance too.

Emotional sobriety encompasses our ability to live with balance and maturity. It means that we have learned how to keep our emotions, thoughts, and actions within a balanced range.

1

Our thinking, feeling, and behavior are reasonably congruent, and we're not ruled or held captive by any one part of us. We don't live in our heads, our emotions don't run us, and we aren't overly driven by unconscious or compulsive behaviors. We operate from a reasonably integrated flow and enjoy a life experience that is more or less balanced and present-oriented. We're not "off the wall," and at those moments when we do fly off the wall, as all of us do and probably need to now and then, we can find our way back again.

FEELINGS CAME FIRST

Emotions came long before thinking in our human evolution. The limbic system developed eons before the prefrontal cortex or the thinking part of our brain.

Emotions are adaptive, telling us all sorts of very important things. They tell us what is important to us and how much attention to give it. Madison Avenue has known about this for a very long time. Advertising often seeks to grab us at the gut level. Our feelings inform and affect many of our decisions.

Darwin felt that our emotional system was highly conserved throughout evolution because emotions are so critical to our survival. The cave woman who loved her babies and felt fear when they were threatened was the one who survived and kept our species alive. She is the DNA strain that led to us.

Developmentally speaking, feelings predate thoughts. The limbic system that governs our emotions develops before the thinking part of our brains or our prefrontal cortex.

FINDING OUR FEELING RHEOSTAT

Emotional sobriety is about finding and maintaining our emotional equilibrium, our feeling rheostat, the one that helps us to adjust the intensity of our emotional responses to life. Emotional sobriety is tied up in our ability to self-regulate and to bring ourselves into and maintain our balance.

But how do we achieve this living in balance? Is it something we can train ourselves to do? If we didn't learn adequate skills of self-regulation in childhood, can we learn them in adulthood? And how do we fall in and out of balance?

Science now can describe in comprehensive detail just what goes on in the body when we experience emotions, or to take it one step further, how our body works with our mind to experience, process, and create our emotional world. Science can also describe in some detail what happens to us, physically and emotionally, when we fall out of balance.

Emotions occur in the body as well as in the mind. When we're scared, for example, we tense up. Who can't relate to this? Maybe we're in fourth grade and the teacher puts us on the spot: we don't know the answer, and we feel a moment of panic. Our palms sweat, our hearts beat fast, we tense up and sit overly alert in our chair. The blood leaves our head and goes straight to our muscles. Our mind seems to turn off, and we can't think of the answer we're sure we know. Our cortex, which is our thinking brain, can freeze up when we get scared. But our emotional or limbic brain keeps operating. If the stressor is momentary, being thrown into this mind/body conundrum is no big deal. We'll take some deep breaths, relax, and come back to normal.

But if the stress is chronic, it can impact our internal regulators. We can get stuck in our prepare-for-stress mode. Our nervous system becomes keyed for overreaction, or underreaction. We move from one to ten and ten to one. We live on the extremes rather than in four, five, or six. Emotional sobriety is about learning to live on middle ground.

IT TAKES TWO TO BECOME ONE

We learn the skills of self or what we call "limbic regulation" from those who surround us when we are young. As children, if we get frightened or hurt, for example, we look to our mothers, fathers, and caregivers to help us to feel better, to sooth us and woo us back into balance.

Children are dependent on their parents for nothing less than their survival. Because of this, what goes on in those primary relationships affects us on a deep level, at that survival level. Who am I in relationship to you? Do I please you? Am I safe in your arms? Do I have a place in the world? Will I be fed, understood, and cared for? These kinds of fundamental issues are part of early life.

Here's an example. We're on the spot again, but this time we're little, we're being blamed for something, and we can't figure out what we did wrong. We did the same thing yesterday, and no one got mad. Our parent is yelling at us. They look out of control, with arms flying around and eyes filled with fury. It's as if another person has taken over their body and that other person is scary. We are two feet tall. They are huge. We are barely able to tie our shoes or open the refrigerator. They can drive a car and buy groceries. We can't run because they would catch us. We can't fight; they'd win. So we freeze, and all sorts of what we call survival responses swing into action. Our bodies start pumping out adrenaline, for example, in case we need to flee for safety or stand and fight. But we can't do either. We're stuck.

What happens when home is scary, when the family we are growing up in becomes a source of ongoing stress? What about when our fight/flight apparatus gets mobilized not because we're staring into the spear of an adversary or a bear is lumbering toward us, but because our mother is depressed and lost in a world where we can't connect with her or our father is on a drinking binge and hurling abuse of all kinds that reverberates around the house and throws everyone's emotional state out of whack? What if our parents are getting divorced and our lives are being turned upside down? How is our development affected, in other words, when the very place that represents home and hearth feels threatening?

The child looks to the parent to learn whether or not he should be scared and how scared he may need to be. Even a barking dog, fireworks, or a thunderstorm can frighten a child out of his wits. The child is completely dependent on his or her parent to act as an external regulator because his or her own internal regulators won't be fully developed until around age twelve or so. This is why the small child is so vulnerable to emotional and psychological damage when the home is chaotic. Not only is what's going on frightening him and throwing him out of balance, but if the parent is the one who is scaring him, the child loses access to his path back to regulation. He's scared, and no one is telling him it's okay, cuddling and reassuring that life will soon return to normal or that he will not, in any case, be abandoned to manage all by himself.

It's time for a caveat, though. I don't want anyone to get the wrong idea. Life can be difficult. It's designed to be challenging. All homes fly out of balance some of the time. All parents lose it occasionally; then they repair the damage and everyone's fine, even better sometimes, having come through a problem and learned a little something or having felt misunderstood and disconnected and found their way back into a comfortable space. Ideally families tolerate moments of imbalance and find their way back to balance.

Evolution favors adaptability and flexibility because life is constantly changing. We're not meant to live by some rigid ideal of perfection. It's not natural. What we want to develop is flexibility, adaptability, and resilience. We want to sink and then swim again, to lose our balance and have some sense of how to get it back, which actually develops a broader and more complex range of skills and abilities in us than trying to live a phony or contrived sort of balance. It even creates new learning and hence new neural wiring.

As I write this it makes me think of how my cat somehow knows that I want to corral her so I can take her into the city with me. Every week, when Monday morning comes, she can just somehow hear me think. She can hear my husband think, too. We are thinking, "catch the cat." And she immediately slinks away, under the bed, into a closet, somewhere hidden, somewhere she feels is safe. If we have been stupid enough to leave the door open, she shoots outside. Then we're really in for a hair-pulling, nerve-bending couple of hours.

Our sweet little kitty's instinct to escape is inborn. She has a brain the size of a couple of walnuts, but still she has all the survival instincts strewn throughout her brain and body that we will read about in this book. Her scanning instinct is so honed that she can truly read our minds. All we have to do is think about catching her and she does one of three things. She puts her back up and hisses, flees the room as fast as her little legs will carry her, or freezes dead in her tracks, like some exotic forest animal that somehow got transported from the branch of a ginkgo tree to our wall-to-wall carpet. These fight/flight/freeze responses are all part of her animal brain/body system, her limbic system.

But what she doesn't have that we humans have is a well-developed prefrontal cortex, a place where she does math or crossword puzzles or plans a vacation to Europe. That's why we can outsmart her, learn all her favorite hiding places, when not to let her have the run of the house. And because she is not complicating her survival responses with a lot of thinking, when she wants to flee, she just flees if at all possible, or tries to fight, or stays absolutely still. She doesn't seem to worry much about consequences, such as "If I leave, will my sister get my room? Can Lilly still come over if I'm in trouble? Or will my parents dock my allowance?" But children do think all these things because their brains are more evolved. They are much bigger than walnuts. They worry and try to come up with solutions to stay out of trouble, even if their solutions are driven by the best thinking of a five-year-old who is scared, immature, and needy. Children who want to preserve their connection with their parents above all else will likely come up with whatever strategy they need to insure that bond. These child solutions can stay with us throughout life if they are never reexamined, especially if they get frozen into place by fear.

Children who repeatedly find themselves in these situations learn some bad lessons, and they miss learning some of the good ones. The bad lessons they learn are that adults can be very frightening and unreliable. The children then learn to hide what they are really feeling. The good things they don't learn are what positive steps they can take to rectify a situation. They don't learn the skills of repair and negotiation: "This is your part, this is mine, this is what you need to do differently, this is what I will do." They feel forced to take all the blame or they want to kick, scream, and throw it all off. So it is not only what the child does learn that creates problems later in life, but also what the child doesn't learn: the skills of self-regulation and relational regulation.

THE DEVELOPMENT OF A SENSE OF SELF

The self is not developed once and for all, as you might construct a statue or a building, but in the ever-shifting sands of the world in which we live. It is a constantly evolving container that's developed in relationship to others (Moreno 1946).

Drawn from the cloth of our parents' personalities and the fabric of our early experiences, the self is a tapestry into which we have daily woven all of our varied perceptions and experiences.

It holds, in its evanescent grip, our thoughts, concerns, dreams, fears, and aspirations. The self and the mind are fluid, adaptable systems. They are penetrable and porous, always interacting with the environment. They are never quite complete.

Trauma can have the effect of shutting down the cortex (van der Kolk 1994). Our thinking mind shuts down when our limbic/feeling mind becomes overwhelmed with fear. Relationship trauma can interfere with our ability to build and consolidate a sense of self.

Stress during childhood, when we have not yet developed to maturity, has a stronger effect than at other times in life. We simply lack the developmental equipment to process stress. We don't have the maturity to understand what's going on around us because the cortex, that part of us that thinks and reasons, is not fully on board until around age twelve. For years when we're young, we have to depend on others to borrow, in a sense, their selves and wear them as our own. We also borrow their emotional regulation and internalize it into our own self system. Who we are surrounded by as children and how we are seen and treated by those people remains with us as a template through which we see ourselves. It becomes who we are.

BRINGING OUR THINKING AND FEELING MINDS INTO BALANCE

At the core of emotional sobriety is the ability to bring our emotions into balance so what we're feeling is within a manageable range. When our emotions are within a balanced range, a few things happen to bring that balance into our lives:

- Our balanced emotions spawn balanced feelings, and thoughts.

- Our balanced emotions, thoughts, and feelings spawn balanced behavior.
- Our relationship conflicts stay within a reasonable, manageable range.
- We're better able to tolerate the intensity of our emotions so we can use our thinking minds to decode our feelings.

When we operate within a manageable emotional and psychological midrange, we cope better with life's inevitable stresses and overloads.

Our cortex helps us to order our emotional and sense impressions and to make meaning out of them. The cortex loves facts. It lives to nail things down—to order, name, codify, and quantify. The limbic brain, on the other hand, feels and senses its way through life. It collects sensory impressions and emotional data that it feeds in great quantities to our thinking brain, to sort through and make sense of. The limbic brain processes our emotions. The cortex draws meaning from them.

Emotions Aren't Necessarily the Same as Feelings

Though we use the terms interchangeably, Antonio Damasio, author of *The Feeling of What Happens,* suggests that emotions and feelings are actually different, that basic emotions such as fear, grief, desire, rage, and love are hardwired into our bodies and happen "atomically" while our feelings are processed by the thinking part of our brain (Damasio 1999). Our thinking, in other words, elevates our more primitive emotions to a conscious level where we can actually experience them. When we can decode and understand the emotions, we can incorporate them into our ever-expanding and evolving sense of self. Once we make our emotions conscious through thinking about them, we can begin to understand our feelings about them.

We're meant to experience our basic emotions in a split second, *before* we have time to feel our feelings surrounding them.

That crucial one-tenth of a second may mean the difference between health or injury. So nature put first things first, safety above understanding. When we're terrified, the thinking part of us temporarily shuts down for some very sound reasons. We aren't supposed to be distracted by random thoughts when danger threatens. We're meant to be flooded with the adrenaline we need to fight or flee, or to freeze, to be absolutely still and remain unnoticed, to become "invisible." This ancient fear response happens before any conscious thought enters our process. It's part of what is referred to as the "automatic response system." Our emotion gets us to fight, flee, or freeze. How we feel and think about being almost hit by that car goes on hold while we do what we need to do to survive. Later, when we can afford the time, we may realize what a close call we had and experience all of the surrounding feelings that went on hold while our survival response took over.

On the other hand, when it comes to the more pleasant drives and emotions, we're meant to make love rather than think about love, which would do nothing to further our species.

THE RELATIONSHIP BETWEEN EMOTION AND ACTION

We cannot simply lie back and feel our emotions . . . the motor aspect of emotion involves both inwardly and outwardly directed discharge processes. Inwardly, the experience of emotions is accompanied by the release of hormones, changes in breathing and heart rate . . . changes in regional blood supply, and so forth. Outwardly, emotion manifests itself in various ways: through changes in facial expression, baring of teeth, crying, blushing, and the like, but also in complex behaviors like shouting, running away and lashing out (Solmes and Turnbull 2002).

This body involvement, this urge to act, is the key to understanding why we act out our emotions when we can't tolerate feeling them. Learning to tolerate experiencing our strong emotions and use our thinking minds to elevate them to a conscious level where we can actually feel the feelings and think the thoughts surrounding them is key to developing emotional sobriety.

UNFELT CHILDHOOD EMOTION

Sometimes emotions from childhood can live within us in a frozen state if they were never elevated to a conscious level. A child who has been raged at over and over again, for example, may simply freeze, though he will not know why he is numbing himself. He may not be able to tell you how he feels. When, as an adult, he is around anger, he may freeze all over again and still not know why.

Therapy, recovery, and support groups are designed to help with this situation. As the frozenness of that inner child, for example, wears off in the safety of a therapeutic environment, he can now process the feelings that never really were processed to begin with, within the safety and support of a healing environment. This process allows him to self-reflect, to witness this situation from the past through his adult eyes of today. In this way he can process the feelings that went on hold, make sense of them through more mature eyes, and bring them into perspective and balance.

Homes that aren't calm—that are in what we might call chronic chaos—undermine our body's ability to maintain a regulated state. When we're scared too much of the time, our limbic system gets stuck at one or the other end of the emotional spectrum; we either feel too much or too little. We lose our ability to fine-tune, to self-regulate, to live comfortably in our own skin. We don't think through what we're feeling and bring it into a state of equilibrium, because we're either running from our emotions, or they are running ahead of us. At the most extreme level, thought and emotion become disengaged. We lose touch with ourselves.

This subject of finding emotional balance has riveted me much of my professional life, both because of my own background and because I have come to understand that curing people is not what therapy is about. Therapy is about helping people to restore the ability to regulate their emotional responses to life.

I came from a happy, successful family that encountered more pain than it could handle. My stable family became unstable, and my husband came from the same setup. On the surface it was alcoholism, but the alcoholism grew out of a family ecosystem that was perpetuating painful emotional experiences by not working problems through toward understanding and resolution. We went through our pain behind closed doors, and eventually those doors became hidden even from ourselves.

It has taken a good part of our adult lives to fully wrap our minds around what went wrong and how to fix it. That's the bad news. The good news is that we figured it out, or let's say we figured enough of it out so we could get out of our own way and lead happy, constructive lives.

WHAT ARE THE SIGNS
OF EMOTIONAL SOBRIETY?

+ Well-developed skills of self-regulation
+ Ability to regulate strong emotions
+ Ability to regulate mood, appetite
+ Ability to maintain a perspective on life circumstances
+ Ability to regulate potentially harmful substances or self-medicating behaviors

+ Ability to live in the present
+ Ability to regulate activity levels
+ Ability to live with both social and intimate connection
+ Resilience, the ability to roll with the punches
+ Ability to regulate personal behavior
+ Ability to own and process unwanted or painful emotions rather than disown them, split them off, or project them outside the self

WHAT ARE SYMPTOMS OF A LACK OF EMOTIONAL SOBRIETY?

+ Underdeveloped skills of self-regulation
+ Inability to regulate strong feelings such as anger, rage, anxiety, sadness
+ Lack of ability to regulate mood, appetite
+ Lack of ability to regulate behavior
+ Not being able to put strong emotions into perspective
+ Lack of ability to regulate substances or self-medicating behaviors
+ Inability to live in the present
+ Lack of ability to regulate activity level (chronically over- or underactive)
+ Inability to live comfortably in intimate relationships
+ Lack of resilience or the ability to roll with the punches
+ Tendency to try to get rid of painful emotions through defensive strategies such as transference (transferring painful feelings from a relationship from the past onto a relationship in the present), projection (projecting unwanted feelings outside the self onto another person or situation, disowning them), and splitting (throwing unwanted feelings out of consciousness)

WHAT ARE THE SOLUTIONS
FOR COMING INTO BALANCE?

✦ Learn the skills of mind, body, and emotional self-regulation
✦ Resolve childhood wounds so they don't undermine self-regulation
✦ Learn effective and healthy ways of self-soothing and incorporate them into daily life
✦ Learn effective ways to manage stress
✦ Maintain a healthy body; get daily exercise, rest, and proper nutrition
✦ Process emotional ups and downs as they happen and learn to consciously shift feeling and thinking states
✦ Learn to use the thinking mind to regulate the feeling, limbic mind
✦ Develop inner resources: quiet, meditation, spiritual pursuits
✦ Develop outer resources: work, hobbies, social life, community

Emotional sobriety is a term originally introduced by Bill Wilson who, along with others, began Alcoholics Anonymous (AA). In his own words he describes what he sees as the next frontier for recovery, not only from addictions of all kinds but also from what lies in its wake. Sobriety is only the first step. "I think that many oldsters who have put our AA 'booze cure' to severe but successful tests still find they often lack emotional sobriety. Perhaps they will be the spearhead for the next major development in AA, the development of much more real maturity and balance."

*T*he Emotional Body

How Our Bodies
Process Emotion

Emotions are the next frontier to be understood
and conquered. To manage our emotions is not to
drug them or suppress them, but to understand
them so that we can intelligently direct our
emotional energies and intentions. . . . It's time for
human beings to grow up emotionally, to mature
into emotionally managed and responsible citizens.
No magic pill will do it.

—*Doc Childre, HeartMath Solutions*

O ur bodies don't really distinguish between physical
danger and emotional stress. The natural fear
response associated with our fight/flight apparatus
causes the body to react to physical or emotional crisis by
pumping out sufficient quantities of stress chemicals, like
adrenaline, to get our hearts pumping, muscles tightening,

15

and breath shortening, in preparation for a fast exit or a fight. But for those for whom the family itself has become the proverbial "saber-toothed tiger," for whom escape is not really the issue, these chemicals boil up inside and can cause physical and emotional problems. In these cases, family members may find themselves in a confusing and painful bind—that is, wanting to flee from or attack those very people who represent home and hearth. For children in these families, escape is more or less impossible and fighting is a losing battle. So they do what they can; they freeze, or they shut down inner responses by numbing or fleeing on the inside. Though this strategy may help them "get through" a painful situation, perhaps for a period of many years, such children suffer within when they lose access to what's really going on inside.

Martin, a little boy who stood in frozen silence because the yelling around him scared him, may well become the grown man who has little access to his emotions. When he wanted to run to his room, he was told to stand there and take it. When he wanted to cry, he was told not to. So he did the only thing he could do: he shut down. As an adult, though he may be a great work mate, when it comes to intimacy, in those relationships that mirror his past, he might tune out the way he did then, leaving his wife feeling alone, like she is talking to a wall. All of us have our emotional walls, but when relationship trauma has sealed them shut, they can feel rather impenetrable.

The ability to escape or take one's self out of harm's way is central to whether or not one develops long-term trauma symptoms or post-traumatic stress disorder (PTSD) (Wylie 2004). It lives inside the body as a state of frozen feelings, needs, or urges—thwarted intentions. And even though we aren't consciously aware of what those intentions are, they may still affect us at a subconscious level. Years later we may live as if the stressor is still present, as if a repeated rupture to our sense of self and our world lurks just around the corner, because our body and mind tell us it does. We become hypervigilant, waiting for the other shoe to drop. When Martin's wife gets frustrated and angry, for example, he might freeze all over again. He'll likely have trouble even accessing what he's feeling, let alone articulating it. Unconsciously he'll become that frozen little boy again. The same taboos against genuine feeling that were in place in his childhood will clamp down around him all over again and he'll become what we might call emotionally illiterate. He won't put words to his feelings, much less talk them over. So the more frustrated his wife becomes, the more he'll withdraw or blow up or freeze. In this vicious circle, a past issue comes to life in the present.

How Our Bodies Hold Our Emotions

Our animal brain is part of what is referred to as our "limbic system" or that part of our brain/body network that governs not only moods but controls appetite and sleep cycles, promotes bonding, stores highly charged emotional memories, modulates motivation, and directly processes the sense of smell and libido (Amen 1998). In short, our limbic system is central to how we feel, sleep, eat, operate in the world, and relate to others. A well-regulated limbic system can allow all mammals to live in balance, eat in balance, sleep in balance, and feel in balance.

Evolution has humans operating in a strange combination of both the animal and human brain. An important part of emotional sobriety is the ability to think about what we are feeling, to translate emotions into words so that we can make sense of them, so that we can bring anxieties and fears into a more balanced place through reasoning them through. But what happens when our emotions aren't available to us, when they're frozen? Or the opposite, when they are so fleeting or

extreme that we can't grab hold of them? Or maybe we act
them out because we don't want to feel them through? The
ability to use our thinking minds to organize the feelings and
sensory impressions fed to us through our limbic system is key
to emotional sobriety. But when the limbic system is out of balance, our ability to self-regulate becomes sorely compromised.
That's why we need to bring our emotional/limbic system into
balance, so that our emotions don't overwhelm our ability to
function.

Addictions and compulsive behaviors reflect, among other
things, problems with self-regulation. We cannot eat, have sex,
work, or exercise in a balanced way. We go overboard and
overdo or underdo. We cycle between extremes.

MRIs and observation of those with PTSD reveal that
repeated experiences with relationship trauma, abuse, rupture, or neglect can have a long-term effect on the limbic system. Studies on children who were raised with maternal
deprivation showed them as having abnormal cortical profiles
and oversensitized stress responses. The heartbreaking thing is
that when we're deregulated in our limbic system, we are at
risk for re-creating in our relationships as adults the kind of
relationship trauma that caused us pain in childhood. That is,
though our parents may have set the groundwork for this condition, we finish the job ourselves. We finish the job by creating painful dynamics in our intimate relationships that make
them disturbing to live in, by organizing our lives in ways that
don't feel good, or by medicating our feelings rather than feeling them. Our inability to manage our emotions in healthy
ways manifests in our lives and in our relationships well into
adulthood.

Also, since feelings generate a sense of togetherness that
allow us to pick up on the subtle signals that are part of what
psychologists call the affective or the feeling environment
between people, our lack of ability to feel in a comfortable,

flowing, and natural way can make being with other people in genuine intimate connection somewhat strained.

But just as painful emotions become physical, so do positive ones. We can learn to use the body's natural healing chemicals to manage our moods in healthy ways, to heal ourselves rather than continue to hurt ourselves, and to live in balance.

THE PATH OUT

Wherever you are starting from, you can work your way toward balance. Maybe you just need some reminders and a bit of extra knowledge so that you can tweak your activities and attitudes a bit and head them in a slightly more balanced direction, because basically your life is pretty good.

Or maybe you are raw, living on the edges, and need to make some major changes in order to get your life back into balance.

Talk therapy may have innocently created a trap, giving the erroneous impression that if we gain insight into what's bothering us, everything else will fall into place. However, trauma sits in the part of the brain that sometimes defies logic. Until we bring the emotions that are locked within the limbic brain/body system into awareness and elevate them to the thinking level, they may drive our behavior in unconscious ways. When I work with clients using psychodrama, the body as well as the mind can tell the story. As the body moves, the mind follows. Our emotions—our urges to move, to say something, to do something—emerge naturally into the present moment where we can witness and make sense of them. We come out of hiding, get to know ourselves, and find words to describe what's going on inside of us. We develop emotional literacy.

We need this emotional language through which we can find our way back to balance, language that allows us to *talk out* rather than *act out* what's going on inside of us.

We can only hope to become emotionally sober and balanced if we can learn to manage our feelings as they arise, if we can learn to create a sort of safe container within ourselves that is large enough to feel through what's going on inside of us without first blowing up, acting out, or shutting down. Acting out is an attempt not to feel, to rid ourselves of our unwanted feelings perhaps through actions such as bullying, withdrawing, stonewalling, hitting, raging, spending, or self-medication. When we act out, we gain no new perspectives; rather, we project our feelings, making them about something or someone else. We drown them in alcohol, drugs, or addictive/compulsive behaviors. Talking out allows the attachment of words to feelings so we can process our emotions consciously. As we feel through and articulate what's going on inside of us, we deconstruct and understand it. We bring it slowly into balance.

HOW EMOTION TRAVELS THROUGH THE BODY

"The body is the unconscious mind," says Georgetown University research professor Candice Pert in *Molecules of Emotion* (1999). "Repressed traumas caused by overwhelming emotion can be stored in a body part, thereby affecting our ability to feel that part or even move it. . . . There are infinite pathways for the conscious mind to access—and modify—the unconscious mind and the body."

Until recently, emotions have been considered to be location-specific, associated with emotional centers in the brain such as the amygdala, hippocampus, and hypothalamus. While these are, in fact, emotional centers, other types of emotional centers are strewn throughout our bodies. Emotions travel through our bodies and bind to small receptors on the outside of cells, much like tiny satellite dishes. There are many locations throughout the entire body where high concentrations of almost every neuropeptide receptor exist. Our "gut," for example, is one of those centers. It is filled with emotional nerves that we might say respond to what we're feeling. That's why our gut can provide us with valuable information as to how we feel about a person or a situation. It is actually a part of our body that processes our emotions.

Emotional information travels on neuropeptides and is able to bind to its receptor cells through the binding substance of ligands. Information is sorted through the differentiation of receptors. That is, certain information binds to certain receptors (Pert 1999). So our emotions are constantly being experienced in and processed by our bodies. Nuclei serve as the source of most brain-to-body and body-to-brain hookups. The brain and body are exquisitely intertwined systems that are constantly interacting with the environment. All five senses are connected to this system and feed information that determines our unique response to anything from snuggling into our parents' arms to being slapped.

All of this explains why our emotional life is physical. It imprints itself on our bodies and on our neural systems. Problems in our deep limbic system can manifest as moodiness, irritability, clinical depression, increased negative thinking, negative perceptions of events, decreased motivation, floods of negative emotion, appetite and sleep problems, decreased or increased sexual responsiveness, or social isolation (Amen 1998). Our neural system carries with it our emotional sense memories from childhood. When the memories are positive, they are likely to propel us toward optimism and self-acceptance; when they're painful, they can color our sense of self with darker hues. Familial trauma can impact this brain/body system in ways that shape our developing nervous system.

THE HEALING POWER OF TOUCH

Touch is part of our regulatory system. Touch triggers the release of oxytocin, one of the chemicals of contentment, bonding, and self-regulation. Being touched helps us to feel held both physically and emotionally. So important, for example, is touch to our sense of well-being that not being touched can lead to sickness or even death. When pediatrician Harry Bakwin took over the pediatric ward of Bellevue in 1931, fear of spreading infection was at a height. There were signs all over instructing nurses to wash their hands and not to touch babies and "spread infection." Bakwin recognized the horror of this, took away the signs that were instructing personnel not to touch, and put up signs instructing nurses to pick up the babies. The infection rates went down. Apparently, touch and caring are more useful to our immune systems than "healing" policies that isolate us from human closeness. Even though being handled by nurses may have elevated exposure to germs, the babies' immune systems were apparently strengthened enough by the added caring touch to ward off possible infection.

Oxytocin may also influence our ability to bond with others. The hormone oxytocin has been shown, in a recent study, to be associated with the ability to maintain healthy interpersonal relationships and healthy psychological boundaries with other people. "This is one of the first looks into the biological basis for human attachment and bonding," says Rebecca Turner, Ph.D., University of California, San Francisco adjunct assistant professor of psychiatry and lead author of the study. "Our study indicates that oxytocin may be mediating emotional experiences in close relationships." (http://home.att.net/~coachthee/Archives/attractiveness.html) Oxytocin is turned on by the kind of touching and closeness between mother and child. It strengthens connections between neurons in the brain that literally make someone more intelligent, fit, and eventually a more successful adult. We need these "brain fertilizers" for the brain and body to connect up properly.

Oxytocin is one of our important chemicals of connection and self-regulation. In the next chapter we discuss how our systems are designed to tune in to each other and to pick up on and even model each other's emotions. Chemicals of connection, mirror neurons, and limbic resonance are all aspects of how we self-regulate through our physiology.

The Biology of Love

Attachment and Self-Regulation

The mother's lap is the child's first classroom.

—Hindu proverb

*A*s child psychologists study the best approaches in child rearing, they are looking less at what parents are doing *to* their children and more at how parents are being *with* their children. Picture a mother and her baby casually interacting so naturally that it seems their actions have been choreographed for closeness, engaging and absorbing both of them equally. Held within a mutual gaze, their movements appear to be synchronized by some invisible force. They smile more or less together; when a door slams and the baby starts, the mother starts a bit too, but quickly she reaches out to the baby's psyche with her eyes, facial expression, and cooing sounds to soothe, contain, and show by her own face and form that there is nothing to worry about. The baby moves her little face and body into the rhythm and expression of her mother.

The baby is reassured and brought back into balance by a phenomenon called limbic resonance: two systems crossing the division created by the individual bodies that seem to divide them, but don't really.

"Our nervous systems are constructed to be captured by the nervous systems of others, so that we can experience others as if from within their skin," says Daniel Stern, an American scientist working at the University of Geneva, who has long been exploring these subtle mother-child interactions (Goleman 2006). Nature has built into us our own tracking systems that are essentially our biological basis for empathy, emotional contagion, and modeling. They allow us to connect in nonverbal as well as verbal ways.

After all, what is a more classic image of one person's contentment being shared and enhanced by another's than the sight of a baby in a mother's arms or lying on a father's shoulder? Dr. T. Barry Brazelton, author and notable childhood development expert, reflects:

> There is a singularly comforting body chemistry to being hugged by a parent who loves you. If a mother monkey scoops a baby close against her chest, heart rates drop. When scientists measure stress hormones, they can chart them dropping away. An identical reaction can be seen in human children. One of the scientists who has done the first and best work on the chemistry of touch is Saul Schanberg of the department of pharmacology at Duke University. Schanberg suggested that our intense response to touch is a primitive survival mechanism. "Because mammals depend on maternal care for survival in their early weeks or months," says Schanberg, "the prolonged absence of a mother's touch triggers a slowing of the infant's metabolism." That allows the infant to survive a longer separation from the mother. Once she

returns, her touch reverses the process. Premature babies, who are stroked for fifteen minutes, three times a day, grow 50 percent faster than standard, isolated pre-emies. The baby who huddles into his crib, or the little monkey who curls up at the edge of her cage, appears hopeless. But we should be aware that some of this hud-dling is actually conservation. As they hunker down, the babies are waiting for their mothers to come home and for everything to be all right. The bottom line is that touch is good for your health, your immune system, your sleep, your anxiety level, your life (Brazelton 2004).

What we call love is not only a feeling; it is part of our biol-ogy, guiding us toward our own survival by making us want to connect and stay connected with those whom we depend upon for sustenance and care.

MIRROR NEURONS

We have the apparatus necessary to tune in to another per-son, literally built into our own biology through the mind/body phenomenon of mirror neurons. Mirror neurons track the emotional flow, movement, and even intentions of the person we are with, and replicate this sensed state by stirring in our brain the same areas active in the other person. Mirror neurons offer a neural mechanism that explains emotional contagion, the tendency of one person to catch the feelings of another, par-ticularly if strongly expressed. This brain-to-brain link may also account for feelings of rapport, which research finds depend in part on extremely rapid synchronization of people's posture, vocal pacing, and movements as they interact. In short, these brain cells seem to allow the interpersonal orchestration of shifts in physiology (Goleman 2006).

In his book on social intelligence, Daniel Goleman describes that mirror neurons were first noticed by accident in research labs where monkeys were being wired with tiny electrodes to study the sensory motor area of the brain. One hot and tired young researcher wandered into the lab after her break carrying an ice cream cone. As the monkey observed the young woman lifting the cone to her mouth, a set of tracking neurons went off in his brain, and he mimicked the behavior. Simply witnessing the act allowed the monkey to incorporate the gesture into his own behavior (Goleman 2006). This lends scientific evidence to the old expression, "Monkey see, monkey do." In fact, it's true not only of monkeys, but of all of us who have the capacity to watch, learn, and model the actions of another and perhaps even sense some of the feelings that motivate them. These invisible message centers were dubbed "mirror neurons" by scientists. They are neurons that allow us to mimic an action either witnessed by us or, even more phenomenally, an action imagined by us but never really taken, such as when athletes improve their own performance by watching films of successful feats or imagining them through guided imagery.

THE RELATIONSHIP BETWEEN ATTACHMENT AND AUTONOMY

The author C. S. Lewis is famous for saying that "it takes two to *see* one." Neurologically speaking, it takes two to *be* one. Children learn the skills of self-regulation through a successful attachment bond. It is also through this powerful, intimate bond that they gain a sense of relationship, self, and eventually autonomy, in that order. A child builds his ever-evolving sense of self within the protected and protracted relational space between himself and his primary caretakers. He strengthens his sense of self a little more each day and wears it increasingly as his own. His autonomy is the product, we might say, of successful dependency.

Children actually absorb the skills of self or limbic regulation from their mothers and fathers and internalize them as their own. A frightened child calms down in the caring arms of her mother. An overly excited child evens out when the strong arms of his father surround him. Children learn to regulate their emotions through being in relationship with a parent who slowly and over time demonstrates what regulation feels like. They absorb the skills through their skin, so to speak, through each one of their senses. Not only do they soak them up, they pick them up through limbic resonance.

Our nervous systems are not self-contained, but interdependent; they connect with those of the people close to us in a silent, holding rhythm that helps regulate our physiology. *Limbic regulation* is a mutually synchronizing hormonal exchange between mother and child that serves to regulate vital rhythms through *limbic resonance*. The nervous systems of all humans—and for that matter, all mammals—are interconnected. "Limbic regulation mandates interdependence for social mammals of all ages, but young mammals are in special need of its guidance: their neural systems are not only immature but also growing and changing," says Thomas Lewis, author of *A General Theory of Love*. "One of the physiologic processes that limbic regulation directs, in other words, is the development of the brain itself—meaning that attachment determines the ultimate nature of a child's mind" (Lewis et al. 2000).

Humans and mammals have the ability to regulate one another through limbic resonance and mirror neurons, which is why we find being in the presence of people and pets or animals calming. It is also why groups can have a regulating effect on us, whether the group is a family, a gang, a faith community, or a 12-step program.

EXPERIENCE BECOMES BIOLOGY:
HOW OUR LIMBIC SYSTEM GETS WIRED

Research in neuroscience has largely put the nature vs. nurture discussion to rest. It is nature *and* nurture—not nature *or* nurture—that wire our neural networks. Alan Schore, author of *Affect Regulation and the Origin of the Self,* puts forward the widely accepted theory that we arrive as babies, only partly hardwired by nature; nurture does the rest. Our early experiences inscribe themselves onto our neural networks. Each tiny interaction between parent/caretaker and child actually lays down the neural wiring that becomes part of our brain/body network, part of our limbic system (Schore 2000). A fully developed human brain would be far too large to make it through the birth canal. Some of our brain growth needs to occur where there is more space. It needs to occur *as we grow.* Because children are only partially hardwired at birth, the rest of the wiring needs to take place after we are born. All of this learning is laid down in neural wiring throughout the brain/body system, becoming part of both our conscious and our nonconscious being.

Early experiences, both positive and negative, have a dramatic effect on the formation of synapses. Children's brains are growing at a spectacular rate in early childhood. Within each of our brains are millions of neurons (nerve cells) that are connected to each other by synapses. These trillions of synapses, and the pathways they form, make up the wiring of the brain. The number and organization of these connections influence everything, from our ability to recognize letters to our ability to bond. Emotions are double-coded with experience. Whenever we have an experience of any kind, whether a trip to the circus or being chastised at the dinner table, our emotional response to the experience becomes coded right alongside the memory of the experience. Our experiences combine together forming a brain/body template, from which we operate throughout our lives. This may be one of the most important understandings we can have. Our early experiences literally weave themselves into our neural systems, becoming a neural basis for self-regulation and emotional sobriety.

But childhood trauma can cause serious disruption in the way in which children learn to self-regulate. "Because children's brains are still developing, trauma has a much more pervasive and long-range influence on their self-concept, on their sense of the world, and on their ability to regulate themselves" (van der Kolk 2007). Childhood trauma can also create problems in the way children learn to relate. Relationships lay the primary foundation for a child's cognitive, emotional, and social development. Consequently, even if the trauma in the child's life stops, their further development has to compensate for missing parts of his or her emotional foundation. This building on unsteady ground can lead to problems down the road.

The family is our first and arguably most significant classroom on emotional development and regulation, and the daycare and school systems run a close second. The obvious emphasis on intellectual learning that is a natural part of the school system, says Stanley Greenspan, M.D., author of *Building Healthy Minds*, blurs the extent to which our ability to experience, process, and regulate our emotions informs and drives our ability to attend and learn and have healthy relationships within our school environment. Our emotional development is not only our foundation for important relational abilities such as intimacy, trust, and attunement, it is also the foundation of our intelligence and a wide variety of cognitive skills. At each stage of our development, our emotions lead the way, and learning facts and skills follow (Greenspan 1999).

Piglet sidled up to Pooh from behind.
"Pooh!" he whispered.
"Yes, Piglet?"
"Nothing," said Piglet, taking Pooh's paw. "I just
wanted to be sure of you."

—*A. A. Milne*

*A*ttaching Words
to Feeling States

Developing Emotional Literacy

In the last decade or so, science
has discovered a tremendous amount
about the role emotions play in our lives.
Researchers have found that even more than IQ,
your emotional awareness and abilities
to handle feelings will determine your success
and happiness in all walks of life,
including family relationships.

—John Gottman, Ph.D.
Raising an Emotionally Intelligent Child

HOW EMOTIONAL LANGUAGE
EMERGES FROM EARLY ATTACHMENT

*W*ords are not our first form of communication (Greenspan 1999). Long before language formally enters the picture, we humans learn a rich tapestry of gestures, actions, signs, and facial expressions to communicate our needs and desires, and each tiny physical gesture is double-coded with emotion (Greenspan 1999) and stored by the brain and body with emotional purpose and meaning attached to it. A child reaches out with both hands to turn his mother's face toward him so that he can enjoy her attentive, loving gaze or arches his back and pushes on her chest to show displeasure. First comes the gesture or the nonverbal communication, then the word is added to it. Language, our ability to name an idea, a feeling, or an object, is built on this initial stage of body/mind communication.

Our emotional unconscious, this web of gesture, meaning, and word, is formed through our interactions in our environment with our family and caregivers. It is how we learn to communicate when we're young, to read signals from others, and to communicate our needs and wishes to them. It lays a foundation for later emotional growth and language development. Schore (1999), in his research on affect regulation, explains that this "automatic emotion" operates in infancy and even into adulthood at nonconscious levels where it shapes communication. The subtle exchange of emotionally laden signals between people, for example, happens so quickly that we hardly know it's occurring. All these unconscious processes help us to regulate ourselves within our environment and our relationships, to operate on automatic. Our first language is a body language rich with gesture and meaning. From the very beginning, our emotions, behaviors, and gestures are coded together.

Evolution has made the processing of emotions and their

communication to others incredibly rapid so that we can pick up on each other's moods and behavioral signals instantaneously. Because the unconscious processing of emotional information is so rapid, the very subtle emotional dynamics that are involved in the "transmission of nonconscious affect" (Murphy et al. 1995) and the spontaneous communication of "automatic emotion" cannot necessarily be consciously perceived (Schore, in press). We communicate as much through our manner, tone, and body as through our words. Volumes are spoken even when few words are exchanged, and this metacommunication can be so fast that we're hardly aware of what we're picking up on, or, for that matter, sending out. But we're still probably registering it at some level.

Parents help children, as they grow, to translate their more automatic emotions into words so that feelings can be more easily expressed and discussed, which is how we develop emotional literacy. People who have lacked this nonverbal form of communication (which contains so much emotional meaning and purpose) or have grown up in environments in which feelings were not comfortably felt (let alone translated into words and talked about) often have a hard time identifying some of their emotions and their intentions when they try to self-reflect. They haven't developed an emotional language in which to think about, much less talk about, what's going on inside of them or in their relationships. Thus, they may lack awareness about why they do what they do or why they feel what they feel. They have not made the unconscious conscious, so to speak; they haven't elevated their unconscious emotions to a conscious level where they have thought and talked about them.

Marla, a member of my group, can have trouble putting her emotions into words. She often finds her own feelings confusing and bewildering, even somehow unavailable to her. She has no clear idea why she feels depressed or wants to remain

in emotional hiding, even though it runs counter to her conscious wish to connect with people. The other night she came
to group very triggered. She had spent some time with her
family over the Thanksgiving holiday. She described a scene in
the living room of her parents' home that had triggered her.
Her little niece sat quietly in a chair drawing pictures, just as
Marla had done much of her childhood. Out of the blue,
Marla's mother screamed at this child to move her things.
There was no warm-up; the child wasn't making any noise or
demanding anything. Marla's mother had simply decided she
didn't want her drawing in the chair anymore. She didn't ask,
she yelled. She didn't accompany her request with a reassuring
tone or even a soft touch; rather, she barked an order from
across the room in an agitated, accusing voice. She didn't
quietly help her granddaughter to move her things to a table
and settle in to continue her drawing; she charged right into
her personal space. While her words were not especially mean,
her tone was lethal, and the expression on her face was filled
with contempt. But she was completely unaware of it. Her
granddaughter was so shocked that she burst into tears. Unlike
Marla, she was not used to being spoken to this way. She had
not learned what Marla learned as a child: that feeling would
get her nowhere, and showing it would only incite her mother
to more aggression. Marla watched the scene, and her gut
began to twist. She had learned from being in group to pay
attention, to wonder if her body was trying to tell her something that her mind was warding off. Finally she took a risk.
She screwed up her courage and spoke up.

"You didn't have to talk to her like that," said Marla. Her
mother simply looked at her dumbfounded.

"Like what?" said her mother. "I just asked her to move her
things."

"You yelled at her," said Marla, trying to get some sense of
reality. "She was just sitting there, and you yelled at her."

"No, I didn't. You're just imagining that. I just asked her to
move, that's all," said her mother without skipping a beat.

"But the way you said it," said Marla, who was beginning to
feel her own perceptions slip.

"I was talking in a perfectly normal voice," said her mother.
"The child was being overly sensitive."

Suddenly Marla saw her own childhood flash across her
mind. Her mother had frightened her in her tone and manner over and over and over again just this way. This approach
was her mother's constant form of communication, but when
Marla tried to say anything or shed a tear, her mother simply
dismissed her in the same manner that she had dismissed her
granddaughter or called her names like "sensitive," "dramatic," or "troublemaking." Growing up in this environment
had made Marla doubt her own perceptions and blame herself
for her "sensitive" or "problematic" feelings, causing her to
shut down her genuine emotional responses. Suddenly Marla
understood why she couldn't cry as an adult and why she was
frozen inside, afraid to express herself through words. She
only felt safe letting her feelings out through her artwork.
Countless times in group Marla said, "Words don't work too
well for me." No wonder. She'd say things like, "I have no story.
Nothing bad ever really happened to me. I don't know why I'm
like this." Years of this interaction had shaped Marla's ability to
feel, name, process, and express emotion. Her mother made
her see herself as foolish for having her own feelings, and her
father, who was himself remote and noncommunicative, had
backed her mother up. Marla felt that she herself and not the
situation had caused her to lose touch with her own voice and
her ability to use it descriptively. Marla had no outward abuse
to point to; she had a home and was cared for as a child. But
year after year of being dismissed by her mother, modeling her
father, having her reality go so unvalidated and her contribu-
tions and gifts go so unseen, had taught her to curl up within

herself, like a turtle, to draw her head into her shell for safety. It affected her emotional development.

Our ability to feel, name, and communicate our feelings is central to developing emotional literacy. When we are able to talk about what we're experiencing on a feeling level, we can use our thinking minds to make sense of our feeling minds. We can use our reasoning to play a role in regulating and lending perspective on our emotional reactions.

Marla, through being in our psychodrama group, had developed experience tolerating being in the presence of strong emotions without shutting down and translating her feelings into words. Her growing awareness of her own emotional responses allowed her to recognize what in her childhood had had such an undermining effect on her emotional development.

As a child, Marla remembers spending lots of time alone in her playpen and little time interacting with her parents. She hadn't had that kind of constant, tactile, and emotional interaction on a regular enough basis to learn what her feelings felt like inside of her, to feel, name, process, and communicate her emotions. Quite the opposite, she had learned to withdraw into herself, to hide what she was feeling first from her mother and eventually from herself. Marla learned that it was less painful for her when she shut down. She felt less lonely, needy, and confused if she dissociated and went off into her own detached world. Therefore, her feelings while growing up were largely unavailable to her. They weren't elevated to a conscious level where they became felt, named, and communicated. By the time she was even aware that problems from her past were interfering with her ability to be close to people in a genuine manner, she was well into adulthood. When she went home for Thanksgiving, she had learned enough to begin to ask herself the kinds of questions that might help her better understand herself. She had learned to tune in to what her body was trying to tell her by asking questions like, "What does my body want to do right now? Where am I holding tension, and what does that tell me about how I'm feeling? Why am I freezing up like this?" These questions helped her to connect the dots, so to speak, to gain insight into her own emotional makeup.

The kind of emotional information that drives and shapes how we respond to our world may be out of sight, but it is definitely not out of mind. It is often still part of our mind/body system, and it affects how we interact with the circumstances of our lives. Some things seem to just "be there" in our bank of learning to be recalled whenever the situation beckons. It's like riding a bike. We remember just how to do it once we grab the handlebars and swing ourselves over the seat, but that memory—the physical skills that go along with it, and our feeling about it—may be largely unconscious much of the time. That is, we don't spend large parts of our day thinking about riding a bike. Our body/mind just remembers how to do it when it needs to. The same phenomenon occurs in adulthood when we enter intimate relationships or become parents. We tend to behave in the ways we learned in our family. If we learned that it was safe to feel what we were feeling and share it, we carry that skill into our adult relationships. If we learned to hide our genuine emotional responses from those close to us, then that is what we bring with us. But emotions don't stay hidden long. They will find a way out. If we don't invite them through the front door and offer them space and time, they will likely come in through the back.

If the family has caused emotional constriction through the creation of an environment that either does not support healthy emotional growth or contains the kinds of problems that regularly frighten children and undermine or interfere with their sound emotional development and learning the skills of emotional literacy, repair needs to occur after the fact.

This is what recovering from relationship trauma is all about. Therapists often focus on untangling complicated relationships with parents, but children who grow up in homes where parents are overly preoccupied with their own problems may be inordinately influenced by siblings or other parts of their social networks as well. It is useful in therapy to explore all of these networks of relationships in order to better understand the full range of influences on a child's development.

THE IMPORTANCE OF INTERACTION IN REPAIR

We needn't fear problems or misunderstandings if we learn how to quickly and conscientiously repair them. Repairing spills, ruptures, or disconnects can even be growth-producing for children. If a child, for example, spills his milk because he isn't looking or is being careless, the lesson needn't be punitive to be instructive.

One way of handling a situation like spilled milk is to make restorations together: take out some paper towel, and let the child help to rectify the situation so that he learns that mistakes can be repaired. In addition, get on the child's level and talk it over; figure out what can be done to prevent it next time, understand, chat, encounter, and solve it together with understanding and respect. Accidents happen; we clean them up and move on. The child will likely already feel he did something wrong from the alarm on his mother's face, the mess on the floor, and his own feeling of ineptness. Yelling only teaches fear, and that fear could go underground and create anxiety. Let the child know that mistakes can be corrected and can even be a source of learning. Mistakes aren't such a big deal that children lose love and closeness because of them.

Repair allows our shame response to become part of personal growth (Schore 1999). We learn from our mistakes. Something went wrong and we learn ways of setting it right, of

mending what was broken or restoring a lost sense of connection. This process that occurs in the context of a relationship
creates new neural wiring just as any learning does. Only this
time we're not learning math or vocabulary, we're learning
how to live comfortably with closeness, we're learning how to
be real, and we're learning the skills of intimacy. We are teaching a child how to restore a momentary relationship rupture
so that it doesn't grow or fester. When opportunities for repair
are not forthcoming, the child does not have a way of restoring her own feelings of self-worth or repairing an emotional
disconnect or hurt. She may carry instead a sense of unresolved shame for a circumstance she could not rectify. In this
case, the learning is not positive or particularly helpful.

Repair allows for a feeling of calm, resolution, and regulation
to be restored. It allows for flexibility to become part of our
personal style of relating. We can relax, experiment, and be
ourselves in relationships if we feel that we can make mistakes.
We can build confidence if we have some sense of how to get
into and out of trouble. We all yell at our kids, for example. If
we feel we've gone over the top, that's a moment of teaching
too, because we can model sincere apology. Contrition on the
part of a parent honors the child. It says, "You are a person
who is important enough for me to care deeply about. I want
to make things right with you." This is good for both the child
and the parent's soul, and it shows the child what it looks and
feels like to take responsibility for one's own behavior. It
teaches the child how to say "I'm sorry," too.

Repair can occur on societal levels as well. During times of
natural disaster, victims have been found to be less likely to
develop PTSD if they participate in repair efforts. Their very
participation in physical acts of repair can actually stave off
feelings of helplessness, rage, and despair, and channel them
into positive, transformative energy and meaningful action.
The mere act, however small, of trying to make things better

rather than collapsing into helplessness and despair is preventative and perhaps even curative.

DEPRIVATION: WHEN WE NEGLECT TO "PRATTLE OR SPEAK"

A truly horrifying illustration of how a lack of interaction and bonding can affect children comes to us from the thirteenth century. Holy Roman emperor Frederick II conducted a strange experiment in which he had a group of children raised without being spoken to in any way, because he wanted to see what language they would "speak naturally." Once their voices matured, he is said to have wanted to discover what language would have been "imparted unto Adam and Eve by God." The experiments were recorded by the monk Salimbene di Adam in his *Chronicles*:

> Foster-mothers and nurses were told to suckle and bathe and wash the children, but in no ways to prattle or speak with them; for he would have learnt whether they would speak the Hebrew language (which had been the first), or Greek, or Latin, or Arabic, or perchance the tongue of their parents of whom they had been born. But he laboured in vain, for the children could not live without clappings of the hands, and gestures, and gladness of countenance, and blandishments.

Apparently interaction, care, and talking are so critical to children that they literally cannot live without them. All of the children in the emperor's experiment died.

Rejection can actually hurt physically. "Social rejection activates the very zones of the brain that generate, among other things, the sting of physical pain," according to Matthew D.

Lieberman and Naomi Eisenberg of UCLA. "The brain's pain centers may have taken on a hypersensitivity to social banishment because exclusion was a death sentence in human prehistory." The researchers point out that many languages use words like "broken heart" or "heartache" to describe the physical pain of rejection(Goleman 2006).

Romanian orphanages offer another chilling example of the effect that a lack of care and interaction can have on children's emotional development. The vast majority of children in Romania's orphanages were, heartbreakingly enough, not actually orphans. When Nicolae Ceausescu was Romania's dictator, he outlawed contraception in order to build the nation; overwhelmed parents left the children they did not wish to care for in state institutions. A BBC news article on July 8, 2005, described conditions:

> At an institution in Timisoara, one nurse and three other staff members were giving round-the-clock care to 65 children. The staff could only keep up with feeding the children and changing diapers. Children did not leave their cribs for years, and sometimes were tied down. They did not cry, because crying did not bring a response. Instead, they sat silently. Investigators also looked at several adult psychiatric facilities that housed children in unspeakable conditions, with teenagers confined to cribs and wearing diapers (McGeown 2005).

Pierre Poupard, the head of UNICEF in Romania, calls these children a "lost generation." Being closeted away from society, often malnourished, and subjected to physical and even sexual abuse seriously impacted their emotional development and their ability to learn how to behave in society. At the age of eighteen, the majority were simply sent out to fend for themselves. Some, the more classically resilient children, those who managed to somehow woo extra bits of attention and sustenance from caretakers, have been able to pull their lives together and now have jobs, apartments, and even families of their own. Though they certainly carry scars, they are better off than many others, who are still so traumatized by their early experiences that they remain on the fringes of society, addicted to drink and drugs.

Sorin Brasoveanu, the head of Bacau's child protection department, agreed that in the past many children "hadn't learned much about the outside world" before they left state care. These children not only lacked basic skills such as how to cook or manage money, they also lacked the kind of emotional interaction and support that would have allowed them to develop a secure sense of self, skills of emotional regulation, and emotional literacy.

"I used to think: 'Why me? What had I done?'" said twenty-seven-year-old Cornel Anton, who grew up in a series of these institutions. In his early teenage years, Cornel was already so out of control he was given to behaviors like stealing and fighting. With no ability to talk about his helplessness and rage, he became the classic tough kid who took his pain out through bullying, violence, and antisocial behavior. At fifteen, he hit someone so hard that the person was in a coma for a week. His acting out, like so much acting out, was probably a misguided attempt to restore his sense of self, fighting against his inner feelings of helplessness by striking out, by externalizing his pain. With the intervention of international agencies, Cornel was able to turn his life around, and he can now even reflect on reasons for his aberrant behavior. "I wanted love and a stable identity. But I couldn't find it," he said. "On the outside I was strong, but on the inside I was crying."

"Another survivor of life in these institutions who has found meaning in his life is Ioan Sidor, a soft-spoken man who works with disabled and disadvantaged children in the Romanian city of Bacau. "I try to offer them something I never had myself when I was a child, affection and attention" (McGeown 2005).

Children need adults to care for them and regulate their world until they internalize those skills and make them their own. They need mature adults to explain the world to them until they have their own psychological equipment sufficiently developed so that they can explain it to themselves.

When Kids Get Scared

I mention the severe trauma that the child Pablo
Picasso underwent at the age of three:
the earthquake in Malaga in 1884, the
flight from the family's apartment
into a cave that seemed to be more safe,
and eventually witnessing the birth
of his sister in the same cave under these
very scary circumstances. However, Picasso survived
these traumas without later becoming psychotic or
criminal because he was protected by his very loving
parents. They were able to give him
what he most needed in this chaotic situation:
empathy, compassion, protection and the
feeling of being safe in their arms.

—*Alice Miller*

CHILDREN'S LIMITED BRAIN
DEVELOPMENT CAN PUT THEM AT RISK

*H*eld close in our parents' arms, we feel secure and grounded although we don't know why. Watching our mother walk out the door, we feel sad and worried, and as much as the babysitter tries to explain that she will be back in three hours, our one-year-old mind has no way of computing that length of time. When she returns, we feel relieved, happy, and safe again, but we don't think about it that way. We just snuggle back into her body for a tactile, sensory reconnection that goes straight into our little self system—straight to our limbic, feeling world. Our ability to feel comes before our ability to think, which is why children aren't in a position to make sense of what they're feeling when they're small. Their thinking equipment isn't as developed as their feeling equipment, as we discussed earlier. To be more specific, the limbic system, of which the amygdala and the hippocampus are part, develops before the thinking part of the brain or the prefrontal cortex. The level of development of the amygdala, the hippocampus, and the prefrontal cortex has a lot to do with a child's experience of his thinking/feeling/sensing world.

Children are capable of a full-blown stress response at birth (Uram 2006). However, a part of the brain, the hippocampus, that helps us contextualize information and form new memories about experienced events is not fully formed till age four or five. Therefore, children don't always remember events in context. Also, the prefrontal cortex, which is where we have the ability to think and reason, is not fully formed until around age eleven (van der Kolk 1987). Because of these three factors, when small children get frightened and go into fight/flight/freeze, they have no way of interpreting what's going on around them or of using reason to understand it. They can't use their thinking mind to process their emotion of fear, think about why they're feeling frightened, and regulate their level of fear, because those parts of their brain are not developed enough to do the job.

Small children have no way of assessing whether or not they need to be scared or how scared they need to be. That's why they need adults to act as "surge protectors" between them and the stimulus of the outside world. Picture a baby in his mother's arms who hears a door slam loudly. For a moment, the baby's body may freeze up; he may cry, flail, or throw his arms and head back. Until his mother coos to him and reassures him that he has nothing to be afraid of, he has no idea on his own if he should be frightened or not. For all he knows, a bomb is going off. Nothing is inherently traumatic in a slamming door, but a child may nonetheless find it a terrifying sound, if the adult doesn't assure him he has nothing to fear.

ARE ALL FAMILIES DYSFUNCTIONAL? OR DOES THE CHILD'S LEVEL OF MATURATION AFFECT THE STRESS EXPERIENCE?

No situation need be inherently traumatic. It is how we experience the circumstances of our lives that determines whether or not we will find them traumatizing. The presence of caring adults who help children decode the ever-unfolding situations of their worlds is a great protective buffer for the child. Recent studies have been done at the University of Minnesota by about the production of a hormone called cortisol in children under stress (Dr. Megan Gunnar 2007).

If levels of cortisol get too high, the heart rate, digestive system, and ability to think are negatively impacted. Since the amount of cortisol in the body can be measured in the saliva, many tests noninvasive have been conducted with children to determine who produces cortisol and when. It was found that the presence of a loving caregiver during a time of stress, such as getting shots at the doctor's office, reduced the production of cortisol. The child may still cry, but the smaller amount of cortisol indicated that the body was not reacting as strongly to the stress. In other words, a loving, consistent relationship can offset even the most stressful situation. Every time a child learns something new, the brain works seven times harder than normal. This in itself is a stressful event.

Once the idea of dysfunctional families took hold in the 1980s and we began to examine our childhoods for sources of our problems today, the line between dysfunctional and healthy families became pretty blurred. Understanding the limited brain development of the child and the dynamics of early emotional development helps us to recognize that the problem isn't that all families are dysfunctional. Rather, the child's lack of brain development puts them at a higher risk for experiencing family problems as traumatic. They are simply too young to cope effectively when the world they depend on goes topsy-turvy, or even when normal life circumstances are beyond their capacity to understand and cope with effectively. Children need our protection throughout their early years. They are like little seedlings that need special environments in which they can thrive and become strong enough so that, one day, they can take root and grow on their own.

When the parent is the source of stress, the child is put at significantly higher risk. Not only are they frightened, but the person they would normally go to for comfort and reassurance is lost to them. The child can feel confused and betrayed when the parent they need is regularly unavailable or is causing pain and fear and denying the impact of their behavior.

"BIG EYES"

Last night I did a workshop on the theme of childhood development. I put a series of numbers along the floor and asked the group members to stand at a number that represented an age when they felt something in their sense of self had been seriously affected. Various people shared about why they were standing at a particular age. A man in his forties stood at four years old.

"I'm standing here," he said, "because it's the first time that I have a clear memory of my father, how mad he used to get at me. I've been wanting to do some work with that; I don't know what. I have no idea; I just feel like there's more there. I'm forty-two, and I can't get any relationship to last. I don't know why, and I don't even want children. Well, maybe I do, but I can't even get close. I have a lot of friends, but not one close person of my own." We decided as a group to do a psychodrama. Gerry chose someone to play his father.

"You look at me like you hate me," he said, the child in him speaking out. "You scream at me, you hit me, then in the morning you act like nothing happened. I come down the stairs and you say 'Hi, little buddy.'" The boy inside of Gerry remained confused about this treatment by his father. As a child, he had no way of understanding that his father's contempt, insults, and violence were part of his drunken stupor and that, by morning, he had no recollection of any of it. So he came to the conclusion that children often come to: "My father, a grown-up, must be right. I must be bad." Because he had not examined this in his adulthood—gotten underneath it, so to speak—he was still living by the meaning he had made out of it as a boy.

"Just tell me what I'm doing wrong, so I can get it right. I never know where I am with you. I can never get it right for you." Gerry described getting "big eyes," watching everything from high above. "My eyes get huge," he made large circles with his fingers to show how big his eyes got. "I just make my eyes huge so I can see everything that's going on. I go up to the ceiling and watch everything." What Gerry is describing here is an experience of dissociation. I walked over behind Gerry and "doubled" the feeling that I thought was in him, but with which he was not able to connect.

"I'm so scared," I said.

"I'm just on the ceiling, I see everything. I don't know what I feel." Here Gerry is articulating what happens. We dissociate so we don't have to feel what's going on, because we're frightened and feel helpless to do anything to change things or defend ourselves.

"You just keep saying, 'Be a man,'" said Gerry to his "father."

"I'm four," I doubled. "I'm four years old."

"Play with me," said Gerry. "Stop telling me I can't do anything. Stop hitting me."

"You're hurting me," I doubled.

"When I go up to the ceiling, it doesn't even hurt."

This is a price children pay. Years after the abuse is over, after they have grown taller and stronger than their parents, they still feel small and scared on the inside. And they still "go away" when the feelings of dependency and vulnerability that are a part of intimacy make them feel afraid of humiliation and rejection.

"I don't know what to do. You just keep telling me to be a man. I just want a dad. I want to know how to get it right so I can have a dad. I try to tell you, but all you say is 'you wrong, you wrong.' That's what you say all the time. And when I ask you why, you say 'cause 'me right,' so I shut my mouth."

"Yeah, that's right, me right," said the man playing his father.

"And Mom just lets you do it. She says, 'Oh, Dad's a genius, he's so smart.' So I'm thinking you're a genius and I'm a dummy who can't figure anything out. Mom never did anything to protect me." I asked Gerry if he wanted to choose someone to play his mother.

"You just went along with everything," said Gerry to the woman taking on the role of his mother. "It was just a mess in here [Gerry motioned to the space between his "parents"]. You knew he was a drunk but you called him a genius. He used to take me to bars, and he'd order me Coke after Coke. I'd be bouncing off the walls with sugar, and then he'd say, 'Don't tell Mom, this will be just between us men.' I was so confused. I was so confused all the time."

Not only did Gerry lack a comfortable relationship with his father, but his secrets with his father kept him from being able to ask for help from his mother, the parent he felt closest to and relied on most. "I'm so confused. I never wanna grow up and have kids and have this come out. I never wanna be a man like you," he said to his "dad." "And I never wanna have a relationship like the two of you have." Suddenly the pieces were falling into place, the unconscious was becoming conscious.

Gerry turned to his "father" and stretched himself up to his full height as a man. "You wrong, Dad. You wrong. You were wrong about me. I'm a good guy; I was a good kid. You were too drunk to be a father. You wrong." At this point, Gerry's face began to look relieved, and his neck, legs, and arms began to relax. "I feel like I'm back in my body," he said. "I didn't realize, I didn't realize that I thought if I got close to someone it would turn into all this." He made a motion that referred to this family dynamic in which he'd grown up. "I've been so scared of repeating my past, I've been stuck in my present."

Unresolved childhood relationship trauma can leave an adult vulnerable to difficulties in forming secure adult relationships. Patterns of attachment continue through the life cycle and across generations. New relations are affected by the expectations developed in past relationships. There is a strong correlation between insecure attachment, marital dissatisfaction, and negative marital interactions. An adult who does not feel safe with others may tend to be rejecting of his or her partner or overly clingy, or to alternate between the two. Attachment problems or relationship patterns are often handed down transgenerationally unless someone breaks the chain. These can impact both our ability to live comfortably in intimate relationships and to parent. As a parent, an insecurely attached adult may lack the ability to form a strong attachment to one's child and provide the necessary attachment cues required for the healthy emotional development of the child, thereby predisposing their child to a lifetime of relationship difficulties.

One important thing to keep in mind is that even well-intentioned parents can cause significant emotional and psychological pain for their children, because the child's limited brain development and total dependency on the parent can make him very vulnerable to being hurt. The self does not develop in an isolated vacuum; it is cocreated. So is relationship trauma. It occurs in the context of a relationship, and it tends to repeat the unresolved contents of its residue in relationships also. That is, childhood relationship trauma often resurfaces in adult relationships.

When we have what we might call unrepaired experiences from childhood that we carry into adulthood, the repair we need to settle our insides needs to occur after the fact. Otherwise, we may not understand how yesterday's experiences are driving our behavior today. One-to-one therapy, 12-step programs, and group therapy are all places where this repair can occur. I have found the role-play techniques of psychodrama particularly useful here. Being able to momentarily inhabit the role of the confused, wounded, or even elated child, for example, allows the child within us to have a voice while the adult in us looks on. The adult can see in concrete form what the child is trying to say, do, or have. The body language emerges alongside the words in the way Gerry was standing, talking, and gesturing as the child's story is being told. In this way the past can be reexperienced, repaired, and reunderstood in the light of today. The child within can finally let go and relax.

JOURNALING

Exercise One: Letting the Child Speak

One journaling exercise that can be useful here is to reverse roles with yourself at any moment in your own childhood where you believe you may have felt as we have described throughout this chapter: disempowered, disconnected, or unheard. Journal in the voice of yourself at that time; journal *as* the child within you, talk from that place. Then journal about what fears you may have developed about relationships that you might still be living out today.

Exercise Two: A Moment of Repair

Journal about a time when repair occurred—how you felt afterward within the relationship and what positive lessons you learned from working something out about relationship repair that you might still be living out today.

*B*ehind Closed Doors

The family. We were a strange little band
of characters trudging through life sharing
diseases and toothpaste, coveting one
another's desserts, hiding shampoo,
borrowing money, locking each other out
of our rooms, inflicting pain and
kissing to heal it in the same instant,
loving, laughing, defending and
trying to figure out the common thread
that bound us all together.

—*Erma Bombeck*

*W*e pick up on each other for better or worse. We are, in fact, designed to do just that, to tune in to each other through our own biological systems. We sense and imitate the motions, moods, and manner of those around us. My bad mood lingers in the air, and your enthusiasm gets me pumped up. In other words, I read you through the various tracking systems that are in me, and you're doing just the same. Mirror neurons and chemicals of connection take the phenomenon of "picking up on each other" out of the realm of new age and put it directly into the realm of science. Between the emotional contagion and mirror neurons, we see a picture of family life emerge that includes an ever-present, powerful, and deep sort of group sync from which we draw much of who we are.

Understanding that emotions—particularly strong ones that are felt by one person—are also anticipated, tracked, and felt by those close to them helps us to wrap our minds around why those with whom we live have such an impact on our minds and our bodies; why, when there is tension or anger in the room, our gut tightens up; and why we can't keep a straight face when someone we love is laughing.

Virginia Satir, author of *The New People Making*, referred to the family as a mobile that will always seek to regulate itself, to constantly adjust its disparate parts in order to achieve that delicate balance that family therapists refer to as homeostasis. When crisis of any kind—whether in the form of mental illness, death, alcohol, drugs, or significant dysfunction—are introduced into a family system, the manner in which the family regulates itself is greatly affected. The family, however, always seeks homeostasis. When relationship trauma enters the picture, that homeostasis may become maladaptive or, to use the vernacular, dysfunctional.

WHAT ARE THE RULES AND PATTERNS IN FAMILIES THAT HAVE EXPERIENCED RELATIONSHIP TRAUMA?

In families where there is relationship trauma, all of the individuals within that system are somehow affected. Both dysfunction and emotional sobriety are contagious. As the family that is holding too much unaddressed emotional pain struggles to retain its equilibrium, it looks for strategies that will allow it to find some sort of balance.

If the family cannot tolerate genuine and authentic expression of the emotional pain and psychological angst that family dysfunction is engendering, pain does not get processed, worked through, and put into any context that might allow the family to move through it.

Members who act out the underlying and unspoken emotional climate may become scapegoats who provide the family with a distraction, giving parents and other siblings something to be anxious about other than what's really happening. They may become what family systems theorists call the "symptom bearer," symptomatic on behalf of the whole family. Children who act out, for example, can have the effect of getting warring parents to pull together in order to address what's going on for the child; thus, the family buys some more time, the focus is diverted from the parent's or the family's underlying problems, and homeostasis, albeit a costly one, is again achieved.

But the family is engaged in a losing battle. Without help, intervention, and treatment, relationship trauma tends to be passed down through the generations. Though this population may not be evidencing wounds that make first responders rush to their sides, they are bleeding from within nonetheless.

Naming and talking about the problem is crucial. While the problem sits unspoken in the emotional underbelly of the family, it affects everyone, but no one is really sure what they are feeling or why they're feeling it. Nor do they necessarily understand why they have an impulse to act out, withdraw, or self-medicate. Family members feel crazy inside. They see one reality being shown on the surface, but they sense and pick up on a very different one that is denied. "No talk" rules and the family's need to look good and present a "normal" face to the world may make pain denied and off-limits.

So key are family and community to survival that nature rewards close, comfortable connections with body chemicals that feel good and punishes stress and rupture with body chemicals that feel bad. Family members who fear experiencing the ever-growing pain that is seeping into their container of connection and disconnection may become very adept at colluding to avoid more pain from erupting and "rocking the boat." Those in the system who have the clarity or courage to act as whistle blowers, who attempt to reveal the truth of the family pathology, may be perceived by the family, which is steeped in denial, as in some way problematic. Naming the dysfunctional behavior becomes the sin, not the dysfunctional behavior itself. These members may be cut off, humiliated, or even hated if they get too close to the truth, though much of this may be unconscious. Simply bringing up the family's problems causes other family members, who cannot and will not see their own pathology, to want to kill the messenger. Again, the message—the truth—threatens their survival as a system.

WHEN A SUBSTANCE ENTERS THE FAMILY

The direct introduction of a chemical into the family system has the power, over time, to radically alter the thinking, feeling, and behavior of all involved. While most likely problems exist in a family before a drug takes over—and the drug is in part a symptom, a way of self-medicating the preexisting problems—this is only part of the story. Addiction introduces a very distinct disease pattern of its own. As with Agent Orange, once exposed, a previously healthy person can present with strange symptoms that mimic a wide variety of other diseases. Someone who is addicted may seem depressed, anxious, obsessive, borderline, or even manic-depressive. The disease itself can induce the symptoms. It is entirely possible that there is a dual diagnosis or an underlying disorder that is being self-medicated, but addiction itself throws the self system so out of balance that until sobriety is established, it can be difficult to know for certain.

Family members may also mimic and absorb this emotional, psychological, and behavioral climate, becoming depressed, anxious, defiant, or erratic in their response to living with the pain and chaos that addiction engenders. "You can tell how sick an alcoholic man is by how crazy his wife acts" is a saying that speaks to the degree of pathology that is internalized and acted out by those who live with the chronic relationship trauma of addiction. Families, even with their preexisting pathologies and dysfunctions, may have made it into healthier styles of relating as the stresses of raising children and supporting a family lessened over time. But with a drug introduced to manage the stress instead of something healthier or less destructive, these families become an accident waiting to happen.

Drugs and alcohol, once they take hold, can change even a saint into a sinner. Wonderful, upstanding, fine people lose their ability to regulate their own behavior and begin to hurt those they love the most. Addiction makes it virtually impossible for the user to heal his own pain; instead he is anesthetizing it and living on borrowed time. Initially, addicts may feel they have found a way to manage a turbulent inner world. Unfortunately, in the long run, they create one. They often lose their sense of what constitutes functional thinking, feeling, and behavior, and their secure hold on the so-called normal world starts to slip.

Because the family's disease or problems are progressive—

they don't get better by themselves and, in fact, get worse—family members seamlessly slip into patterns of relating that become increasingly dysfunctional by the day. They may adopt elaborate defenses designed to look good or seem normal, withdraw into their own private world, or compete for the little love and attention that is available. In the absence of reliable adults, siblings may become parentified and try to provide the care and comfort that is missing for each other, or they may become co-opted by one parent as a surrogate partner, filling in the gaping holes and massaging the sore spots of a family in a constant low level of crisis. This is on-the-job training for codependency.

Such families become characterized by a kind of emotional and psychological constriction. There is a lot of fear in the way they relate. They do not feel free to express their authentic selves for fear of triggering each other; their genuine feelings are often hidden under strategies for keeping safe, like pleasing or withdrawing. The family becomes organized around trying to manage the unmanageable disease of addiction. In their desperate attempts to maintain family equilibrium, they invent a novel strategy at each new turn of the disease progression. Some members overfunction to restore order and dignity while others underfunction, providing an alternative focus for their ever-growing problems or defending against their deep fear of ultimate disappointment and failure. They yell, withdraw, cajole, make jokes, harangue, criticize, understand, get fed up—you name it. They become remarkably inventive, trying everything they can come up with to contain the problem and keep the family from blowing up. They develop novel and highly inventive ways of managing the unmanageable. Actually, some of these qualities can become part of the family member's unusual gifts and strengths, particularly if they are able to recover from their relationship trauma. But the alarm bells in this system are nonetheless on a constant and annoying low hum, causing everyone to feel hypervigilant, ready to run for emotional (or physical) shelter or to erect their defenses at the first sign of trouble.

Because family members avoid sharing subjects that might lead to more pain, they often wind up avoiding genuine connection with each other. Then, when painful feelings build up, they may rise to the surface in emotional eruptions or get acted out through impulsive or controlling behaviors. These families become systems for manufacturing and perpetuating relationship trauma. Trauma affects the internal world of each person, their relationships, and their ability to communicate and be together in a balanced, relaxed, and trusting manner. It affects their emotional sobriety or ability to self-regulate.

Due to the trauma-related defenses of dissociation and numbing, and the active avoidance and denial that characterize addicted or dysfunctional family systems, family members may not attach words to the powerful emotions they're experiencing. Consequently they often have trouble talking about, processing, and working through the pain that they are in. In this way they lose one of their most available routes to processing pain and developing emotional balance and sobriety. Individuals in addictive or abusive systems may behave in ways consistent with the behaviors of victims of other psychological traumas; in other words, they are traumatized by the experience.

Passing on the Pain: Trauma and Addiction as an Intergenerational Disease Process

Children of addiction are four times more likely to become addicts themselves and these statistics don't include multiple addictions such as food, sex, gambling, work, and so on. Nor do they include those who marry addicts.

Many feel that there is a genetic predisposition to addiction, and there is certainly evidence for this possibility. However, even putting genetics aside, the types of emotional, psychological, and behavioral patterns that are traumatizing put each generation at risk for perpetuating the kind of painful dynamics that lead to psychological problems and addictions of all kinds, if rigorous treatment doesn't intervene. Even if the generation beneath the addict doesn't evidence drug or alcohol addiction, they may well be passing on the types of dysfunctional relationship dynamics that put the next generation at risk. In this way, addiction and dysfunction become a family illness that is intergenerational. For this reason, in addictive family systems, each person in the family needs to undergo a rigorous recovery effort in order to arrest the disease progression in its path and learn to adopt new, healthy patterns of relating.

TRAUMATIC BONDS

The intensity and quality of connectedness in families that contain repeated painful interactive patterns can create the types of bonds that people tend to form during times of crisis, referred to as traumatic bonds.

Alliances in dysfunctional families may become critical to one's sense of self and even survival. As the family members' fear increases, so does their need for protective bonds. This situation can be played out in bonding with the abuser because, as the victim's dependency grows through abuse, so does the need for perceived protection. Or one parent may co-opt a child and form a bond against the other parent. Additionally, children who are feeling hurt and needy and who lose access to their parents as a source of reliable support may turn to each other to fill in the missing sense of security. This can develop into a traumatic sort of bond among siblings. Siblings and other children may form a trauma bond with each other, much as soldiers or prisoners do, in a phenomenon referred to as "twinning." Children who are lost and frightened may "rescue" each other, increasing their sense of loyalty. These bonds carry with them a sense of "surviving together" and may create a feeling that loyalty should be maintained at all costs, even if this bond becomes problematic or dysfunctional.

Traumatic bonds formed in childhood tend to repeat their quality and contents over and over again throughout life.

Abusive bonds can become traumatic bonds that pass through the generations. For example, the bond between an abusing parent and the abused child may repeat itself when the abused child grows up and becomes or marries an abusing spouse or reverses roles and becomes an abusive parent to his or her own child. These bonds find new homes in willing hosts. They get revived, repeated, and relived over and over again. Traumatic bonding can also come from feeling dehumanized and robotized by abuse or neglect. Because we dissociate from our real selves, we may lose the ability to direct our own destiny and temporarily get co-opted by a person who seems in charge. Factors that can contribute to bonds becoming traumatic are:

+ If there is a power imbalance in the relationship.
+ If there is a lack of access to outside support.
+ What sort of meaning is part of the bond—for example, "You can only trust me; other people are out to get you," "We have to stick together or we will fall apart," "I'm the only person who really cares."
+ If there are wide inconsistencies in styles of relating.

A confusing aspect of these types of relationships is that they are neither all good nor all bad. Their very unevenness can make the nature of the bond all the more difficult to unravel.

In the case of addiction, this is an all-too-familiar dynamic. The addicted parent, for example, may swing between being attentive, generous, and caring to being abusive, neglectful, and rejecting. This is a setup for traumatic bonding for both children and spouses as the addicted person becomes an unreliable but still very important source of caring and closeness. One minute they are everything one could wish, and the next they are miserably disappointing. It sets up a cycle of excitation vs. disappointment, or of gratification vs. withholding, which is yet another manifestation of the seesawing from one end of the emotional spectrum to the other that is so common in addicted/traumatized families. This pattern also sets up inconsistent relationship models for the entire family and demonstrates a lack of continuity and responsibility.

Trauma can put us in the double bind of both wanting to withdraw from close relationships and to seek them desperately. The profound disruption of basic trust—the common feelings of shame, guilt, and inferiority, and the need to avoid reminders of the relationship trauma that might be found in social or intimate life—may all foster withdrawal from close relationships. But the terror of rupture and emotional, psychological, or physical abandonment intensifies our need for protective attachments. The traumatized person therefore frequently alternates between isolation and anxious clinging to others.

NOT KNOWING WHAT "NORMAL" IS

In homes where relationship trauma or addiction is present, behavior may be inconsistent. The rules that apply one day don't always carry over to the next. The same rules that are laid down on Monday may no longer apply by Tuesday and then suddenly on Friday, Monday's rules may be enforced as if there was never any interruption in continuity. Children may see behavior that sails past normal, mocks normal, and feels normal all in the same day. It can be mind-boggling, to say nothing of discouraging, for the child in this system just to figure out how to act to stay out of trouble. Some children may just give up trying and lose all respect for family rules; others may drive themselves nuts trying to read their parents' minds (codependency in the making); while others may muster up their own independence and self-reliance (a sign of resilience), realizing that their parents are asleep at the switch.

Still another crazy-making dynamic may be that punishment gets doled out based on the parent's mood rather than on the child's behavior. Children can become deeply confused as to how to maintain an intimate connection within which they can relax and be themselves, retaining a sense of self while allowing another person to do the same. All of this contributes to "not knowing what normal is" (Woititz 1983).

Not knowing what normal is can lead to emotional deregulation and problems with emotional sobriety. We lose our sense of what represents balanced "normal" behavior. We're not sure what to pay attention to or what to dismiss, what to aim for and what to avoid. Our emotional compass is off, and our fuel gauge can get broken too. We no longer know what full and empty feel like. We can get and get and get, but we don't ever feel filled up. Or we can be very empty and not know how to let in what would help us to feel full inside.

All of this, of course, is undermining to one's developing a well-consolidated sense of self, as the self is an ever-evolving interface between external reality and one's inner world. Development and maintenance of a sense of self is a fluid rather than static process. It requires that we have the space to feel our way in and out of situations and emotional states so that we develop a felt sense of a normal range of functioning.

WHEN CHILDHOOD PAIN
SURFACES IN ADULTHOOD

Within those who have experienced trauma in childhood may be a child who is frozen in place, afraid to move and afraid to feel. Through recovery, this inner child often wakes up and begins to feel. This reawakening of parts of the self that have been, shall we say, frozen or out of reach can feel threatening to the adult self. The adult self wants to be in charge, and letting the child self wake up threatens to upset the apple cart. What if they feel more than the adult self has the ability to handle? This is where the adult self needs to seek help, and create a support network, so that as the child self wakes up, the adult can be steady enough to allow emotions that were shut down in childhood to emerge. Within the support of a recovery network, we can face and work with our more hidden selves. As we do this and come to new insights surrounding our intense emotional reactions, we feel the relief of experiencing banished emotions. We see that they are part of another time and place, that we no longer need to live today by the meaning we made out of circumstances when we were young and helpless. We take our life back a feeling or thought at a time. As each of our feelings arise and we make sense of them with our adult mind, we grow up on the inside, becoming emotionally more mature. Emotional maturity rather than an act of will is, in this sense, a natural outgrowth of deep, emotional work, an awakening into another point of view, a letting go of the past in order to live more fully in the present.

TRANSLATING OUR FEELINGS INTO WORDS

Emotional literacy is the ability to translate our emotions into words so that our feelings and thoughts can be held out in the intellectual space between two people, shared and reflected on, so that we can think about what we're feeling. It is a natural outgrowth of sound emotional development. To attain and maintain emotional sobriety, we need to learn to tolerate our strong feelings and translate those feelings into words. *The ability to use our thinking minds to organize the feelings and sensory impressions fed to us through our limbic mind is key to developing and maintaining emotional maturity, balance, and sobriety.* If we cannot tolerate our strong emotions and the physical sensations that accompany them, we will want to somehow get rid of them, to make them go away. When we can tolerate our powerful emotions and sensations without blowing up, withdrawing, or self-medicating, we can use the information that we gain from them to inform our thinking. Simply stated, if we don't know what we feel, it's hard to make sense of ourselves and make sense of another person. And it's hard to communicate what we feel and tolerate listening to another person communicate what they feel.

When we can use our thinking mind to make sense and meaning of our limbic mind, we develop a feeling of mastery and self-confidence, knowing that we can find a way to deal with what life throws in our direction. We feel we have the skills necessary to cope with our lives, and at those moments when we can't, we know how to ask for help.

$\mathcal{R}$elationship Trauma

Suffering has been stronger than all other teaching,
and has taught me to understand what your heart
used to be. I have been bent and broken, but—I
hope—into a better shape.

—Charles Dickens

Our bodies, minds, and hearts are designed by nature to want to be in relationships of all kinds. We're wired for connection, wired to *desire* closeness and to *fear* abandonment. Our impulses to relate and read each other's subtle signals, so that we can cooperate, live, and work together, are hardwired into us at a profound mind/body level; they inform and create our drive to attach. Without this hardwiring for closeness and love—and the feelings of need, fear, pain, and protectiveness that surround it—our species could not survive.

Nature has painstakingly evolved this *biology of love and fear* in us, in order to assure that couples pair-bond, parents attach to their children, and children attach to their parents. Our very survival depends on our ability to form and maintain sustaining relationships. That's why the emotions associated with these "survival relationships" are so very powerful and intense, and why we will go to such extraordinary lengths to keep these relationships intact; because our sense of self is interwoven with our sense of relationship at a fairly fundamental level; because relational dynamics that we experience with those who raise us literally become part of our neural wiring. That is why losing someone we love can feel like we are losing a part of ourselves; why when our family fragments, we feel fragmented inside. These emotions associated with attachment are literally coded into our DNA to ensure our survival. And that's exactly why ruptures in these "survival relationships" can shake us at our roots; they can be, in other words, traumatic.

WHAT DO WE MEAN BY "RELATIONSHIP TRAUMA"?

Human connection is high on the evolutionary scale for selected traits. We need to feel each other's pain in order to attend to it. We need to share the experience of hunger or rejection in order to be motivated to reach out and share what food we have, or drag out of harm's way another person who is wounded. Without this ability to feel for and with each other, we would have long ago become extinct. This profound level of connection is present in the underbelly of families, communities, and society itself. People affect other people. We share in an emotional world that is constantly vibrating beneath the surface of any group, any relationship. The extent to which we are conscious of this and willing to become responsible for what we put into this silence that is not so silent may go a long way toward creating the emotional world that we live in.

Because we are so sensitively wired to pick up on each other's evocative signals, the emotional atmosphere in which we are raised has a powerful impact on how we experience ourselves and our world.

Over the years I have come to call what I work with "relationship trauma," or trauma that occurs exactly because we care so much and are so deeply connected with those we love. I deal with the unresolved pain, hurt, and resentment that people carry long into adulthood when those they live or grew up with and depended upon leave them prematurely, hurt them physically, wound them with a barrage of words that strip them of their dignity and twist their sense of reality, or demonstrate the kind of behavior that is traumatizing even to be near. *Relationship trauma is the kind of emotional and psychological trauma that occurs within the context of relationships.* Because we experience and hold emotion in our bodies, relationship trauma impacts both the mind and our emotional or limbic system in ways that can last for many years after the stressor is removed.

When the Vietnam War ended, veteran hospitals across the nation were confronted with soldiers who, long after the war was over, were still experiencing emotional, psychological, and physical disturbances as a result of the terror they lived with during combat. As their symptoms of post-traumatic stress disorder became better known, the mental health field began to realize that it was seeing similar characteristics in its clients who had experienced family abuse and neglect: terror over circumstances that were frightening and out of their control. Eventually brain scans confirmed what mental health workers suspected: clients who had lived in homes where there was chronic chaos or abuse showed some of the same brain changes that soldiers of war exhibited. In just the same manner that a shell-shocked soldier flinches or drops to the floor when he hears a car backfire because it is reminiscent of the sounds of war, a child who grows up in a family where rage is out of control and turns into emotional or physical abuse might flinch or shake when around intense anger, because it is reminiscent of his or her early family experience. It feels dangerous.

Our thinking mind makes sense out of the emotional and sensory input from our limbic mind. This is how we make meaning out of experience. But trauma is all about *not* experiencing what we are experiencing. It is about splitting off (pushing out of conscious awareness) or numbing out what we're feeling because what we're experiencing is frightening us. When our environment is chaotic or fear inducing, we may have a hard time tolerating what we're feeling, a hard time "staying in our bodies." When we cannot remove ourselves from what is frightening us or fight it off, we may go numb or shut down. We cannot take action on our own behalf, so we freeze in place. Our bodies carry the imprint of this action never taken or thwarted intent.

Why do we freeze? We freeze because we're scared, because something is overwhelming us. And what happens when we freeze? When we freeze, we don't process normally what's going on around us. We experience an altered state of consciousness. Time may be slowed down or feel fragmented. Our senses go on high alert while the thinking part of our brain shuts down. "It can be quite disturbing to the individual experiencing it, because aspects of this altered state are substantially different from ordinary consciousness. For example, one's perceptions may be affected and altered, and the location of consciousness may be outside the body or in a phantom body" (Gant 2003). This is what Gerry was describing in our previous chapter when he said he "went up to the ceiling."

UNPROCESSED EXPERIENCE

Remember, emotion came before thinking, evolutionarily speaking. We have all the instincts of an animal when we're scared, but the part of the brain that makes us uniquely human and think about the situation rationally shuts down in moments of threat. The cortex, which is where thinking, reasoning, and long-range planning take place, was developed later in human evolution. The two systems were developed thousands of years apart and can operate somewhat independently. We call the first our survival system, our reptilian or animal brain, or our limbic brain. The second, the prefrontal cortex, represents what makes us more human, what allows us to think, dream, imagine, and process our emotions so our thoughts and feelings become elevated to a conscious awareness, so we can make sense and meaning out of the events of our lives.

Because our cortex shuts down when we're frightened, the content of the experience that would normally get thought through and processed may get more or less flash frozen or thrown out of consciousness instead. It gets stored as a frozen sense memory (body memory) with little reason or understanding attached to it. These painful memories may not get processed, understood, and placed into the overall context of one's life. They may become banished from consciousness by one of our psychological defenses of dissociation or numbing. They may get "forgotten."

But unfortunately, what we don't know can hurt us. What we can't consciously feel or remember can still have great power over us. As children from families that contain trauma, we may find ourselves moving into adult roles carrying unconscious or only partly conscious burdens that we aren't fully aware of, that interfere with our happiness. In other words, unresolved pain from yesterday gets transferred onto the relationships and circumstances of today without our knowing how or why. Part of what gets us into trouble is that our honest and genuine reactions to previous painful events may be unavailable to us, hidden even from ourselves. Consequently, we may be unable to trace back to their origins our strong reactions to the circumstances in the present. In other words, we don't know that we don't know. We really think that our intense emotional reactions to circumstances in the present belong entirely to the situation that is triggering them, and we are unconscious of what might be driving them from underneath. Our overreactivity in the present goes unrecognized—that is, we don't connect today's trigger with events from the past. We may get anxious or angry or go into a panic state or even a panic attack without any recognition of what from our past is getting triggered by our present. Key fragments of the original traumatic event have become inaccessible to ordinary remembering (Grant 2003). Experience needs to be processed so that we can let it go. If a person goes into an instinctual trauma response, the likelihood of developing PTSD symptoms is great. Often PTSD takes some months or even years to become full-blown (Grant 2003).

HOW RELATIONSHIP TRAUMA DEREGULATES OUR LIMBIC SYSTEMS

When we cycle back and forth between feeling the very intense emotions that flood us when we're scared and shutting down, it's like revving up a car and slamming on the brakes over and over and over again.

Chronic stress can get us stuck in fight/flight mode. Here's how that happens. The constant release of the stress hormone cortisol has some serious and long-term effects on our brain and body. Too much cortisol tends to shut down the hippocampus. The hippocampus is the part of the brain that helps us to accurately perceive and read our environment. Cortisol also impairs the cortex's ability to regulate fear signals coming from our fear center, the amygdala. So at the same

time that we are being oversensitized to stress, we lose some of
our ability to regulate our fear and anxiety and put into proportion and context what's going on around us. There is a
threefold impact on the body of too much cortisol. First, the
impaired hippocampus begins overgeneralizing fearfulness to
details of the moment that are irrelevant (such as a change of
expression or tone of voice). Second, the amygdala circuitry
becomes overactive, and third, the prefrontal area is unable to
modulate and accurately interpret signals from the overreact-
ing amygdala. The result is that the amygdala starts reading
everything as scary or threatening, and the hippocampus
mistakenly perceives too many triggers for that fear. This condition of hypervigilance and overreactivity is part of post-
traumatic stress disorder. The brain/body becomes oversensitized to stress, reading signs of potential danger, and may
overreact to even perceived slights, humiliation, or threat.

Our neural networks can become oversensitized to stress if
we've been traumatized. Distorted thinking, hyperreactivity,
mistrust, and ambivalence can be some of the issues that
become part of being in close relationships. Dysfunctional patterns of relating that are the direct result of relationship
trauma literally wrap themselves around our emotional and
psychological development and imprint themselves on our
neural networks. If our pain occurred in the context of our
primary close childhood relationships, the most likely place
that our post-traumatic stress reactions will surface is in our
primary close relationships in adulthood. In partnership, the
very closeness we feel, along with feelings of dependency and
vulnerability that are part of intimacy, can bring up our previous experiences around early primary relationships.

For these reasons, recovery from relationship trauma that
has imprinted itself onto our self system takes time. We are
changing the body as well as the mind. Trauma that occurs
within the context of our early relationships not only affects

our relational patterns, but it also impacts our mind/body system through the phenomenon of neural patterning. These patterns set the foundations from which we operate in our relationships throughout life. The more we play out patterns in our relationships of today, the more engraved and ingrained the patterns become.

A DOUBLE WHAMMY

Relationship trauma as well as the ACOA syndrome can be seen as being a twofold condition. *One, it is a post-traumatic stress syndrome in which our reactions to relationship trauma that occurred in childhood are surfacing in adulthood. Two, it is a developmental disorder in which problematic self-concepts and patterns of relating become incorporated into the developing self throughout childhood, adolescence, and young adulthood.* ACOAs and those who grew up with relationship trauma are adults who are seeking help for an unresolved childhood condition.

When the ACOA movement began, many people identified with it, even those who had never lived with addiction. They were identifying with symptoms or the patterns of thinking, feeling, and behaving that they learned growing up in stressful families; they found these emerging in their adult relationships as a post-traumatic stress reaction. Long after the stressor was removed, they were still living as if the stressor was present.

Gradually the word "codependent" evolved in a grassroots sort of attempt to give a broader applicability to the syndrome. For this reason, I gradually evolved the term *relationship trauma* to describe what I work with because it was a clearer way of explaining what I was really seeing clinically. I was not only treating the effects of living with addiction, but I was also treating the effects of being traumatized within the context of primary relationships.

TRAUMA AND THE SENSES: WHY TRAUMA SINKS INTO THE DEEP LIMBIC SYSTEM

The more senses involved in an experience, the more the brain remembers it. The first responders on the scene after the attack of September 11, 2001, for example, were most at risk for developing PTSD symptoms because all of their senses were involved; that is, they saw, smelled, heard, and touched the chaos and devastation at Ground Zero firsthand. Their brains and bodies just soaked up the experience through the direct involvement of their senses.

All of our senses are alive and functioning in the home environment. Family is a uniquely sensorial experience from day one. The home is a tactile environment alive with sounds, textures, sights, smells, and tastes. It is kinesthetic in every way, a body/mind proprioceptive experience. Proprioception is linked with our ability to sense ourselves and our bodies in space. It involves the sensory nerve endings in muscles, tendons, and joints that, through internal signals, help us to find ourselves within our environment by responding to stimuli from within the body. Because our senses are so alive in the home, what goes on in the home is absorbed straight into the bloodstream, so to speak, inscribed into our neural networks. This makes relationship trauma a body/mind phenomenon.

A Body/Mind Combustion

Lanie grew up with a mother who was psychotic and flew into rages at the drop of a hat. Lanie could never figure out how to adjust her behavior to keep these flights of rage from happening; she personalized them (and so did her mother). Lanie really felt that if she could only address her mother's constant litany of complaints, she might be able to curb her outbursts. Lanie had a lot of the physical symptoms of someone who had been under lifelong stress, who had had too much cortisol in her bloodstream for too long. Her hair was thinned and brittle, she looked pasty and tense, she self-medicated with food, and though she was always trying to eat well, she was chronically overweight. In group she was terrified just sitting in her chair. From the moment she walked into the room she began to feel caged and anxious. She was so afraid of not being accepted that she was suspicious and fearful much of the time. If someone looked askance at her, she began to create scenarios in her mind of impending rejection. The more fearful she became, the more her body began to feel tense and anxious. Her gut churned at the thought of not ever feeling able to join easily and readily into the group, her head pounded when she looked around the room, and her legs felt shaky when she talked. She frequently shifted in her chair to relieve the pain expanding in her lower back. The more fearful Lanie became, the more those disturbing sensations went through her body. And the more her body felt disturbed, the more fearful she became. She felt exhausted and disheartened by her own internal combustion. All it took was a look, vocal tone, or sideways comment to send her straight to the ceiling, or down through the floor.

Because trauma is stored by the body as well as the mind, when we get triggered, we may experience disturbing body sensations as well as disturbing thoughts and feelings. These unintegrated and unconscious trauma memories may resurface in the form of somatic disturbances such as headaches, back problems, and queasiness, or as psychological and emotional symptoms such as flashbacks, anxiety, sudden outbursts of anger, rage, or intrusive memories.

The person experiencing these swings in her physiological, emotional, and psychological inner world may find herself in an intense bind in which painful mental imagery or memories stimulate disturbing physiological sensations *and* disturbing physiological sensations stimulate painful mental imagery or memories. This combination can create an internal combustion, a psychological, emotional, and physical "black hole" that can send us into an ever-intensifying downward spiral fraught with fear and anxiety. We may experience this as panic, feeling stuck in or flooded by intense emotions.

As Lanie felt increasingly out of control, her mind went into mental handsprings trying to figure out what was going on. She tried hard to tell the group how to behave so that she would feel less triggered. Needless to say, the group could never quite get it, nor did they particularly care to. Lanie saw the solution to her problem as getting her environment to change and adapt. Unfortunately for her, one of the skills of self-regulation lies in the ability to balance and regulate our own behavior and adapt it to our environment. Lanie's ability to read the subtle signals sent to her by various group members and adapt her behavior accordingly was very impaired by years and years of stress and living with a mother for whom there was no "normal." Her father had died when she was a child, and she lived a great distance from close relatives. She grew up in a narrow and distorted world in which she could never quite find her footing. She needed to spend much time in a secure one-to-one therapy relationship so that she could gradually take in a new attachment figure—a new therapeutic mother or "constant object," as psychologists call it. But the thought of that made her feel physically ill. She cycled between feeling deeply needy of therapists and wanting to rage at them and tell them to get lost. Lanie described having trouble feeling true to herself while in the presence of others. Her sense of self was not developed enough for her to hang on to it in the presence of another person. She needed to slowly and methodically rebuild a reliable sense of self that could eventually become portable.

CHARACTERISTICS OF TRAUMA AND RELATIONSHIP TRAUMA

Trauma has the potential to affect many different aspects of a person's life. In this section we review a number of possible outcomes of experiencing trauma.

Problems with self-regulation and emotional sobriety. Trauma survivors are susceptible to swings on the emotional scale from zero to ten and back again. These swings might go from one extreme to the other bypassing intermediate stages. The intense emotional reactions of people who have experienced trauma result from a loss of neuromodulation—that is, the ability to regulate moods, which is at the core of posttraumatic stress disorder. "Traumatized people go immediately from stimulus to response without being able to first figure out what makes them so upset. They tend to experience intense fear, anxiety, anger, and panic in response to even minor stimuli. This may lead them to either overreact and intimidate others, or to shut down and freeze" (van der Kolk, van der Hart, and Burbridge 1995).

Numbing of responsiveness/emotional constriction. Numbness and shutdown occur as a defense against overwhelming pain. The result may be a restricted range of affect or lack of authentic expression of emotion. "Aware of their difficulties in controlling their emotions, traumatized people seem to spend their energies on the avoidance of distressing internal sensations, instead of attending to the demands of the environment. In addition, they lose satisfaction in matters that previously gave them a sense of satisfaction and may feel 'dead to the world.' This emotional numbing may be expressed as depression, anhedonia [inability to experience pleasure in normally pleasurable acts] and lack of motivation, psychosomatic reactions, or as dissociative states" (van der Kolk, van der Hart, and Burbridge 1995).

Learned helplessness. Learned helplessness is the feeling that a person can do nothing to affect or change one's own situation. Overwhelmed by the feeling that change will never come or that they can do nothing to change their situation for the better, the trauma survivor simply gives up, remaining passive and inactive, they collapse into helplessness.

Loss of trust and faith. In the case of relationship trauma, one's personal world and the associations within it often become unpredictable and unreliable. The result may be a loss of trust and faith in an orderly world and in relationships. In addition, the concept that one can repair and renew one's own life is undermined (van der Kolk 1987).

Hypervigilence. In a state of hypervigilence, a person experiences a persistent low level of anxiety, always scanning the environment and one's relationships for signs of potential danger or repeated insults and ruptures to one's sense of self. A hypervigilent person may over read signs and signals from other people. Common program phrases used to describe this state are "waiting for the other shoe to drop" and "walking on eggshells" (van der Kolk 1987).

Hyperreactivity. In some ways a combination of many of the previous symptoms, hyperreactivity is a condition in which a person typically overresponds to stress—particularly if that person is feeling vulnerable—they may blow out of proportion conflicts that could be managed reasonably. The brain and body of someone who has experienced a certain level of trauma may become oversensitized to stress. As a result, reactions to stress are intensified.

Depression. As mentioned earlier, one of the results of trauma is deregulation of the part of the nervous system that regulates mood: the limbic system. People with a deregulated emotional system may have trouble handling feelings such as anger, sadness, and fear, which can also contribute to a clinical state of depression. High levels of cortisol, associated with the fight-or-flight response, are also found in people who report feeling depressed. Cortisol is important in helping us get going, we typically have elevated levels in the morning, for example. But stressful lifestyles may be causing too much cortisol to circulate through the body. Notably, working women have shown higher levels in the evening, more than their male partners which may reflect the mother's trying to do two jobs. Production of excessive amounts of cortisol has many possible negative health effects, such as weight gain, thinning hair, bone loss and brittle nails.

Learning difficulties. Trauma's hyper arousal can affect one's ability to attend in the present—that is, to pay attention to one's current circumstances and surroundings. Physiological hyperarousal interferes with the capacity to concentrate and to make sense of, draw meaning from, and learn from current experiences or teaching, thus linking trauma and the possibility of experiencing learning difficulties (van der Kolk, van der Hart, and Burbridge 1995).

Aggression/self-mutilation. Van der Kolk and other researchers have linked the previous experience of trauma to an aggressive personality and a predisposition to self-mutilating activities, such as cutting: "Being abused as a child sharply increases the risk for later delinquency and violent criminal behavior. In one study of eighty seven psychiatric outpatients (van der Kolk et al., 1991) we found that self-mutilators invariably had severe childhood histories of abuse and/or neglect. There is good evidence that self-mutilative behavior is related to [chemical] changes in the secondary [central nervous system, resulting from] early traumatization" (van der Kolk, van der Hart, and Burbridge 1995).

Distorted reasoning. Many people experience trauma within their family unit, rather than from an external source. When one's family unit is spinning out of control, people are prone to adapt all methods of coping mechanisms—whatever they have to do to maintain feelings of connection. Distorted reasoning—which may take the form of rationalizing and justifying bizarre or unusual forms of behavior and relations—can be immature and can also produce core beliefs about life upon which even more distorted reasoning is based. For example, "he is only hitting me because he loves me."

Loss of ability to receive caring and support from others. Based on the characteristics already discussed, this reaction seems almost a natural result. Along with mistrust, hyperreactivity, hyperarousal, depression, and aggression, the numbing response and emotional constriction that are part of the trauma response may lead to the loss of ability to accept caring and support from others. As mistrust grows, so does the ability to accept love and support (van der Kolk 1987).

High-risk behaviors. By engaging in high-risk behaviors such as speeding, sexual acting out, spending beyond one's financial means, fighting, excessive drinking or drugging, or other behaviors done in a way that puts one at risk, trauma victims act out of an intense emotional and psychological pain. Their desire is to alter their mood and stimulate a rush of feel-good body chemicals perhaps in order to replace or cover the pain and suffering that they are experiencing, or perhaps to "jump start" an otherwise numb inner world (van der Kolk 1987).

Survival guilt. A person who escapes from an unhealthy family system while others remain mired within it may experience what is referred to as "survivor's guilt." The guilt one feels of being the one who "got away" while others may not have been able to.

Tendency to isolate. People who have experienced trauma may have a tendency to isolate or to withdraw for safety into a lonely world of their own in order to avoid pain. Reaching out may make them feel too vulnerable or rejection sensitive, or they may be out of touch with their need for connection and support or not know how to bring it into their experience.

Development of rigid psychological defenses. People who feel emotionally, psychologically, or physically wounded and who are not able to address their emotional and psychological pain openly and honestly, may develop rigid psychological defenses to manage their pain. Examples of such defense mechanisms include dissociation, denial, splitting, repression, minimization, intellectualization, idealization and projection.

Reenactment patterns. It is a natural phenomenon of unresolved and unconscious pain that gets recreated over and over again in what psychologists call an attempt to "master pain." Memory is state dependent, so we tend to re-create familiar patterns when confronted with like circumstances. Thus, with intimacy, vulnerability, and dependency acting as memory primers, people who have experienced trauma in past relationships, especially from childhood, may re-create these painful patterns in their adult relationships.

Somatic Disturbances. Because the body processes and holds emotion we may experience our unconscious emotions as somatic disturbances or body issues. Some examples of emotional pain affecting the body are back pain, chronic headaches, muscle tightness or stiffness, stomach problems, heart pounding, headaches, shivering and shaking (van der Kolk 1987).

Memory disturbances and dissociation. In the words of researchers van der Kolk, van der Hart, and Burbridge, "Increased autonomic arousal not only interferes with psychological comfort, anxiety itself also may trigger memories of previous traumatic experiences. Any arousing situation may trigger memories of long-ago traumatic experiences and precipitate reactions that are irrelevant to present demands."

Relationship issues. The effects of relationship trauma tend to reemerge in one's present relationships. Some of the ways that trauma reemerges are through *unconscious transferences,* bringing old dysfunctional patterns of relating from the past into new relationships in the present; *projection,* emotional pain is projected onto another person in an attempt to disown or get rid of it; *hypervigilance,* in which an emotional atmosphere of anxiety and suspicion is created; or being *easily triggered,* hence creating instability and unnecessary pain within the relationship. Mistrust and the loss of ability to take in caring and support from others can also make intimacy challenging.

Traumatic bonding. Traumatic bonds may develop between parent and child or among siblings in alcoholic or dysfunctional homes. For example, parents may coopt a child as their surrogate partner or confident pitting them against their other parent, children may be left to care for each other in ways they are not mature enough to handle, or older siblings may have too much power over their younger siblings. Traumatic bonds tend to repeat themselves throughout the life cycle.

Desire to self-medicate. The use of drugs, alcohol or food to mask and manage a painful inner world or compulsive activities done to excess such as sexual acting out, debting, over spending or gambling may represent misguided attempts to quiet and control a turbulent, troubled inner world. These behaviors represent an obsessive or compulsive desire to achieve a form of pleasure or mood modification that the person feels they cannot achieve on their own in more functional and life enhancing ways. They are self-destructive rather than self-constructive.

Factors That Impact How We Experience Trauma

✦ The ability to escape is central to whether or not we develop PTSD. When we can't get away from a traumatizing circumstance, when we can't "escape," we're more likely to develop long-term effects in what is now called a post-traumatic stress reaction (Wylie 2004).

✦ If a person goes into the instinctual trauma response of dissociation, the likelihood of developing PTSD symptoms is great. Often PTSD takes some months or even years to become full-blown.

✦ The basic genetic makeup of the person—that is, the biological strengths and vulnerabilities we're born with—affect how we experience painful events (Krystal 1968).

✦ The length and severity of the stressor: how long did stressful events persist and how serious were they? (Krystal 1968).

✦ The developmental level of a child or person at the time stressful events were occurring: young children are more vulnerable to being affected by stress than older ones.

✦ The quality of attachment with the mother/parent (Schore 1999): a secure attachment with a parent can act as a buffer to stressful events.

Self-Medicating
Trying to Feel Better Fast

Everything in moderation.

—*Aristotle*

*M*ichael came to group last night raw and frustrated. "Most of my life is going so well," he described, "I'm doing more successful things at work than ever. . . . I'm living my dream. My wife and I are trying to get it together, and it's working. I'm so happy about that. I want to show up for my kids. I want to be a good father." As he was saying this, he made physical movements almost as if he was dodging a cloud of gnats swarming around his head. "But I can't shake this compulsion. I'd say I spend 30 percent of my time obsessing about what other people think of me, reading my performance reviews, manipulating other people to talk about me. When I give talks for work, I ask at least ten people what they thought of me, and I'm convinced that if they don't say they loved my talk, I failed miserably. I'm driving myself crazy, but I can't stop."

Michael is about seventy-three days sober. His two medicators are sexual acting out and alcohol. Between the two, he
previously managed to keep this inner world he describes
from surfacing. He kept both compulsions at a low enough
hum so they didn't destroy either his very active and successful
work life or his family. However, as his behaviors grew worse,
he became gradually unable to manage his life. His relationship with his wife and children began to deteriorate, he got
into serious debt, and his work life was beginning to show signs
of unraveling. His life, in short, was spinning out of control,
and his wife demanded that he seek some help; his family had
had enough. Michael went to treatment, got sober, and began
the long and arduous process of trying to bring his life back in
balance. On the surface, he was taking the steps he could to
restore equilibrium, but his insides hurt. Without his ready
medicators, the needy, wounded part of him was acting up. He
was now *feeling* what he had previously been *medicating*. He was
awake and conscious rather than sedated, and it hurt. He
found himself trying to live a balanced life without balanced
insides.

WHAT IS SELF-MEDICATING,
AND WHY DO WE DO IT?

Self-medication is an attempt to self-administer what
amounts to emotional, psychological, and physiological
painkillers. We self-medicate because we want to feel more
pleasure and less pain. We want to feel better fast, to make
pain that we don't want to feel go away. We achieve inner quiet
through chemical means, or we engage in certain behaviors in
a way that makes them self-medicating, achieving a strong
enough adrenaline rush that we feel no pain. Adrenaline is as
addictive to the brain as cocaine. Certain high-risk behaviors

or behaviors done to excess can become addictive partly because of the makeup of our brain chemistry.

Some of the most common substances used to self-medicate are:

+ alcohol
+ food
+ tobacco
+ drugs

Some of the most common behaviors used to self-medicate are:

+ excessive work
+ high-risk behaviors
+ compulsive exercise
+ excessive busyness/compulsive activity
+ sex
+ gambling/spending

Addictions of all kinds may be seen as misguided attempts to regulate the self. The words "addiction" and "compulsion" have often come to be used interchangeably because they both represent behaviors over which we have little control. Compulsive self-medicating, whether with a substance or a behavior, represents a lack of self-regulation, a lack of emotional sobriety. For example, it's not food itself that's the problem, but our compulsive, unregulated use of food as a mood regulator (e.g., eating too much or too little) that gets us into trouble. It's not work itself that is addictive, but the compulsive manner in which we work that turns it into a problem. Gradually these compulsive uses and abuses come to have a life of their own.

ADDICTION AND THE PREFRONTAL CORTEX

The prefrontal cortex and its role in the process of decision making and hence regulating behavior has become a subject of interest in research circles. The two observations that have caught researchers' interest that apply to the world of addiction are that people with damage to the ventromedial prefrontal cortex (VMF) may be especially prone to impulsive decision making in their daily lives. The other observation of interest is that these same people are impaired on laboratory decision-making tasks that require balancing rewards, punishments, and risk—that is, they don't seem to understand the consequences involved with high-risk, feel-good behaviors the way other people do.

Another study conducted at Harvard Medical School found that patients with frontal lobe damage had a harder time directing their attention to and responding in novel ways to test situations. They also showed greater apathy than the test group without damage.

Studying the neural bases of human decision making has the potential to provide insights into the brain processes underlying self-defeating behaviors or compulsive and acting out behaviors. Trauma, we remember, has the effect of temporarily shutting down the prefrontal cortex.

HOW COMPULSIVE BEHAVIORS COME TO HAVE A LIFE OF THEIR OWN

Compulsive behavior is generally defined as an irresistible urge to perform a certain act, regardless of the rationality of the act. We engage in compulsive behaviors because they can produce a positive and pleasurable mood change. They remove us from our real feelings and provide a form of escape.

We all want to live with the least amount of pain and the most amount of pleasure possible. This is natural and human. But a person who has low self-esteem or unresolved issues that are causing emotional pain, or who has learned that other people are not to be trusted and therefore has difficulty developing healthy relationships, may be more likely to develop compulsive behavior patterns as a way to cope with stress in his or her life. These patterns develop slowly over time.

In the *initial stage*, we're discovering that an activity or behavior, whether drinking, gambling, shopping, or eating, feels good. To begin with, there may be no bad effects from these behaviors, so we repeat them, feeling as if we have found our escape or a solution to feeling out of sorts. The seduction of the behavior lies in its ability to produce good feelings on a consistent basis, allowing escape from problems, pain, or anxiety. In other words, they work to make us "feel better."

The *second stage* of developing a compulsive behavior occurs when the behavior we're engaged in, instead of creating good feelings and providing us with a feeling of comfort and release, begins to create new problems. As our compulsion continues, we may develop some concern and worry about the behavior and our apparent inability to control it. As a result, our self-esteem suffers even more, which may in turn reinforce our compulsive pattern. The more we feel bad or out of control, the more we engage in the compulsive behavior to escape from those feelings.

The *chronic* nature of the behavior is the final stage in this process. In this stage, the compulsive activities are repeated so frequently and continuously that the compulsive behavior is now controlling our lives. What began as a way of gaining a sense of control is now causing us to lose control in very real ways. Our compulsive behavior begins taking priority over friends, family, and self.

WHEN PAINFUL FEELINGS
DON'T GET FELT AND INTEGRATED

Self-medicating is all about not feeling pain, whether that pain is because of a recent breakup, unresolved childhood issues, or low self-esteem. Many people, for example, use substances to manage a level of social anxiety. They discover that a few drinks give them "liquid courage," that sexual exploits make them feel empowered, or that food soothes them or helps them to go numb. But when we medicate our feelings, we don't feel them. And when we don't feel our feelings we don't process them, think about them, and come to understand what's going on inside of us. We don't integrate into our self system the information we would get from understanding what we're feeling. This weakens rather than strengthens the self.

The compulsive person may show a hyperfocused and overcontrolled cognitive style that does not allow for the integration of experience as a whole. Compulsive busyness or work, for example, can be a way of shutting out a painful inner world. Or the compulsive person may intellectualize her emotions because feeling them feels too scary. She is looking for an intellectual solution, an insight, a magic bullet to make pain disappear or to represent a miraculous solution to problems. Compulsive people don't have a relaxed style of processing what's going on in their lives or their inner worlds. This hyperfocused processing style, in which the compulsive person can take only a myopic view of their world, can also mean that they aren't able to adequately process, integrate, and resolve their feelings of pain, shame, and remorse around their compulsive uses and abuses. This may make them feel even more desperate and out of control, which can lead to more use and abuse. It further undermines the compulsive person's ability to reflect on their own behavior and make the changes necessary to get into better habits. Medicating feelings rather than feeling them is a vicious circle. Compulsive behavior leads to life complications, and life complications lead to increased use and abuse.

HOW WE SEEK PLEASURE AND AVOID PAIN

Evolution has selected our most intense and powerfully motivated behaviors from those actions that have proven beneficial to the survival of our species. To ensure that we continue to do these beneficial behaviors and to ensure that we do them a lot, nature has evolved specialized systems in the brain that work to give us pleasure each and every time that we engage in these activities.

Reward and Punishment

The brain operates on a reward and punishment system: it rewards behaviors that it wishes to encourage, and it punishes behaviors that it wishes to discourage.

The two major pathways in the brain that activate these "helpful" or "unhelpful" behaviors are the reward circuit, which is part of the medial forebrain bundle (MFB), and the punishment circuit, or periventricular system (PVS).

The MFB pathway or circuit operates through the desire/action/satisfaction cycle. The PVS pathway or circuit operates through the successful fight-or-flight response. Together, they form what's referred to as our behavioral approach/avoidance system (BAS).

Finding Healthy Ways to "Feel Good"

There is no use in fighting nature. Because we're wired to want to seek pleasure and avoid pain, we need to learn healthy and life-enhancing ways of giving ourselves pleasure and efficient and intelligent ways of managing pain.

Studies done on both animals and humans have shown that stimulation of the reward bundle produces an intense pleasure that some researchers have associated with that experienced during sex and orgasm. Stories exchanged by researchers anecdotally even suggest that some of the animals in these experiments have developed strong feelings of attraction for the researchers in charge. The research implies that the same stimuli that reinforce behavior in animals also produce intense pleasure in humans.

This desire/action/satisfaction cycle is clearly at the base of all sorts of what we might refer to as addictive or self-medicating types of behaviors. We have a desire perhaps to feel better; then we learn an action that leads to the satisfaction of that desire. The more consistently that action leads to the state we want to achieve—the more it wipes away pain, regulates our mood, and makes us feel good—the more we want to do it. This is how compulsive behaviors take hold in the brain. They are highly rewarded, working with our own brain chemistry to make us feel good.

Here is a key point in understanding the link between addictive behaviors and the reward system. When a particular behavior is rewarded with feel-good chemicals, that behavior becomes reinforced. This is called "positive reinforcement." Dog trainers offer a kibble to their pups whenever the pups perform successfully the behavior the trainer is teaching them. People like kibbles too. Addiction is all about getting bonded to kibbles that eventually make you sick. Recovery is about just the opposite.

Psychologists also use the term "negative reinforcement" to refer to eliminating a behavior we wish to stop. Antabuse would be negative reinforcement because that medication makes the addict sick when they drink. Losing a job, spouse, friends, family, or money are negative reinforcements when it comes to addictive substances or behaviors. Feeling overweight and unable to wear what we'd like to wear or do what we'd like to do is a negative reinforcement when it comes to overeating. Going into debt is a negative reinforcement for compulsive spending or gambling. Getting caught in compromising behaviors or having brushes with the law are negative reinforcements for sexual acting out.

Learning alternative methods for creating what we might call "natural highs" is key in turning addictive/compulsive behavior around and achieving emotional sobriety. We need to know how to satisfy our natural desire to feel good in functional, life-enhancing ways rather than dysfunctional and debilitating ones. We need to learn how to make ourselves feel good, how to soothe ourselves and come into a state of balance and well-being without the use of mind-altering chemicals or behaviors.

If we have issues with self-medicating, regaining control of our lives begins with recognizing our compulsive tendencies. Our desire to control these tendencies reflects a self-affirming step toward personal growth and greater self-awareness. The actions we take toward this goal gradually build self-esteem. We need to understand that our negative behaviors developed slowly and over time, and that some of the issues that we are self-medicating may have begun as far back as childhood. Our solution will also be slow and require long-term commitment.

REREGULATING THE LIMBIC SYSTEM: BOTH THE BODY AND MIND NEED HEALING

I am constantly hearing clients say things like, "Why isn't this over yet?" or "I know I should be past this." But we don't leave our bodies behind when we grow up. We bring them right with us into adulthood. We live in them, sleep in them, eat in them, and love in them. Our bodies contain a sort of neurological template that informs and guides us, a flesh-and-bones root system from which we flower into life. In addition to bringing our compulsive uses and abuses into balance, we will need to address the issues that got us to abuse in the first place. This may be childhood pain, interpersonal problems, or a deregulated limbic system.

Changing habits of thinking, feeling, and behavior doesn't happen overnight. These habits have become part of our neural wiring and have been laid down over a period of years. Physical mechanisms or sensory impressions are what produce our experience of the world, and we need new sets of physical impressions to change or alter those impressions (Lewis et al. 2000). We need to log the hours in healing activities and relationships that will, over time, create new wiring. That takes time. This is what a new design for living is all about. We create the life that will give us a new body to live in, a new neural network that allows us to tolerate painful or uncomfortable feelings without blowing up or acting out. Part of strengthening our limbic systems is to learn new and healthy ways to self-soothe and to bring ourselves into balance.

$\mathcal{R}$esilience

Thriving in Spite of the Odds

The truth is, young people are not saved by
bureaucrats sitting behind desks
in Washington, D.C., or, for that matter,
Atlanta, Georgia. They're saved one at a time by
people like you, by volunteers in churches
and boys clubs, and by teachers and coaches in
schools. And most importantly, they're saved at
home. Abraham Lincoln said it simply,
"The hand that rocks the cradle rules the world."

—*James O. Mason, U.S. Assistant Secretary for Health, 1991*

*W*hen I was in fifth grade, my family was probably on
its last year of anything that resembled itself. We
were treading water, losing our grip on the rest of
the world, and sliding into a drunken sort of oblivion, with our
father leading the charge and our mother running after him

with the keys, his sport coat, and his tie.

When my fifth-grade teacher announced that we needed to bring toothpicks to school on Wednesday, I asked her what we should do if we didn't have any toothpicks, if we'd run out a year ago, for example, and hadn't had them around for a while. She said not to worry, everyone had toothpicks. I knew differently. I went home anyway, armed with this knowledge about everyone always having toothpicks, and went basically nowhere with it. My teacher apparently hadn't come from an alcoholic family. An audience with my mother at that point was about as hard to come by as an audience with the pope, and Dad was "not available" that particular week. He was lost somewhere in his addiction, which could mean anything from passed out to simply too preoccupied with his next drink to focus on anything else, and Mom was too preoccupied with him to focus on anything else. I tried to talk up to her height through the fog of frustration that surrounded her constantly and ask her if we had any toothpicks.

"Look in the kitchen drawer, we may have some colored ones."

"I looked. There weren't any there."

"Then look in the dinette cupboard, maybe you'll find some."

"None there either. I tried."

"Then I have no idea. Put them on the shopping list."

"We need them by Wednesday."

"Oh."

So, having gotten nowhere, which was where I had expected to get, I tried to figure out what to do that wouldn't get me in trouble but would fill the assignment. I went to my Dad's shirt drawer, for years a reliable source of cardboard. I took a shirt cardboard and cut it into tons of little strips. When we were asked to take out toothpicks on Wednesday, I pulled out my little cardboard sticks and hoped that I would somehow become invisible. Instead, Poufie, our fifth-grade teacher, came over to my desk and asked me why I didn't have toothpicks. I said we didn't have any, so this is what I thought of. Poufie maybe had the picture, as I was the third Barbatsis girl she'd had in her grade. We all loved her and she loved all of us. She held up my little cardboard sticks much to my mortification. If she'd loved the Barbatsis girls, this might be the day all that ended. I might be breaking that happy tradition, along with so many others that seemed to be dying out around me.

"Class, look here for a minute" *(Deliver me, God, teleport me out of this fifth-grade class into the cosmos anywhere else, the dark side of the moon, even)*. "Class, I want you to see an example of what we call resourcefulness" *(What's resourcefulness, God?)*. "Tian's mother didn't have any toothpicks, so Tian cut these little cardboard sticks out of cardboard, and she can do the assignment just as well. Tian was being resourceful" *(Thank you, God, for helping me to be resourceful instead of an idiot, which was probably the other possibility)*. The other girls' toothpicks looked a lot better at the end of the exercise, not bent and crinkly like mine, but Poufie had elevated me to a new level. If my family was falling apart and I couldn't depend on them the way I used to, maybe I could be this new thing called resourceful. Thank you, Poufie.

Unusual upbringings can and often do create unusual strengths—which we need to pay attention to during our recoveries, along with identifying pathological dynamics. Over the past two decades I have witnessed the mental health field and, more specifically, the field of addictions go through many organic changes. In the 1980s, we probably overpathologized the family of origin, specifically parents, and neglected to sufficiently look at other factors such as siblings, family order, and culture. There was perhaps an overemphasis on feeling all of our negative emotions, as if that would lead to a sort of automatic healing. But studies of those who thrive, in spite of conditions that would put many under, reveal that many factors go into creating resilience. While it is critical to go back and rework significant issues as we've discussed throughout this book, focusing exclusively on the negative qualities of others and the damage others wreak can have the adverse effect of weakening the self rather than strengthening it. It can create the illusion that if we can get everything right on the outside, happiness will inevitably follow, or that if we can identify our needs and state them clearly, they will always be met. But life and relationships are much more complex than this. Life may still not conform to our idea of what it should be, even when we state our needs clearly and confidently, share our feelings with all "I" statements, or forgive those who have hurt us. We may still go through hard times. What we want to learn to identify and develop is the resilience that is necessary to thrive and even become stronger, better people through adverse as well as good times. The truth is probably more like: happiness comes to those who see beauty in things as they are without requiring life to meet them on their terms, but living, as we say in the program, "life on life's terms." Happiness seems to follow those who have "an inborn sense that life will work out," who look around them and see not only what is missing but what is there.

Overly sheltered childhoods can actually undermine resilience. Ever wonder why the guy who seemed to have life handed to him on a silver platter spills it? Does he not appreciate all his good fortune, taking it for granted, and tossing it over? Is he spoiled or lazy? Well, think about it. Emotional and psychological muscles are a lot like leg muscles. We need to walk on them in order to strengthen them. The little child who is overattended to by a coterie of nannies, who are paid to keep him happy by removing any obstacles, may not be learning the basics: to tolerate frustration, to share, to read the social signals from other kids. Kids who are busily engaged in play have no interest in adapting their world to little Jimmy and will demand from him that he adapt himself to the situation if he wants to stay in the game. So will teachers who are managing and balancing the needs of many kids at once. And eventually the work force will require that he be a team player. Social isolation does not build the skills of resilience. For growing kids, a little hardship that they can overcome may be more developmentally valuable than a seemingly perfect world that they can control. And to add to a weakening of the self, they may be spending too little time with the people they want to be with most, namely, their parents, and too much time forming strong attachments to people who can be fired or may quit. Further, they may live in a sort of splendid isolation, an empty world filled with high expectations, but lacking in the family support to develop the strength to meet them.

Resilient Qualities of ACOAs

Neural plasticity allows us to constantly improve ourselves in both body and mind throughout our lives. We can do so much to make life better. Part of making ourselves better is to consciously build new strengths, and the other part is to identify and build on the strengths we already have. One silver lining of family dysfunction is that we're not necessarily surrounded by models we feel we can't live up to, which can actually free us up to take risks to improve our lives because we're less ingrained in patterns and molds that are working "well enough."

Those who have lived with relationship trauma can develop qualities that Wolin and Wolin (1993) identify as associated with resilience. They may develop strategies for managing chaos that can become real assets in life if they can work through their downside. The *inventiveness* of those who have thrived in spite of the odds can be quite remarkable in dealing with problems. Because we have had to think outside the box to solve complex family situations, we can be highly *creative* and original, which are real assets both at home and in the workplace. This group has also had to develop *courage* and grit. We don't expect to be handed things and have long ago absorbed the reality that we don't always get just what we want in life, that life isn't always fair. Those who grew up with emotional trauma can sometimes be quite *dogged*, working hard even if the rewards are not always forthcoming. People for whom life has always gone smoothly tend to expect that to continue. This has both an upside and a downside. The upside is that they don't expect problems; they can let life work out without sabotaging it. The downside is that problems might throw them. Adults who have grown up with relationship trauma are used to problems; in fact, we may thrive on them and manage crisis very well. Remember that "normal," not crisis, hard for the ACOA or the adult child of relationship trauma. Crisis is what has come to feel normal.

Humor is another asset that those from problematic backgrounds often develop. Out-of-the-ordinary circumstances we have had to cope with can give us a real sense of the fringe of life. Our humor can be hilariously zany, biting, or insightful. We have used humor for very specific reasons: to manage the unmanageable, to lighten the family's emotional load by breaking tension, and to find alternative ways of bonding and feeling good. Norman Cousins refers to laughter as "inner jogging." Laughter is good for the soul and the body.

Many ACOAs and adult children of relationship trauma have learned to be *self-reliant* and *independent.* We have had to make decisions on our own and manage in the absence of parental assistance or sometimes even for our parents. ACOAs can be very *loyal.* We know what it feels like to be left out in the cold, and our own need for caring and protective bonds may make us loyal. Lastly, many ACOAs develop deep, *spiritual* lives. We learn compassion from seeing the other side of life. Life has brought us to our knees, and we have looked to other sources for support. As authority figures in our families became less available to depend on, we may have turned to a Higher Source, one that is outside of the human realm, for a sense of guidance, comfort, and security. In other words, we can be deeply spiritual people.

Problems, if they don't sink us, deepen us. We develop *insight* and *wisdom* from meeting life on life's terms rather than asking that it meet us on our terms, as we recognize the strengths and limitations of those we love or need and move beyond them. *Morality* is often developed as much from seeing what should not be done as what should. Those who have been wounded can have clear life lessons on what hurts and can feel determined to try not to hurt others as they have been hurt or even to dedicate parts of their own lives to helping others.

ATTITUDES OF RESILIENT PEOPLE

Resilient people, according to *The Resilient Self: How Survivors of Troubled Families Rise Above Adversity,* by Wolin and Wolin (1993), tend not to let adversity define them. They often move their lives forward by establishing goals for themselves, reaching them and moving beyond them, continually marshaling their strengths and propelling themselves out of their present circumstances. Additionally, they see their problems as a temporary rather than a permanent state of affairs and tend not to globalize; they find reasons and ways— whether religious, creative, or just good common sense—to place a temporary framework and perspective around the problems in their lives. Resilient people have the capacity to see beyond themselves into a different kind of life. They have an inborn feeling that life will work out. My own more resilient clients often report relatives, neighbors, and even television shows that showed them a different way to live. And when they saw it, they somehow believed it was possible for them too.

Wolin defines resiliency as the capacity to rise above adversity, to be hurt and rebound at the same time, to keep hacking away at the thorny underbrush and moving through life. Victor Frankl, in what is arguably one of the finest examples of rising above circumstances, developed his own, very unique understanding of the meaning and purpose of life in the most dire and forbidding of circumstances. During World War II Frankl was interned at Auschwitz, Dachau, and other concentration camps. Amazingly, even in these forbidding circumstances, Frankl was able to track and reflect on a distinct manner of adaptation that inmates experienced in response to the incredibly harsh conditions of life in the camps. There was a pervasive and understandable emotional numbing that occurred. But even in these cruel conditions, he saw that inmates with a sense of purpose, with loved ones whom they believed they would see again, or with unfinished tasks that they felt compelled to complete survived better and longer than their counterparts without them. Frankl noted that "a man who becomes conscious of the responsibility he bears toward a human being who affectionately waits for him, or to an unfinished work, will never be able to throw away his life. He knows the 'why' for his existence, and will be able to bear almost any 'how.'"

Frankl turned questions on the how and why of survival around in order to find meaning in what most would consider a hopeless world. Ultimately, he explained his incredibly courageous and generous attitude toward life in this manner:

> It did not really matter what we expected from life, but rather what life expected from us. We needed to stop asking about the meaning of life, and instead to think of ourselves as those who were being questioned

by life—daily and hourly. Our answer must consist, not in talk and meditation, but in right action and in right conduct. Life ultimately means taking the responsibility to find the right answer to its problems and to fulfill the tasks which it constantly sets for each individual. (Frankl 1959)

Frankl's ability to self-reflect allowed him to create his own meaning in life, to conceive and come up with this incredibly resilient strategy to manage life and sustain a sense of self in the most horrific of circumstances.

Resilient people do have emotional and psychological scars that they carry from their experience. They indeed struggle, but they keep going, staying engaged with life and continue to function as a part of the world. Resilience is not the ability to escape unharmed. It is the ability to thrive in spite of the odds.

QUALITIES OF RESILIENT PEOPLE

Resilience, Wolin and Wolin (1993) observe, seems to develop out of the challenge to maintain self-esteem. Troubled families can make their children feel at fault or bad about themselves. But resilient children find ways to feel good about themselves and life in spite of powerful influence to the contrary. They understand that everything is not their fault, that there are other forces at work beyond them, and they are not to blame for all that goes awry. They tend to internalize their successes, taking responsibility for what goes right in their lives. The research on resilience helps to counter what Wolin refers to as the "damage" model, or the idea that if you've had a troubled childhood, you are condemned to a troubled adulthood or you are operating without strengths. In fact, resilience helps us to understand that adversity can actually develop strength.

But resilient people don't operate alone. They tend to have engaging personalities from birth and have the natural capacity to attract mentors to them. One of the cardinal findings of resilience research is that those who lacked strong family support systems growing up sought and received help from others—perhaps a relative, a teacher, a neighbor, the parents of peers, or eventually a spouse. Those who thrived had one secure bonded relationship, usually within the family system. Resilient people are able to talk about their own hard times with someone who cares, who can help, or who will listen.

In their research, Wolin and Wolin discovered that resilient children tended to have the following characteristics:

+ They had likable personalities from birth that attracted parents, surrogates, and mentors to want to care for them. They were naturally adept recruiters of support and interest from others, and they drank up attention, care, and support from wherever they could get it.

+ They tended to be of at least average intelligence, reading on or above grade level.

+ Few had another child born within two years of their birth.

+ Virtually all of the children had at least one person with whom they had developed a strong relationship, often from the extended family or a close community member.

+ Often they report having an inborn feeling that their lives were going to work out.

+ They can identify the illness in their family and are able to find ways to distance themselves from it; they don't let the family dysfunction destroy them.

+ They work through their problems but don't tend to make that a lifestyle.

+ They take active responsibility for creating their own successful lives.

✦ They tend to have constructive attitudes toward themselves and their lives.

✦ They tend not to fall into self-destructive lifestyles.

Wolin and Wolin in studying resilient adults found that they tended to:

✦ Find and build on their own strength.

✦ Improve deliberately and methodically on their parents' lifestyles.

✦ Marry consciously into happy, healthy, and/or strong families.

✦ Fight off memories of horrible family get-togethers and create new, more satisfying holidays.

✦ Live outside a "magic two-hundred-mile" radius from their families of origin, enabling them to be connected but somewhat apart from the daily fray of potential family dysfunction.

Researchers found that the price these people tended to pay were:

✦ Stress-related illnesses.

✦ A certain degree of aloofness in their interpersonal relationships.

HOW CAN I FOSTER RESILIENCE IN MYSELF?

Recently I did a large psychodrama workshop. We began with a couple of experiential warm-ups in order to bring the group together and to see who wanted to become the protagonist, to explore their issues in more depth. Three people said they'd like to do a drama that evening. I asked each person to

say a few sentences about what work they'd do if they were chosen by the group. The group members listened carefully and
then walked up and stood next to the person whose work drew
them, the person with whom they felt identification. All three
people had lots of choices and support from the group. We
started with the protagonist who received the most identifying
choices, and it became rather involved. Most of the drama was
internal; the protagonist chose people to represent aspects of
herself like her own fear, for example, and her own resistance.
After the first drama came to closure, we had a little time to do
a short vignette with the person chosen to be second. The second drama was quite brief but still went well, and much was
accomplished for the protagonist. When this drama came to
closure, we spent the rest of the workshop letting the group
share with the protagonists.

All three possible protagonists shared. The first person,
Katherine, had felt challenged and somewhat surprised by the
depth of the work she had done. The second person said, "I
was getting so much out of Katherine's work that I wasn't sure
I could even do my own, but it worked really well for me." I
asked him what he meant. "Well, all of the dynamics she was
playing out, my head was spinning I was identifying so much. I
could really see myself and the way I deal with things, in her
work." One of the qualities that Wolin and Wolin (1993) found
resilient children have is the ability to soak up support and
attention even surreptitiously. If it's around, they use it. Chuck
was expressing a variation on that quality; he was able to learn
from what was available and make use of it for himself. Last,
Karen expressed that she hadn't really been able to pay much
attention to anything because she was upset she hadn't gotten
to work. "It's the story of my life. I don't get chosen. I get
screwed over." Neither Chuck nor Karen were necessarily
going to get to work, but they were both highly chosen and
supported by the group. Chuck absorbed that support, let go

of his need to be the protagonist that evening, and opened himself to the rest of the work that was very absorbing. He wound up getting so much out of Katherine's work that he could apply to himself that he felt he'd already come away with plenty from the workshop. Karen became stuck in her feeling that it was all just happening all over, that her life script was just being played out again. She wasn't able to take in the support and choice she did have, and she seemed to get nothing out of the work that went on the rest of the evening. She went away angry and empty.

While both Chuck's and Karen's responses are completely understandable, one is more resilient than the other. The world doesn't run after us to make sure we get all our needs met. I have little doubt that Karen has good reason for feeling as she does, but one of the tragedies of relationship trauma is that it can make us unable to take in caring and support from others, with the result that we reject the good that may be coming our way. I can surely try to meet Karen's need to work and help her to get loose of the life script of always being the victim, which is, in fact, keeping her a victim. But the world probably won't. I can help to get her ready to meet life on life's terms so that she can make use of opportunities without sabotaging them, but the world may not. While Chuck needs help with his chronic feelings of depression, he is already successful in the world of work, and he is working things out with his wife and children. The world favors joiners; it tends to come to those who are willing to jump in and make use of what it offers. It favors those who adjust and adapt to it rather than the opposite.

We can consciously develop the kinds of qualities that will allow us to make use of the world we already live in and the opportunities that may already be surrounding us. Following are some suggestions of ways that you can develop resilience.

Reframe life issues. Reframing is at the heart of resilience.

Resilient people use it as a way of seeing the glass as half full rather than half empty, seeing life as a challenge rather than taking a defeatist attitude toward it. Wolin sees this reframing as central to "survivor's pride."

Don't avoid life. Learning to tolerate small amounts of stress and manage them builds resilience both in children and adults. Retreating from life and playing it safe so that we can avoid pain doesn't teach us how to handle it and move along. It can actually make problems get larger rather than smaller in our heads.

Get honest with yourself. Be willing to ask yourself penetrating questions and answer them honestly.

Take meaningful actions. Remember initiative. Take charge of your life and take meaningful, sensible actions toward ensuring your present and future. We build emotional and psychological strength just the same way we build a muscle: slowly, steadily, and daily.

Find and maintain relationships. Relationships actually foster resilience. Do what's necessary to find and maintain a solid network of relationships.

Look for the lessons. All situations have lessons and silver linings. Looking for the lessons is a way of seeing life as a challenging journey of unfoldment. It allows us to use the circumstances of our lives to grow from, as well as to build strength and self-esteem.

Develop inner resources, strengthen your inner self. When we mobilize through recovery, we are consciously developing inner strength and mastery. We are learning a language of emotional literacy that allows us to take on more of life.

Work through past issues. Unresolved issues from the past can interfere with our ability to have successful relationships in the present. Take active steps to work through those issues so the past can be understood and integrated and lessons can be learned that help us in the present.

Maintain good boundaries. Keep your desired life and way of being in front of your eyes and don't get into situations or even conversations and thinking patterns that head you down a self-destructive path.

Stay away from "victim thinking." We need to understand that we may not have been to blame for being children in painful homes. However, we need to guard against getting too comfortable in the victim role. Change doesn't happen by accident. Victim thinking can become entitled thinking and can interfere with our motivation toward change.

Find other family models. Resilient children seek out other types of families as models. They often spend time with and marry into strong family networks.

$\mathcal{M}$ind/Body Memories

The Dynamics of Conscious and Unconscious Memory

We cannot change anything unless we accept it.
Condemnation does not liberate, it oppresses.

—Carl Jung

I t can be difficult to wrap one's mind around the idea of an
unconscious—that there are, indeed, parts of ourselves
that are outside of our conscious awareness that nonetheless have significant impact over how we operate in our lives.
Hopefully, when you read about the dynamics of memory, the
concept of an unconscious that drives our thinking, feeling,
and behavior will become clearer.

THE THREE TYPES OF MEMORY: IMPLICIT, EXPLICIT, AND SENSORY

There are essentially three forms of memory, *implicit* or
unconscious memory, *explicit* or *conscious* memory, and *sensory* or

body/kinesthetic memory. Much of our childhood experience becomes part of our *implicit* (unconscious) memory and our *sensory* (body) memory.

Our families are our first classroom on relationships. The lessons we learn in the arena of family relationships become sewn into the very fabric of our conscious, unconscious, and biological selves. This self, as it were, comes with us into our lives and affects our patterns of relating. When we meet someone with whom we want to pursue a deeper connection, for example, what part of us knows that they are a fit with us? Or when we take care of our children, why do we act as we do?

Explicit memory includes all that we are fully aware of, like directions to a restaurant, a recent conversation with a friend, or an article in the newspaper. Most research around memory has focused on explicit memory. Research subjects, for example, might be asked to memorize a tray of items, a list of words, or a collection of small objects and then recall them verbally or to recollect a situation or conversation. These test our conscious memory, what we observe consciously and can recall at will. The cortex or the thinking/reasoning part of the brain is involved in *explicit* memory. We remember something because we have elevated it to a conscious level. We're aware of what we're trying to recall.

Implicit memory, on the other hand, is the kind of memory that we are not aware of, but that nevertheless influences our thinking, feeling, and behavior. Advertising is based on the principle of implicit memory. Throughout the day, we're bombarded by media messages that are more or less beneath the level of our awareness. Then when we go shopping, even though we may think our choices of shoes, laundry detergent, or blue jeans are not influenced by these images that have worked themselves down into our memory storage, research reveals otherwise. Experiments have shown that when we're in a store and have to choose among similar products, we tend to buy the ones that have been featured in ads.

One of the best known of the various types of implicit memory is called procedural or kinesthetic memory, which is basically the memory of movement. Procedural memory enables us to acquire motor skills and gradually improve them, like when we learn how to ride a bike. Procedural memory is part of sensory or body memory. It involves proprioception, our sense of being alive and functioning within our environment. It is largely unconscious, not in the Freudian sense of repressed memories, but because it is made up of automatic sensory motor behaviors that are so deeply embedded within our memory systems that we are no longer even aware of them. Psychiatric patients with profound amnesia often retain their procedural memory, which argues for a system of separate neural pathways. While they may not remember who they are, for example, they can still raise a fork to their mouth to eat or tie their shoes.

Sensory memory, what we pick up through our senses, is essential to our overall ability to perceive what's around us. Sensory awareness and memory provide us with a gestalt or an overall impression of the unity of our environment. Sensory memory does not require our conscious attention. Our senses pick up information "automatically" and then place it in our short-term memory storage. If sensory information gets downloaded into our long-term storage, through repeated exposures, it becomes part of what we might call nonconscious memory. Implicit and sensory memory systems are the storehouse for our conditioned responses and reflexes, our knee-jerk reactions. They are why, if you were hit by your parent as a child, you might hit your child when you become a parent. Sensory memory also explains why people who have been traumatized, sexually abused, or hit repeatedly can sometimes describe bright colors, smells, or body sensations, but they can't really piece together, order, and make sense of the situation. This is why their trauma-related memories are spotty. The thinking part of their brain may have shut down at the time of the trauma so they never wove together the various elements of their experience into a coherent picture, but their sensory memory was being stimulated and functioned normally. Their body may remember the sensation and their mind the context, but their thinking mind doesn't know exactly how it all connects.

PRIMING: HOW OUR KNEE-JERK REACTIONS GET JERKED

Conditioned Emotional Responses

We are constantly forming implicit and sensory memories without being aware that we are doing so. When attempting to study such memories because they live beneath the level of our awareness, scientists often try to uncover them by indirect methods, called "priming."

Our human memories are primarily associative. That is why we remember a new piece of information better when we can associate it with a piece of knowledge that we've previously acquired and which is already firmly anchored in our memory. The priming experience can be sensorial—a smell, sight, or feel of something—or it can be a word that reminds us of another word, like "dog"/"cat" or "soft"/"silky." Test subjects will remember the word "north" faster if they see the word "south" as a priming word. If testors use nonsense words such as "nana" as primers, memory will not happen as well. The more meaningful the association is to us personally, the stronger our association.

Memory Is a Mental Reconstruction: Reframing, Changing the Construction

Interestingly, contrary to the image that many of us have of memory being a vast collection of archived data, most of our memories are actually reconstructions. They are not stored in our brains in clear paragraphs, images, or even permanent constructions. Consequently, whenever we want to remember something, we have to reconstruct it each and every time from elements scattered throughout various areas of our brains. That's why scientists now view remembering not as a simple retrieval of fixed records, but rather as an ongoing process of reclassification resulting from a series of continuous changes in our neural pathways and our parallel processing of the information stored within our brains. In recovery we learn to "reframe" past experiences. As the adult in us replays a situation from childhood either in our minds or through role-play, we see the childhood situation through adult eyes. As we do this, we may come to see it differently. As we reframe, we are making new mental constructions so that we actually remember things differently. This puts scientific data behind the recovery expression, "it's never too late to have a happy childhood." Through reframing we actually reprioritize memory; we see the same situation through different eyes as we reinterpret events of childhood through our adult minds.

Traumatic Memories

When we have a traumatic experience, the implicit memory systems of our amygdala and the explicit memory systems of our hippocampus each record different aspects of the event that is frightening us. This is why we are able to recall some parts of the event while others remain trapped in our unconscious.

But the hippocampus provides the context for these memories. The hippocampus specializes in processing groupings of stimuli rather than simply individual stimuli—in other words, the context of a situation. Hence, because of the hippocampus and its close connections with the amygdala, the entire context associated with a traumatic event can provoke anxiety. When the amygdala registers danger and fear, the hippocampus can make everything associated with the scary situation scary. If a child fears a policeman because one arrested her father, a policeman may always be scary even when trying to help. Memories get generalized. A loud sound, like the slamming of a door, can barely disturb one person who has no particular negative associations with it, while it sends another person, who grew up with rage, door slamming, and abuse into an anxious state. Our association with the sound, not the sound itself, becomes a problem and triggers our fear response. If a wife was sexually abused in a particular way, being again touched in that way or in that part of the body by her husband can cause her to freeze up all over again, even though other parts of her body might enjoy being touched or the idea of sex generally seems appealing. Lying on her back or engaging in foreplay may be a trigger. Or sex may provoke feelings of guilt, rage, or an urge to fight or flee, to take the action that was denied to her as a child.

Deconditioning Emotional Triggers

Beverly shudders when there is arguing and tension in our group. It makes her want to run out of the room. Even in group therapy, elevated voices and conflict make her shake inside because they trigger her fear that they will lead to what conflict led to in her own home, namely slamming doors, hitting, tears, and isolation. In other words, if pieces of her past reappear in her present, she assumes the rest will follow; her unconscious wants to fill in the rest of the picture, with its associated context.

The cortex, or the thinking part of Beverly's brain, can learn that there is nothing to fear if Beverly is willing to sit through these group conflicts, feel the anxiety they bring up in her, and talk about what she is feeling as she is feeling it. Major connections to the amygdala come from the medial prefrontal cortex. Through these brain pathways, we can use our thinking minds to recondition our fear response. We can reframe the past and bring it up to date with the present; we can learn new ways of thinking, feeling, and behaving. This is one way that we use our thinking mind to bring our feeling mind into balance. Our thinking mind helps us to elevate the experiences of our sensory and implicit memories into conscious thought. Our more highly evolved mental structure—our thinking, reasoning cortex—is what allows us to manage our system of rapid, automatic responses.

Priming: Remembering the Forgotten Known

When we become adults and create our own homes, the very acts of setting up house, having children, and raising a family are "priming" experiences for our past experiences.

Early memories get restimulated in a variety of ways. Perhaps they are being warmed up because we are entering into an intimate relationship as an adult where feelings of closeness, dependence, and vulnerability stimulate experiences associated with emotional intimacy in our childhood relationships. Another common trigger is parenting. We reverse roles and become the parent rather than the child. We play out what we learned in the role of child through our role as parents. Another powerful trigger is what is referred to as an *age correspondence reaction*; when our children's age (and their feelings and actions at that age) stimulate memories of our own experiences from around that time in our own life. Still another trigger can be the work environment, which can stimulate issues related to authority and collegiality.

A trigger that is part of the healing process is recovery itself. During recovery, we "remember" what we have "forgotten." For a moment it hurts all over again. But if we can get through that reexperiencing of the pain with the help of a solid recovery support network, there is freedom on the other side. Actually the fear of the pain is often worse than the pain itself.

Most people feel relieved and renewed when they can reawaken the parts of themselves they have shut down. It is not easy, but it is worth the work, because when we unblock our ability to feel painful feelings in the context of intimacy, we also unblock our ability to love, to care and be cared for, to be vulnerable and find strength in that vulnerability. We stop blocking everything associated with close connection. In this way intimate relationships can be a path to a better us. We become adept at experiencing more of who we are and more of who another person is. This ability makes us more available to all of life. It builds self-confidence and inner strength.

The Stabilizing Effect of Intimate Relationships

Only in relationships can you know yourself,
not in abstraction and certainly not in isolation.
The movement of behavior is the sure guide
to yourself, it's the mirror of your consciousness,
this mirror will reveal its content,
the images, the attachments, the fears,
the loneliness, the joy, the sorrow.
Poverty lies in running away from this.

—*J. Krishnamurti*

I remember taking Alex to the playground when we lived in London. He was just under a year and a half old. The moment we arrived, he began his routine. First he placed his folded arm on my crossed legs, leaning against them as if they were a coffee table as he perused the scene at the playground. After a couple of minutes he headed out for his first excursion, say, to the big slide, a group of children playing with a toy that appealed to him, or maybe just a slow walk across the sand. Once he'd arrived at his destination, whether the top of the slide, the branch of a tree, or settled in the midst of a group of children, he would turn around, get me in his line of vision, and wave or look. Eventually, maybe twenty minutes or so later, he'd come back, lean against my legs to "refuel," and then the whole thing would start all over again.

The British psychoanalyst John Bowlby spent his life studying mother/infant attachment and separation. He studied what a secure child looks like and the stages of loss that child goes through when separated from those to whom he is attached. Securely attached children, he observed, are more likely to embrace small challenges than those who are insecurely attached. It concerned him that adult attachment was little studied, and that being deeply dependent in our adult relationships was even sometimes viewed as regressive. He felt this was an unfortunate view of one of life's great stabilizers— that, in fact, we benefit from and need a secure base throughout our lives.

Adults are really not much different from children when it comes to needing deep attachments. We all need to feel as if we belong somewhere, as if we have a place to call home. Stable relationships offer us the courage and freedom to take little forays into the world knowing that we can return to our secure base. Here's a bit of research that studies an adult version of the pattern I described with Alex. Couples were asked to spend time talking about the hopes, dreams, and ambitions they had for their own lives. The researchers found that the more empathic and supportive the couples were when listening to each other, the more each member of the partnership was inclined to take on increasingly complex life challenges. The reverse was also true. The more controlling or unsupportive each person was, the more their partner was likely to minimize or give up on trying to accomplish their dreams. Controlling behavior apparently carried with it an implicit lack of faith in the abilities of the other partner and their ability to actualize their own plans. It had the effect of undermining their self-confidence and resolve. Supportive couples, on the other hand, experience a positive ripple effect in other areas of their lives.

The family is that arena where our passions run wild. Jealousy, deep love, rage, and forgiveness entwine themselves in and around family systems. In them we become our best and our worst selves. When we try to live only in the light, pretending our baser instincts and emotions aren't there, we foreclose not only on our pain, but on our joy and creativity as well. We deny ourselves the possibility of spinning straw into gold; of mining our darkness for our own, unique illuminations and light; and of using our creative intelligence to see life circumstances through an inspired lens.

Learning to use our relationships as mirrors that cast light onto our own inner world turns them into a journey of spirit. It allows us to use them to grow, to expand our understanding of ourselves and others, and to become better, more balanced, and fairer people.

THE SELF-OBJECT

Most good partners are what psychologists call a "self-object." This means that the person we're with is not only the person we're with, but also the living representation of a part of our inner and outer world. They are part of what steadies us and helps us to feel planted in the ground where we can sprout roots and grow. Our relationship with them provides us with a sense of belonging somewhere; it is part of who we are and how we balance ourselves in the world. This is a primary function of any reasonably good relationship. When we don't understand this very critical function that a relationship plays for us, we risk underestimating its fundamental importance in our lives, our hearts, our psyches, and yes, our bodies, too.

BONDING CHEMICALS

Anthropologist Helen Fisher from Rutgers University has divided love into three systems: *lust, romantic love,* and *attachment* (1999). These types of love each have their own emotional and motivational systems. They have evolved to enable mating, pair-bonding, and parenting.

Lust is the form of love that represents our biological drive to have sex. It's passionate and sensual and comes with desire and longing that involves a craving for sex. An exciting mix of chemical changes occurs when we're in a lust state. It includes increases in the levels of serotonin, oxytocin, vasopressin, and endogenous opioids, which amount to the body's natural equivalent of heroin. "This may serve many functions, to relax the body, induce pleasure and satiety, and perhaps induce bonding," reflects Jim Pfaus, psychologist at Concordia University in Montreal (2005). Dr. Pfaus says the aftermath of lustful sex is similar to the state induced by taking opiates. This biological bonus system helps us understand why sexual addiction and Internet porn sites are on the rise. They offer a quick fix, as they are both intoxicating and very self-medicating. The ancient Greeks referred to this type of love as "eros."

Romantic love is nature's way of ensuring pair bonding. When we "fall in love" we're focusing all of our attention on one person, and our body is releasing the same "love chemicals" that are associated with closeness and desire. We're inclined, when we're in love, to ignore the annoying little traits of our love object, which explains in neurological terms why "love is blind." Nature wants us to fall head over heels so that we will want to mate and reproduce. This is evolution's way of ensuring that we mate with one person so we actually do produce a child. It involves attraction, romantic and sometimes even obsessive love, and is characterized by feelings of exhilaration, as well as intrusive, sometimes even compulsive, thoughts about the object of one's affection.

As important and wonderful as romantic love or "agape" is, it is too unstable for child rearing. For this awesome task nature has evolved the final stage of love, long-term attachment, which allows parents to cooperate in raising children.

Attachment is the system that bonds people long and well enough so that we raise a child. It is also the parenting system, or the attachment that a parent feels toward a child, and vice versa. This state, says Dr. Fisher, is marked by feelings of calm, security, social comfort, and emotional union. All of the chemicals of connection that we referred to earlier in this chapter are also part of what bond us to our children and our children to us. Our psychological need for belonging that is at the base of Maslow's hierarchy of needs is well met by this "familying" state.

RELATIONSHIPS CAN BE GOOD OR BAD FOR THE BODY

We are entering a new age of scientific research in which we're beginning to consider the physiological effects of relationships. The presence of regular relationships in our lives actually has a stabilizing effect on our nervous systems because the nervous systems of all humans and even all mammals are interconnected. We seek out relationships of all kinds as mood stabilizers whether with people on the Internet, at work, or with animals. Relationships of all kinds serve as mood stabilizers.

Our limbic systems connect and resonate with those of others, and this resonance helps us to stay in balance. These bonds help us to self-regulate so that we experience the circumstances of our lives from a secure base.

Relationships can be either good or not so good for our overall health. They can help us to face life with confidence or withdraw and feel less good about ourselves. In a *New York Times* article, Dr. Daniel Goleman writes, "The emotional status of our main relationships has a significant impact on our overall pattern of cardiovascular and neuroendocrine activity. This radically expands the scope of biology and neuroscience from focusing on a single body or brain to looking at the interplay between two at a time. In short, my hostility bumps up your blood pressure, your nurturing love lowers mine. Potentially, we are each other's biological enemies or allies . . . Physical suffering aside, a healing presence can relieve emotional suffering" (2006).

Facing a stressful or even threatening situation with a partner can ease tension and fear. In a study of the brain scans of women facing a scary situation, researchers observed that they showed immediate signs of relief when holding their husbands' hands. James Coan, a neuroscientist at the University of Virginia, studied sixteen married women who were subjected to mild electrical shocks while holding, first, their husbands' hands; second, a stranger's hand; and third, no hand at all. MRI scans of the women's brains clearly showed a large decrease in the brain's fear response when the women held their partners' hands and a limited decrease when holding a stranger's hand. This drop in threat-related brain activity also included a decrease in activity along the neural pathways and circuits that process our emotions. Coan asked each of these couples to rate their level of satisfaction within their marriages. Here he found that the largest decrease in threat-related brain activity was found in women with the highest satisfaction in marriage. Apparently, the more comfortable we are with our partners, the more comforted we are by them. Love and security are good for the body as well as the soul (Janov 2006).

The opposite is true, too. Acrimony in our relationships can contribute to problems with our health. Psychological factors, for example, are now recognized as contributing to the development of heart disease. In a study presented at a meeting of the American Psychosomatic Society, the connection between hardening of the arteries and the emotional climate of a relationship was examined and compared. "Some 150 older, married couples were asked to pick a topic that was the subject of disagreement in their relationship. The topics ranged from money, in-laws, children, and vacations to household duties. Each couple was asked to discuss their topic for six minutes while they were videotaped." The comments exchanged between the husbands and wives were then categorized by words like "friendly," "hostile," "submissive," "dominant," or "controlling." A comment that was seen as dominant or controlling might be, "I don't want you to do that, I want you to do this instead," while a comment that was seen as both hostile and dominant might be, "You're too negative all the time." An example of a friendly and submissive comment could be, "Oh, that's a good idea, let's do it." Hostile and submissive could be, "I'll do what you want if you get off my back."

After the discussion, each couple had a CT or CAT scan of the chest to look for evidence of hardening of the arteries.

The researchers found that the more hostile the wife's comments, the more evidence there was of hardening of *her* arteries, and her arteries were even worse if she had a hostile husband, too. On the other hand, husbands who displayed more dominant or controlling behavior, or whose wives displayed dominant behavior, were more likely than other men to have more severe hardening of the arteries.

The implication is that for women, hostility increases the risk of heart disease, and for men, dominant or controlling behavior increases that risk. Interestingly, the women were unaffected by their own or their husbands' dominant behavior, and the men were unaffected by their own or their wives' hostility. "We still don't have enough information to be certain," says Senay, the researcher in charge of the study. "Exercise and good diet can help reduce stress and the risk factors for cardiac disease. Perhaps marriage counseling will eventually be added to the list of heart-healthy advice!" (CBS 2006).

TRANSFERENCE: HOW WE LAYER YESTERDAY'S PAIN ON TODAY'S RELATIONSHIPS

One of the ways that historical pain gets layered onto our relationships in the present is through a phenomenon called "transference." Essentially, transference means that a relational pattern from the past, along with all of its surrounding feelings, meanings, and mentations, gets transferred onto a relationship in the present without our awareness of what is actually happening. The past is re-created in the present, and if there is no understanding or processing of these historical issues, the past repeats itself in the present. If pain-filled memories are the source of the transference and those memories are largely unconscious, there can be little or no awareness of how this dynamic of transference is being played out.

When those of us who have grown up with trauma in close relationships give ourselves over to deep caring and connection, we may unconsciously fear that chaos or out-of-control behavior might be looming just around the corner, because this was our early experience. The natural feelings of dependency and vulnerability that are a part of intimacy may act as triggers that bring up all that we have experienced in the arena of close relationships. The anxiety and hypervigilance that we bring with us into intimate relationships can make sustaining deep connection challenging. Beneath the level of our awareness, we may be so convinced that distress is at hand that we may experience mistrust and suspicion if problems are solved smoothly. This can even lead us to push a situation in a convoluted self-protective attempt to ferret out potential problems until, through our relentless efforts to avoid them, we actually create them.

Unconsciously, we're expecting what we get. We're transferring our unresolved pain from childhood onto our adult relationships, thus bleeding from the past into the present. We're feeling what we had to shut down yesterday within our relational world of today through the phenomenon of transference.

It is the nature of things that what is inside wants to come out. A sliver will work its way through the skin until our system has gotten rid of it. Our body knows it doesn't belong; it is disturbing, and we want it out of us. Emotional pain can operate along similar lines. The psycho/emotional system wants to get unresolved emotional and psychological pain up and out, to see it, to make it concrete, and to work it through and bring it to closure. This is one of the reasons we get caught up in playing out the unconscious contents of our previous relationships in the relationships of our present-day world. We shadowbox with our pasts through our relationships of today, and so the emotional patterns from the past are reinforced and passed along.

Our unconscious drives our thinking, feeling, and behavior in ways that never cease to amaze me. Through clients' stories, I am ever privy to the strange and often circuitous path that intergenerational pain takes. It leaks into the emotional atmosphere of the family. Mercifully, intergenerational strength and resilience also flow downward. But of one thing I am sure: just because something isn't spoken doesn't mean it isn't there. In fact, what isn't spoken can have even more power;

putting something into words and sharing it tends to diminish its power. Unresolved pain or anger floating around in an unnamed, unacknowledged state is the most confusing to deal with.

Intimacy may feel unsafe to someone who has lived with emotional trauma. When relationships make us hurt too much, we get scared and we may not want to feel the pain we're in. So we get rid of it somehow, we turn it off. But it doesn't disappear. It lives within the self system as a land mine waiting to explode. One of the scariest parts of therapy and deep intimacy is to learn to tolerate our own powerful emotions that get triggered in intimate situations while we're actually in them. Part of the trauma response is an attempt to depersonalize what feels overwhelming or frightening; it is natural and even protective. But as far as intimacy goes, this unconscious drive to depersonalize obviously doesn't bring a couple any closer. They deal with each other in ways that are distancing rather than intimacy building.

But if we can tolerate these feelings, literally allow these unmodulated memories to float to the surface where we can make sense of them in the light of today, healing can happen. When we do this, the feelings of fear and vulnerability pass. Then the feelings we have been defending against emerge. They may be hurt, anger, or fear. We may want to flee or fight all over again. As we come in touch with how we really felt about our early experiences, pieces of the puzzle begin to fit together. We begin to make sense of ourselves. Self-assuredness grows when we no longer have to avoid huge pockets of our inner world or run from deep connection. Like a frightened child who, when the parent turns the light on, realizes there are no monsters under the bed, we can calm down and return to a state of equilibrium. Our thinking minds can be used in service of understanding and regulating our inner world. We meet our tiger in the night.

THE EMOTIONAL SUBTEXT: META-EMOTIONS

John Gottman has named what he calls "meta-emotion."
"Meta" is from the Greek word meaning "later or behind."
Meta-emotion encompasses such things as how people feel
about feelings and what their history is with specific emotions
like pride, respect or disrespect, love, fear, anger, and sadness,
along with what their philosophy is about emotions, and why
they have this philosophy. The whole category of meta-
emotion is critical to parenting and to couple relationships as
well as underlying and determining the emotional meaning
that might drive behavior in families.

Gottman and Levinson (1988) found that by reading the
emotional signals between a couple, they could predict, with
over 90 percent accuracy, what was going to happen to a relationship over a three-year period. They examined their physiology and behavior during a conflict, and again later during
an interview about how the couple viewed their past. Initially
they thought it might be just chance, but they found from
doing study after study that very simple patterns repeated in
sample after sample. "You could tell from just looking at how
a couple talked about how their day went, or talked about an
area of conflict, what was going to happen to the relationship
with a lot of accuracy," said Gottman. "It seemed that people
either started in a mean-spirited, critical way, talking about a
disagreement, or started talking about a problem as just a
symptom of their partner's inadequate character, which made
their partner defensive and escalated the conflict, and people
started getting mean and insulting one another. That pre-
dicted the relationship was going to fall apart. Ninety-six percent of the time, the way the conflict discussion started in the
first three minutes determined how it would go for the rest of
the discussion." Four years later it was like no time had passed;
their interaction style was almost identical. Gottman and
Levinson also observed that 69 percent of the time they were

talking about the same issues over and over again, which the researchers saw as "perpetual issues" that they would never solve. These issues reflected basic personality differences that never went away.

Some couples, they observed, were "caught by the web of these perpetual issues and made each other miserable; they were 'gridlocked' like bumper-to-bumper traffic with these issues, while other couples had similar issues but coped with them and had a 'dialogue' that even contained laughter and affection. It seemed that relationships last to the extent that you select someone whose annoying personality traits don't send you into emotional orbit. Once again, conventional wisdom was wrong. *The big issue wasn't helping couples resolve their conflicts, but moving them from gridlock to dialogue.*"

The researchers found that allowing each member of the couple to talk about their dream within the conflict was what got them unstuck. Once people talked about what they wished and hoped for and why this was so important to them, in 86 percent of the cases they would move from gridlock to dialogue. "Again a new door opened," said Gottman. "Not all marital conflicts are the same. You can't teach people a set of skills and just apply them to every issue. Some issues are deeper, they have more meaning. And then it turned out that the very issues that cause the most pain and alienation can also be the greatest sources of intimacy and connection." When couples understand that the areas of their deepest conflict can also spur them into their most gratifying and freeing growth, they can learn to use their relationship to grow as individuals and to plumb their own and each other's depths in service of healing.

Another surprise according to Gottman:

> We followed couples for as long as 20 years, and we found that there was another kind of couple that didn't really show up on the radar; they looked fine, they

weren't mean, they didn't escalate the conflict—but about 16 to 22 years after the wedding they started divorcing. They were often the pillars of their community. They seemed very calm and in control of their lives, and then suddenly they break up. Everyone is shocked and horrified. But we could look back at our early tapes and see the warning signs we had never seen before. Those people were people who just didn't have very much positive connection. There wasn't very much affection—and also especially humor—between them.

These are the people you see in restaurants who've been married a long time and they're sitting there not talking to each other throughout the whole dinner and they don't look very happy about the vast chasm between them. Those are the couples where you say to your partner, "Let's never become like them, okay?" These sorts of emotionally disconnected relationships were another important dimension of failed relationships. We learned through them that the quality of the friendship and intimacy affects the nature of conflict in a very big way (Gottman 1988).

Gottman's work brings us back to the day-to-day reality of living in relationships. They were discovering "a hidden world in the ordinary everyday moments. These moments were the key to how people build friendships and even sexual intimacy. Foreplay really happens all the time. Eventually in our theory there were three circles having to do with conflict, friendship, and sense of purpose and meaning that were interlocked here. That became our theory we called the 'sound relationship house theory.' It also worked for the gay and lesbian couples that Levenson and I studied for a dozen years."

The emotional climate that we grew up in becomes part of

our meta-emotions. It shapes the very feelings we are used to or even capable of feeling, our philosophy of intimate life, and how we feel about what we feel.

LEARNING HOW TO USE OUR RELATIONSHIP TO HEAL OURSELVES: TRADING IN BAD HABITS FOR BETTER ONES

Couples have an opportunity to become deep healers for each other if they can use their moments of conflict constructively rather than destructively. This doesn't mean that conflict both outside and inside of the relationship doesn't occur; it means that the couple is willing to work with it in order to deepen intimacy and understanding rather than use it as fuel for distance and disconnection. While couples who have experienced relationship trauma enter intimate relationships carrying significant baggage that needs to be faced and worked through, they may also enter relationships with a clear and realistic picture of just how much damage we can do if we don't watch our own behavior. Some of the most impactful lessons we learn are by what we might call negative example. We learn what not to do by watching the mistakes other people make that get them into trouble.

We choose our partners with our unconscious as well as our conscious minds. The issues they bring often tend to mirror at least some of what we carry inside of ourselves. If we are genuinely interested in growing from our conflicts, of using our triggered moments to better understand where our own wounds lie, conflicts become moments of self-discovery rather than blame. If each partner is willing to back up and self-reflect, miracles can happen.

Decide to Change the Legacy Together: Get Motivated to Break the Chain for Your Own Children

Couples who value the happiness and well-being of the generations beneath them enough to motivate them to do deep, healing work contribute greatly to their families, communities, and their own happy futures. Love for our children and grandchildren can be a powerful motivator for change. Good relationships take a tremendous amount of work, and the work is constant. What changes isn't that they are work, but that we get better at it. We spend less time in conflict and blame and more time in constructive interaction and negotiation. There is no greater wealth than family love, a safe harbor, a place in this world that is always held for you, and for those you love.

Build Relationship Resilience

To use your relationship to build personal and interpersonal resilience, try getting challenged by relationship issues and tackling them head on. Take pride in your relationship and your willingness to pull together on behalf of your kids and your future as both a couple and a family. In the same way that you get motivated and pull together to build a nest egg, build a nest in which to enjoy it—a nest that can hold your children, your grandchildren, and each other.

Use Moments of Conflict to Grow from Rather than to Deepen Negative Patterns

The patterns we get absolutely stuck in are often indicators of where our wounds lie. That's why we get so stuck; neither party wants to feel what's going on underneath, neither party wants to accept responsibility, and each party wants to blame. Step back at these moments and self-reflect. Is anything from your past gluing you to this psychic spot? How do your wounds interface here? How can you use this moment to help each other heal rather than drive the pain further down?

Seek Out Help

None of us see ourselves clearly all the time. There is so much help to be had these days, there is really little excuse for not accessing some of it. With couples and family therapy, my experience is that a little can go a long way. Partners who are willing to do the work to change their own negative patterns build a legacy for the futures of several generations. They invest in both the present and the future.

Stay in Touch with the Larger Community; Don't Isolate as a Couple

We need a community in which to operate, have fun, and build friendships. It's wonderful for children to witness their parents having fun and enjoying themselves and those around them. This is how we teach our children social skills. Build a community of family friends and play together.

Incorporate Novelty

In long-term relationships, novelty can stimulate the types of body chemicals that are linked with romantic love. That's one of the reasons that vacations can be great for intimacy. Dinners out to new places, little forays to do something you don't normally do together, or changing your routine for a day or two can all add a bit of passion to your relationship.

Healthy Romanticizing

Sometimes looking at our partners through those slightly tinted rose-colored glasses can be a predictor of long-term success. Psychologists at the University of Texas in Austin have spent a decade following 168 couples who were married in 1981. They are finding that idealization of a kind can help people stay happily married. "Usually, this is a matter of one person putting a good spin on the partner, seeing the partner as more responsive than he or she really is," said Ted Huston, the study's lead investigator. "People who do that tend to stay in relationships longer than those who can't or don't" (Carey 2005).

In another study, psychologists at the State University of New York at Buffalo followed a group of 121 dating couples. The couples answered questionnaires designed to determine how much they idealized their partner and how well the pair was doing every few months. "The researchers found that the couples who were closest one year later were those who idealized each other the most. The idealizing seemed to help carry these couples through the inevitable rough spots. 'Intimates who idealized one another,' concluded the researchers, 'appeared more prescient than blind, actually creating the relationships they wished for as romances progressed'" (Carey 2005).

Be a Tortoise, Not a Hare

Taking time to really get to know who you're about to spend your life with is worth it in the long run. Through his research on couples, Ted Huston identified three patterns of early courtship: *fast and passionate, slow and rocky,* and *in-between*. The fast-track group, about 25 percent of the total, usually were interdependent within weeks. This group tended to ignore or forget their initial problems and were committed to marriage within several months. The slow-motion group, on the other hand, took an average of two years to become committed.

Thirteen years later researchers found that the slow and steady group won out. "The more boring and deliberate the courtship, the better the prospects for a long marriage. People who had very intense, Hollywood-type romances at the beginning were likely to have a big drop-off later on, and this often changed their view of the other's character" (Carey 2005).

THE SCENT AND FLAVOR OF INTIMACY

Learning how to self-soothe and modulate our own emotional reactions will help our relationships. If each member of the couple takes responsibility for regulating their own emotions, the emotional atmosphere of the couple will likely improve.

Intimacy is a delicate balance between too much and too little. It requires countless subtle shifts in the range of four, five, and six all throughout the day. It also encompasses a capacity to go to extreme ranges of emotions, now and then, and to successfully find our way back into midrange.

Relationship trauma, remember, tends to make us live on the edges rather than the middle. This is not intimacy enhancing because it puts too much pressure on the relationship and uses up all the breathing room. But those who have lived on the edges and learned how to come back from them into day-to-day stability have a unique vision of life and ability to tolerate emotional intensity, which can add aliveness to love and make ordinary life seem extraordinary. They have the capacity to enter the mystery.

$\mathcal{P}$assing on the Pain

What Am I Bringing into My Parenting?

Stay, stay home, my heart, and rest;
Home-keeping hearts are happiest.

—Henry Wadsworth Longfellow

Our children don't become who we tell them to be, they become who we are. As a therapist, I need no convincing that children live in the affective space between their parents. They live in their unspoken and sometimes unfelt emotional world. Much of parenting is implicit rather than explicit, which is why children become who we are rather than who we tell them to be. Our children drink us up like little sponges. They watch us, they sense us, they model who we are and what we do. Each moment we are parenting or, for that matter, living in front of our children, we are showing them who we want them to become. There is no such thing as creating a comfortable emotional atmosphere for your child while being constantly at war with yourself or your spouse. The family is the family. It operates as a whole. Every time we resolve our own unconscious conflicts, generations of people benefit. Tending to our relationships, our personal lives, and our bodies are all the right thing to do, not only for us, but for our kids.

When Janet Woititz wrote *Adult Children of Alcoholics,* grown people came literally out of the woodwork with boxes of Kleenex and sad little stories of hiding in closets while their parents tore into each other. These children in adult bodies talked about feeling isolated in their pain, like frauds who felt that they had to constantly hide their authentic feelings for so long that they had themselves lost touch with those feelings. These were children marooned at various stages along the continuum of maturation walking around in the bodies of thirty-five-year-olds. They weren't necessarily the screwups or those who couldn't seem to get it together. In fact, they were more often the ones who could get it together because they'd been functioning like little adults much of their lives. They were the ones who'd gone into bars to drag their fathers home. Or, in the higher socioeconomic groups, who'd quietly undressed their drunk mothers and tucked them into bed. Perhaps they had tiptoed around on Sunday morning getting breakfast for younger siblings while parents slept off the night before or the help was off duty. Maybe they went to school, got As, and were captains of teams and cheerleading squads, functioning to keep the family from falling apart and restoring a sense of order and dignity. But later, when these little adults grew up, they carried unattended emotional wounds that were triggered in their adult relationships. Confused and disheartened, they came in droves when the problems that they had been carrying in silence finally got a name.

It is exactly this group that often swore off booze and avoided drugs, sincerely thinking that this would mean that their children wouldn't have to go through the pain they endured. But all too many of them also carried more than significant denial and ignorance as to how much growing up with addiction had traumatized them.

The truth is, ACOAs and codependents who have trauma-related issues need to undergo a comprehensive, long-term treatment approach that is tailored to their specific needs. Without it they are likely to engender the kinds of issues in their intimate circles that have gone untreated within themselves. They repeat the patterns that they learned growing up. They reenact the unresolved pain that they carry. Unfortunately, their years of living in denial about family problems all too often are played out in the form of denying just how out of balance, both emotionally and psychologically, they themselves have become. Living with addiction and relationship trauma has long arms that wrap themselves around generation after generation until they are consciously and methodically addressed.

One of the other sad things that can happen for children in alcoholic homes is that they lose connection with each other. The children wind up playing out the parents' pain in their own relationships, or they become co-opted by one parent and pitted against each other. This is a double loss because it is wonderfully healing to be able to compare notes and process together. Siblings share a very special bond. No one else can quite make you double over in laughter the way a sibling can, recounting nonsense memories of crabby car trips, funny uncles, or warm memories of the closets and kitchen at Gramma's house. Siblings and cousins remember you when, and they knew you in ways that no one else quite does.

Some Things to Watch Out For

Parents with a family history of trauma and/or addiction may tend to:

+ Have trouble tolerating their children being rejected by anyone.
+ Have problems with their own self-regulation that impact how they deal with their children's ups and downs.
+ May violate their children's boundaries by being unnecessarily intrusive and overly curious about their children's affairs.
+ Either read too much into situations that bother their children or block them.
+ Overprotect their children even when it is not in their children's best interest.
+ Not know what normal is and consequently have trouble understanding which behaviors to accept or foster as normal in their children and which behaviors to discourage.
+ Have trouble having relaxed and easy fun with their children.
+ Have impulsive features that they act out in their parenting.
+ Feel somewhat different from other families.
+ Attempt to overcontrol family life and the lives of their children.
+ Have trouble establishing healthy boundaries with their children, positioning themselves either too close or too far.

GRANDCHILDREN OF ADDICTION AND TRAUMA

Many ACOAs swear that they will never do to their children what was done to them. By now, the reader hopefully understands enough about the unconscious nature of traumatic memory to realize that this is not possible. What sits within the brain body is very likely to get triggered and emerge when we are presented with like situations, namely, families. ACOAs tend to pass along their pain in one of two ways: exactly in the form they received it—for example, that battered son becomes the battering father, or, in its direct opposite, the ignored daughter becomes the intrusive or overly protective mother. ACOAs often don't know what normal is. If they felt rejected as children, they may tend to compensate with their own children by being overly involved. They lack an innate sense of how much involvement is appropriate and how much is too much. If the ACOA/T (adult child of trauma) doesn't get help, his children may well inherit his unresolved issues.

GCOAs (grandchildren of alcoholics) often report feeling that they carry the burden of healing their parents' wounds. They are very much aware of their parents' "painful pasts," and they can feel guilty about adding to their pain. Or they just sit underneath their parents' histories, underneath the parents' overly intense reactions to life. This can mean that the GCOA takes on too much of her parents' "stuff." The GCOA may feel guilty individuating because she doesn't want to abandon her parents. She can get caught in a bind: it feels good to have her parents' undying love, but it comes at a price. The GCOAs I have worked with sometimes carry anger around this. They are angry that their parents haven't done their own work and look to their children to heal them, angry that they feel in this love-lock and angry that they feel they can't get angry because their parents cannot tolerate it.

When ACOAs do not do the long-term personal work that they need to recover from their trauma-related issues, they risk passing along their own distorted and unresolved relationship dynamics to their children. ACOAs may look to their own children to fill the emotional void left by pain from their own past.

+ GCOAs may carry a sense of guilt for their parents' painful past.

+ GCOAs may feel "crazy" because, while there is nothing like addiction or abuse occurring in their families, their parents are passing on pain through their own unexamined and unregulated behavior.

+ ACOAs may pass on their tendency toward traumatic bonding to their children; they may become overclose or cycle between over- and underclose, because they themselves lack a sense of normal.

GCOAs have no obvious addiction or abuse on which to pin crazy-making relational dynamics. Their parents may love them to bits, and need them, but the style of parenting may reflect a lack of regulation. The ACOA's parenting style may seesaw, for example, between enmeshment and disengagement or chaos and rigidity. The same unregulated family dynamics that the ACOA learned while growing up get recreated in the ACOA's own parenting. Thus, the GCOA inherits the dynamics that are trauma-related without the obvious trauma; they feel guilty over their parents' tough past but confused about how their parents' pain is being passed right along to them. In this way, the torch of dysfunction gets transmitted to another generation and may set the GCOA up for wanting to self-medicate. Addiction, in other words, skips a generation.

TIPS FOR RAISING KIDS
WHO CAN SELF-REGULATE

Teach Resilience

Overprotecting our kids, raising them so that nothing bad happens to them, doesn't equip them for what's ahead. They need us at their side teaching them to manage the kinds of problems that are part of any life. Sharing toys, sticking up for themselves, taking turns, listening to the other guy, not dominating but not retreating either, are all skills that our kids need to learn in order to live a balanced life. Our kids are much better off if they can learn to regulate their intense emotions and manage their inevitable states of stress and the challenges they meet in their daily lives than if they grow up in a hothouse. We want to teach our kids to roll with the punches, to build their own resilience and strength so that they can live life on life's terms rather than retreat from it. Protecting our children from anything bad happening is probably less useful to them than to help them learn to manage stress and conflict as they come up.

When You're with Your Kids, Be with Them

We live in a world of distractions, but what children need is our full attention. They need our attending to them so that they can learn to attend to themselves. If we can learn to be with them when we are with them, we will create a baseline of connection that we can draw on throughout the day, and they will internalize this energy of calm and attuned attending. Even as we drag them along behind us, rush them into their clothes, push them into their next activity, and settle them into some pursuit so that we can have them occupied for a while, we can be with them as we do it. These are all points of connection that can add up to wonderful little moments of attending and learning throughout the day if we really make the effort to connect in a nice, even flow. This approach turns the day into a kind of relational experience that will teach our kids more than anything else can about how to live in a happy, intimate connection.

Laced into these days needs to be a sense of actually being with our children, because if we aren't, they will know it. If we don't really cultivate the habit of being with them on what we might even call a heart-to-heart level, they may feel unimportant. They will try in every way they know to grab our attention, and if they cannot, they may come to the conclusion that they are not important enough to deserve it. When we truly attend and are present with our children, it sinks into their pores. When we laugh at their sweet attempts at jokes, they feel funny. When we admire their little works of art, they feel they have talent; when we make them special foods, they feel special; and when we listen to them with our eyes and our heart, they feel heard, seen, and as if they have a right to be here.

Get in Sync with Your Child

Studies have shown that even at birth the child responds positively and specifically to the tones of the human voice, reports Peter Russell in *The Brain Book* (1979). "A high-speed film of a newborn baby when slowed down many times and examined frame by frame shows that tiny gestures on the part of the child are synchronized with specific tones and syllables from the parents. Sounds other than the human voice, however, produce no such response. While he is in the womb the child learns the sound of the mother's heartbeat, and after birth the sound of a human heart will have a very soothing effect on the baby."

"The mother's emotionally expressive face is, by far, the most potent visual stimulus in the infant's environment," points out UCLA's Alan Schore (2007), "and the child's intense interest in her face, especially in her eyes, leads him/her to track it in space to engage in periods of intense mutual gaze." The result is that endorphin levels rise in the baby's brain (and the mother's), causing pleasurable feelings of joy and excitement. But the key is for this joy to be interactive. We now know that the baby's participation is crucial to creating a solid attachment bond. The loving gaze of parent to child is reciprocated by the baby with a loving gaze back to the parent, causing both their endorphin levels to rise, thus completing a closed emotional circuit, a sort of love loop. Now parent and baby are truly in a dynamic, interactive system. "In essence, we are talking less about *what* the mother is doing *to* the baby and more about *how* the mother is being *with* the baby and how the baby is learning to be with the mother," says Schore. The final aspect of this developing interactive system between mother and child is the mother's development of an "emotional synchronization" with her child. Schore defines this as the mother's ability to tune in to the baby's internal states and respond accordingly.

Keep Your Emotions in a Balanced Range

Our emotional reactions with and around our children actually give each sensory experience texture and meaning. "As we've watched many babies develop over the years, we've come to realize that what have traditionally been described as separate emotional and cognitive (or intellectual) reactions are not so separate after all. In contrast to existing notions, we believe that each time your baby takes in information through his senses, the experience is double-coded" (Greenspan 1999), as both a cognitive and an emotional reaction to those physical sensations. Our emotional reactions, in other words, are interwoven with the experience itself and recorded that way in our memory bank.

Touch Your Children

Not accidentally, the opiates that are our biological reward system are turned on by touch. The "opiates of attachment" or "brain fertilizers" that are turned on by the kind of touching and closeness between the mother and child strengthen connections between neurons in the brain that literally make someone more intelligent, fit, and eventually a more successful adult. They are food for the brain and body. Without these chemicals coursing through us, the brain cannot connect properly. This is why nature rewards mother/child intimacy so strongly by making it a pleasurable experience, because without it, our children can't survive and thrive.

Talk to Your Kids

The power of early adult-child interactions is remarkable. Researchers found that when mothers frequently spoke to their infants, their children learned almost three hundred more words by age two than did their peers whose mothers rarely spoke to them. However, mere exposure to language through television or adult conversation provided little benefit. Infants need to interact directly with other people. Children need to hear people talk to them about what they are seeing and experiencing in order for their brains to fully develop language skills.

When an infant is three months old, his brain can distinguish several hundred different spoken sounds. Over the next several months, his brain will organize itself more efficiently so that it only recognizes those sounds that are part of the language he regularly hears. During early childhood, the brain retains the ability to relearn sounds it has discarded, so young children typically learn new languages easily and without an accent.

Have Positive Expectations for Your Child

Research suggests that positive expectations yield positive results and negative expectations yield negative results. This, in parenting, is a bit of research that goes a long way.

Expecting good things from our children can become a self-fulfilling prophecy, as can expecting negative things. Cultivating positive expectations for our children can actually help them lead more constructive lives.

Build Emotional and Relational Skills

Put the "stuff" on hold. You are your child's best toy. Studies suggest that pushing your baby to learn words, numbers, colors, and shapes too early forces the child to use lower-level thinking processes, rather than develop his or her learning ability. "It's like a pony trick at the circus: When the pony paws the ground to 'count' to three, it's really not counting; it's simply performing a stunt." Such "tricks" are not only not helpful to a baby's learning process, they are potentially harmful. Tufts University child psychologist David Elkind makes it clear that putting pressure on a child to learn information sends the message that he or she needs to "perform" to gain the parents' acceptance, and it can dampen natural curiosity. Instead, focus on building your child's emotional skills (Elkind 2001).

"Emotional development is not just the foundation for important capacities such as intimacy and trust," says Greenspan (1999). "It is also the foundation of intelligence and a wide variety of cognitive skills. At each stage of development, emotions lead the way, and learning facts and skills follow. Even math skills, which appear [to be] strictly an impersonal cognition, are initially learned through the emotions: 'A lot' to a 2-year-old, for example, is more than he would expect, whereas 'a little' is less than he wants."

Don't Deny Their Reality or Yours

Kids sense what their parents are feeling both within themselves and within their parents' relationship. Pretending that the emotions that are present in the house aren't there makes kids feel crazy and teaches them to doubt their own perceptions. If there is denied pain and anger, kids are likely to feel it's about them, that they did something or are being something that displeases their parents or is causing problems. This erodes their self-esteem and undermines their ability to make sense of a situation, work through it, or rise above it. "Clearly, the emotional state of others is of fundamental importance to the infant's [child's] emotional state," says Harvard child psychiatrist Edward Tronick (2007). Children form many important relationships with adults. Infants may also scan their parents' faces for signs of what they are feeling. Babies send their parents nonverbal messages, too. Infants smile when they are pleased, cling when they need contact, and follow with their eyes when they are worried that we may leave (Brazelton 2000).

Help Your Kids Learn to "Tolerate" Their Strong Emotions

The capacity to feel—to be empathic, attuned, and engaged with our children during all points of their development—is at the crux of being a good parent. Helping our children to develop the ability to tolerate their strong feelings and translate those feelings into words so that they can be held out in the intellectual space between parent and child, thought about, and reasoned through, is central to developing the ability to integrate our personalities and regulate our body/mind emotional systems and learn to self-reflect.

Codependency Revisted

I wanted to call it Codependent,
Not So Much. The publisher said
it would never sell and suggested
Codependent No More; which is
obviously impossible on a practical level.
Sometimes in recovery we have to
bow to the demands of accounting.

—*Melody Beattie*

O ur ability to read social signals and adjust accordingly, to fit ourselves into a group and work together for the common good, is at the core of our enormous success as a species. In spite of war, disease, and famine, we're breeding and thriving on every corner of the earth, and in time, maybe even in outer space. Dependence is central to our resilience as human beings. It is programmed into our DNA. Dependency is actually completely natural; we're built to want to touch, nurture, sustain, and comfort each other. Our biology is, in fact, programmed to flood with feel-good chemicals when we connect and nurture and with stress chemicals when we rupture that secure connection. We run into tricky territory, then, when and if we pathologize our natural need to depend. America's constant preoccupation with rugged individualism and perhaps even aspects of the codependency ideology may inadvertently have given dependency a bad rap. This was, however, never the original intention of the codependency movement.

A BIT OF HISTORY

Codependency grew out of the term "co-addict." The codependent person, or the co-addict, was that person who got sick through *living with* the distorted, unregulated, and out-of-balance thinking, feeling, and behavior that surround addiction. Codependency was a grassroots movement that grabbed its name as it ran headlong down a path that had been opened by the ACOA movement. When the terms "codependent" and "ACOA" went public, they became a movement, almost overnight. Codependents became the new neurotics. If neurotic was *intra*personal, referring to problems in relating to ourselves, then codependent was *inter*personal, referring to problems in relating to others. Finally there was a name to describe what many of us were living with in silence and frustration. Current research in neuropsychology is helping us to comprehend why codependency may grow out of homes where relationship trauma is present and why it is a developmental disorder with long-term implications. What we understood by instinct, experience, and clinical trial and error two decades ago may today have science behind it.

Codependency is generally seen as a set of maladaptive patterns in relating to others. In the early 1980s, codependency became a catch-all word for people with relationship issues of all kinds. But seeing codependency as a set of behaviors means that we tend to think that changing our behaviors is the solution to becoming less codependent. While behavior changes are always a part of recovery, it may be useful to reexamine the roots of codependency in light of neurological findings.

It was through the door of the ACOA and codependency movement that I arrived at the door of relationship trauma. This is what, I feel, people were looking to answer when they flooded the movement in the first place. Why do relationships hurt and what can I do about it? One of the most freeing things that we can pull from research is that relationships, at times, are meant to hurt, that nature evolved this particular pain so that we would stay connected and survive.

The task of our generation, then, is to learn how to manage our relationships so that the hurt becomes constructive, so that we learn and grow from it. This kind of understanding can let us spend more time in the other side of what nature has evolved relationships to do, and that is to nourish and sustain us, to give us pleasure and a sense of purpose and belonging. We need to learn how to let ourselves be dependent in ways that are perfectly natural and healthy. Healthy ways of depending are part of emotional sobriety. Relationships are key to our emotional balance. Countless studies correlate strong relationship networks with physical health, reduced doctor visits, and longevity.

I think that understanding codependency as a trauma-related loss of self that happens slowly throughout our personality development is the most helpful way to conceive of it, and that's the thesis I am putting forward in this chapter. Codependency, I feel, is fear based and is a predictable set of qualities and behaviors that grow out of feeling anxious and therefore hypervigilant in our intimate relationships. It is also reflective of an incomplete process of individuation.

THE LINK BETWEEN CODEPENDENCY AND CHILDHOOD TRAUMA: WHY CODEPENDENCY IS DESELFING

As we've discussed, when we get scared, our left brain, the language part of the brain, becomes overwhelmed and shuts down. That's why we get speechless when we're stunned.

What remains very active, however, is the emotional scanning system in our right brain. The part of our brain that scans and remains hypervigilant is, in fact, working overtime when we are scared—codependency in the making. Children who regularly experience relationship trauma often learn that they can fend off trouble if they can stay hyperfocused on reading the other person's emotional signals (van der Kolk 1997). They can become very adept at reading other people's moods, often to the exclusion of their own. They become more in touch with what those around them are feeling than what they are feeling. They become habitually outer-focused and may lose touch with what is going on inside of them.

But here is the key: *The very fact that when frightened we lose access to our thinking function where we integrate our emotions, think them through, and consolidate our sense of self is why being in a constant state of fear interferes with our ability to develop a sense of self.*

Codependents spend a lot of time managing the world around them so that they can feel less anxious. One of the ways they do this is to try to anticipate danger and head it off at the pass. Growing up in codependency-making families, like those we have been discussing in this book, can cause us to lose touch with who we are on the inside, at the same time as we are overly preoccupied with other people and their moods. Though codependency seems to be about caretaking or being overly attuned to the other person, it is really about trying to fend off our own anxiety. Codependency is, in this sense at least, fear based: the result of relationship trauma or being in a frightened enough state enough of the time so that our fear-based survival apparatus gets repeatedly mobilized. Codependency and hypervigilance go hand in hand. For this reason, traumatized people can be thoughtful of therapists and other attachment figures. They learned from having drunken or disorderly parents that they didn't get hurt as much if they could anticipate parents' wishes and moods and thus could fend off some of the trouble. The fear structure of codependency may also be why giving up our codependent postures can feel like our survival is being threatened, because those very beliefs and relational dynamics were set up right alongside our survival responses. Our scanning, for example, is tied in with our fear response, which is tied in with our survival response. We get scared, we freeze, we scan. It's the codependent dance.

Another link between codependency and trauma is that when we numb out or dissociate from experiencing what is happening around us, we cannot make sense of that experience. Numbing or dissociating has a protective function and can even be useful if it can act as a buffer when reality becomes too overwhelming. But the kind of emotional numbing that goes on in dysfunctional homes where our fight/flight apparatus is turned on too much of the time is detrimental to the development of self and subsequent individuation. The boundaries we so desperately try to find and maintain in recovery actually grow quite naturally out of a successful, attuned attachment. But when the attachment is fraught with fear, the child self submerges and the child becomes overly preoccupied with getting it right for the parent rather than himself or herself. There is not enough of the kind of negotiation that allows for each person to feel heard and seen. The child is not free to explore, to be, to feel what he is feeling and work his little way into a new state. His energy gets devoted to strategies for pleasing or placating those who are in charge of his young life rather than exploring his own reactions so that he can better understand himself, or negotiating so that he can learn useful strategies and styles of relating. This constant outer preoccupation and hypervigilance is codependency-making. It is deselfing because the parents' moods take up all the oxygen. It can also create a sort of sibling competition because the first concern becomes reading the parents' moods rather than interacting as a family. The focus is hierarchical rather than lateral.

CARETAKING

Caretaking is commonly associated with codependency. Children who are worried about their parents may become anxious little caretakers of them, constantly scanning their parents' faces and moods for what they need or want. These children may develop a habit of scanning other people's moods in order to establish their own equilibrium and balance. This interferes with developing a sense of self because our sense of self, over time, becomes enmeshed with that of another person.

Caretaking may also be seen as a grief reaction (more on that in our chapter on grief). It is a classic symptom of codependency—or caring and concern gone awry—to be constantly focusing on the needs of the other person to the exclusion of our own, and it may be a misguided attempt to assuage our own anxiety and grief. But caretaking does not necessarily feel good to the person being "care taken." Attention from someone who is acting out of codependent instincts doesn't necessarily feel attuned or nourishing. The codependent may be projecting her own anxiety outward and attempting to fix in someone else what may need fixing within herself. Though the codependent may experience herself as putting the needs of others before her own, a look underneath may reveal other, more complex motivations.

Over the past two decades, the mental health field has focused a lot of attention on self-care. Sayings like "take care of yourself" have become second nature. Certainly taking care of ourselves is central to emotional sobriety, but is it the whole story and the whole solution? Intimacy is not black and white; it asks us to learn to balance our needs with those of others, so that each person can have a sense of autonomy alongside a sense of connection. This emphasis on self-care may have created a few problems along with solving others. It may create the impression that we should be able to solve all of our problems internally. But our sense of self, for better or worse, is impacted by our relationships so we need to factor our needs for interdependency into what we call self-care. In other words, part of taking care of ourselves may be learning how to live comfortably in relationships.

WOMEN AND STRESS

Codependency is maladaptive and is not to be confused with women's natural and biological need to tend and befriend. Research on stress and women reveals that women may respond to stress somewhat differently from men, in what researchers call a tend-and-befriend response. Oxytocin, the "touch chemical," is released in men and women under stress, but the testosterone in men tends to override it. In women, however, estrogen enhances the effects of oxytocin, making women want to gather together, "grab the children, and run for safety." The more they gather, the more they want to gather as oxytocin levels increase through continued physical closeness. Women under stress may thus exhibit different behaviors from men; that is, under stress, as men flee or fight, women may connect or even cling. Some of the symptoms of codependency, seen in this light, may have a biological component for women. Under stress, women's natural tendency to connect may become exaggerated or even maladaptive. But we should not read women's natural desire to tend and befriend as pathological. It is, in fact, nature's way of ensuring the survival of our species.

Real codependency represents a loss of self and an outer focus that is somewhat maladaptive. Women are wired for relationships, which is a wonderful thing. Relational connection at its best allows for each person to be connected with the other while retaining a sense of self. This sense of co-relatedness is inborn in women and very much represents a feminine strength. It is when it becomes maladaptive and fear based in women or in men that it creates identity problems and throws our relationships out of balance. Even though it appears to grow out of care and concern for others, codependent behavior is not really in the other person's best interest any more than it is in the codependent's best interest. Fear-based relating doesn't really serve anyone well.

In her book *The Female Brain,* Louann Brizendine (2006) describes the unique characteristics of the brains of women. Developing girls are wired for connection and relationship. During the early years of a little girl's development, her brain is soaked in estrogen while the brains of her male counterparts are soaked in testosterone. This biological makeup subsides during the middle years and then comes into play again in adolescence when estrogen and testosterone take over the brains of their respective sexes.

Little girls are born with a particular ability to read faces and vocal tones that little boys miss. Any mother who has raised each sex can make this observation. When Marina was a little girl, I could show her how to pick up glass or china objects, look at them, touch them, and put them back in place unharmed. Baby proofing was unnecessary. She read the expression on my face and the tones in my voice, understanding "intuitively" what I expected of her because of her ability to read tone and expression. Imagine my surprise when, upon showing Alex exactly the same things I had shown Marina, he grabbed my precious glass bird around its neck and I caught it just as he was leaning back and heaving it across the room. Alex was clearly wired for different kinds of activities.

Codependency, then, if we take recent research into account, may be influenced by both relationship trauma and gender. Chronic states of fear that mean we are doing less thinking and more hypervigilant scanning of those in our environment can set us up for becoming what is oftentimes seen as codependent in our thinking, feeling, and behavior.

The Biology of Fear

Why Do I Think I Can't Survive My Feelings?

Have patience with everything unresolved in your heart and try to love the questions themselves as if they were locked rooms or books written in a very foreign language. Don't search for the answers, which could not be given to you now, because you would not be able to live them. And the point is, to live everything. Live the questions now. Perhaps then, someday far in the future, you will gradually, without even noticing it, live your way into the answer. Perhaps you do carry within you the possibility of creating and forming, as an especially blessed and pure way of living; train yourself for that—but take whatever comes, with great trust, and as long as it comes out of your will, out of some need of your innermost self, then take it upon yourself, and don't hate anything. . . .

—*Rainer Maria Rilke*

The only thing we have to fear is fear itself.

—*Franklin D. Roosevelt*

I look around the room and see ten or twelve frightened faces. Some people seem frozen in place. Their faces look immobile. Their bodies look stilted and tense. Maybe one or two have bonded and are talking with each other. Someone else is cracking jokes, trying to relieve the mounting tension. A couple of people are smiling recklessly. They are scared stiff, afraid of what might come up in the course of a week.

When I work in treatment centers, the first evening people arrive they often look terrified. They are afraid of what feelings might well up inside of them that they won't be able to handle—that will overwhelm them, take over their heads and hearts, leak into their bodies, and make them shiver inside. Their fear is of feeling just the way they felt at those indelible moments when they have been hurt, helpless, misunderstood, or resentful. They want to flee, to noiselessly disappear into themselves, to pick a fight. So what if that happens here? What if everyone knows that they are only big on the outside but that deep inside of them is a little person craving attention, a nine-year-old dying to please, an adolescent wanting to tell everyone to get lost, or just a scared adult who is, at moments, barely holding it together?

LEARNING TO OBSERVE

There is no outsmarting the symptoms of relationship trauma, codependency, or the disease of addiction. Even if our mind "forgets," our bodies have recorded and will remember and react to situations that have frightened us. If we never processed those frightening scenes, elevated our fears and anxieties to a conscious level where we made sense of them and let them go, they will live inside of us, an emotional accident waiting to happen. People often want some sort of magic bullet that will relieve them of the pain they carry as quickly and painlessly as possible. But when it comes to emotional healing, the quick way can be the slowest. It can be just what locks us into shallow, defensive, and superficial solutions that never quite work. We go for novelty rather than cure, for momentary relief rather than long-term change and gain. This is why it is critical that we undertake recovery as a rational and long-term process. In group therapy and one-to-one, old locked-down fears can get triggered. But this time we are in a situation designed to help us observe ourselves in action so that we can say, "Wait a minute. I'm doing just what I do at home, with my son, daughter, or partner. I'm closing down, my body is flooding with all sorts of feelings that make me want to race out of the room, scream at someone, or shut down and disappear. I'm queasy and shaky. Wow, I'm scared. And this is what I'm like when I'm scared. And this is what scares me, where my tender spots are."

Wanting a quick fix is natural. We feel stupid when we can't figure out our own emotions. We feel like kids who can't get it, and that feeling of ineptness doesn't fit with the fact that we may be fully adult in all other ways. So we want to hide this part of ourselves, to read a book that will fix the problem, to get an insight that will make it all go away. But if we can understand that having these blind spots is perfectly natural, that we all, in fact, have them, we can begin to use our mature reasoning to slowly and patiently work our way out of them. Once we accept this fear reaction as nature's way of protecting us from harm, we can stop feeling embarrassed by it and start to heal our own sore spots. We want quick fixes, but through understanding we can find a better way, the way of understanding.

WHY DO WE WANT QUICK FIXES
AND WHAT GETS IN THE WAY
OF OUR ABILITY TO CHANGE?

✦ We're wired to seek pleasure and avoid pain, so it's natural to want to minimize what hurts. Our body doesn't recognize that we are choosing to let ourselves feel hurt in the short term for a long-term gain; our thinking mind needs to convince our limbic brain that recovery is worth it.

✦ We get emotionally, psychologically, and physically run-down and stressed-out and we want to feel better now, *fast.*

✦ We simply don't understand how the unconscious fear/stress response works, so we project pain from yesterday's relationships onto relationships today, which gets us stuck all over again. We reenact rather than heal our pain.

✦ We have a degree of "learned helplessness." When our fear gets mobilized, so do old feelings of helplessness to get anything to change.

✦ We freeze or dissociate. We're not in our bodies. We're gone. We're frozen in our limbic mind and have no access to our thinking mind.

✦ We lose the ability to conceptualize change, to envision a different solution or future outcome. Our thinking gets frozen.

✦ Our low frustration tolerance makes us want to change fast, and if we don't, we want to give up.

✦ There is a loss of trust and faith that accompanies trauma. We lose faith that things can work out for us. We lose hope that we can change our lives.

✦ Rigid defenses that we have relied on to keep us safe can

get in the way of our making changes. We hunker down, dig our heels in, and do whatever we have always done. We don't want to feel out of control or overwhelmed with the kinds of feelings that we imagine change will engender.

Back to the treatment group from the beginning of the chapter. It's five days later, or six, eight, or twenty-eight depending on the program. The group has had a time of opening up, of communal living, of letting people see them as they really are, warts and all, and of seeing others in the same way. They look like a different group of people. They're loose and relaxed. Their faces are easy and open. They hang out together, laugh a lot, and take the day as it comes, enjoying each other's company. They have cried together and let their pain out. They've laughed until the tears rolled. They have felt their deepest fears, met their most vulnerable selves, and are experiencing a sense of self-confidence and self-assurance that they can stand on their own, face their inner demons, and watch them melt away. They are motivated to make the kinds of life changes that will allow them to maintain their new sense of emotional freedom and sobriety.

Not only do they no longer wish to flee from the room, they want to stay here for weeks, months even. They're looking forward to going home and trying out their newfound selves, but the feeling of openness, acceptance, and connection that they have experienced from opening up, from working through painful historical feelings and accepting caring and support from others, is almost intoxicating. They want to hang on to it. They don't want to forget how good it feels to break their own denial and work through the fear and pain that they have been carrying in silence.

HOW THE THINKING MIND
DECONDITIONS THE FEAR RESPONSE

Our fear response needn't run us. In animal studies fear was induced and then extinguished in lab rats. Excuse the invidious comparison, but these studies clearly spell out how relatively easy it might be to recondition a fear response if the stimuli are changed. Rats normally freeze with fear when they hear a tone they have been conditioned to associate with an electric fear-inducing shock, just like we freeze with fear when we get scared. Dr. Gregory Quirk and Mohammed Milad of the Ponce School of Medicine, Puerto Rico, while doing research funded by the National Institute of Mental Health (NIMH), have now demonstrated that stimulating the prefrontal cortex extinguishes this fear response by mimicking the brain's own "safety signal" (www.nih.gov/news/pr/nov2002/nimh-06.htm) Dr. Quirk explains that "repeated exposure to traumatic reminders without any adverse consequences causes fear responses to gradually disappear. Such reduction of fear appears to be an active rather than passive process. It doesn't erase the fear association from memory, but generates a new memory." The new memory creates a sort of safety zone in which the fear can dissipate; eventually we forget to be afraid. The thinking mind tells the feeling mind that it no longer needs to freeze up at the same stimuli that previously were scary. As rats were shocked, the researchers recorded electrical activity of neurons in their prefrontal cortex. The rats were literally taught to fear a particular tone because it was paired with a shock over and over again. The researchers then deconditioned the fear response by presenting the tone without the shock; eventually, the animals no longer froze when they heard the tone.

People in psychodrama and group therapy learn through repeated exposure to others expressing their intense emotions that they no longer have to fear the expression of strong emotion—that the expression, in fact, can lead to calm resolution rather than out-of-control behavior. In psychodrama, we trigger old fear but put a new memory beside it that allows us to decondition the fear memory. We learn that we are safely past the danger zone, that we are adults now who are no longer helpless and stuck, that we can take care of ourselves.

FEAR AND SURVIVAL

Why Feelings Associated with Relationship Trauma Can Feel So Overwhelming

In the next few paragraphs, I have reviewed some of the dynamics of fear that can create problems for us.

Fear itself is coded into our survival system. The body doesn't really know the difference between a physical threat or emotional fear, stress, and anxiety. Both mobilize the deep defenses associated with our trauma response, namely, fight, flight, and freeze. The painful or scary emotions that we experience in our primary "survival" or family relationships go to our very core, to that mind/body fear apparatus. That's why they feel so huge.

Fear is one of evolution's most necessary and adaptive emotions, it warns us of danger and was designed to keep us safe. But we need to develop discrimination so that we can figure out when we're in real danger as opposed to when our fear apparatus is being activated in ways that just needlessly wear us out both emotionally and physically. We also need, in relationships, to learn how not to get stuck in defensive positions that keep us from being able to work things out in comfortable ways.

Fear leads to biological changes induced by adrenaline. As we learned in our chapter on memory, our sense of danger performs the task of activating the amygdala, which is the unconscious or implicit fear pathway in the brain/body system. When we get scared, anxious, or highly stressed, the amygdala's discharge patterns activate our body's fear circuits, which increases our heart rate and blood pressure; we get sweaty hands, dry mouth, and tense muscles. In order to respond quickly to a threat, the body tries to divert blood flow from the digestive areas and the face, head, and neck so that it can be used in preparation for fleeing or standing and fighting.

Fear can get stuck in our bodies. If we can't flee or fight a situation that is throwing us into an acute stress state, those biological urges can get frozen in the musculature and fascia of our bodies as *thwarted intentions,* or what we call in psychodrama *act hungers.* It is these urges to flee or fight, these actions never taken, that get triggered repeatedly throughout our lives when our old unresolved fear and hurt from past relationships gets triggered by relationships in the present. They emerge as transference reactions or projections, or they drive reenactment patterns. It's why an abused child might become an abusing parent.

Fear can be unconscious or conscious. Evolution evolved our fear circuitry to do its job in a split second, far faster than our conscious mind operates. These split seconds can mean life or death; our ability to recognize danger almost before it hits might just save us or those we love from harm. So our fear apparatus has to operate beneath the level of our awareness. We need to sense danger, get scared, and run for safety, or stand and fight. Because all of this happens so fast, it happens beneath the level of our conscious awareness. That's why our fear reactions can be unconscious. Sometimes we can be scared, in other words, but not really know we're scared. We can get locked into defensive positions without even knowing exactly why.

Unprocessed fear scenes from one situation can get triggered without conscious awareness. The hippocampus is particularly sensitive to the encoding of the *context associated with aversive or stressful types of experience*. We might remember sights, sounds, smells, textures, tastes, and so on, but not know what they are connected to exactly. This is a small bit of information that has large implications in terms of relationship trauma. It is because of the hippocampus that not only can a stimulus become a source of conditioned fear, but so can all the objects surrounding the frightening situation. And this can happen without our conscious awareness. This is how fear memories get generalized.

FEAR'S VICIOUS CIRCLE

If we are regularly exposed to frightening situations and we aren't able to process, understand, or gain comfort for our fears, if we become stuck in chronic fight/flight state, our bodies can become sensitized and wired for overreactions. We become easily triggered into a fear state and experience physiological changes associated with the fear response; then we become afraid of the physiological changes. That is, our bodies may tighten up or shiver and shake, our heart may race, our stomachs get queasy, and our palms sweat. But this can then trigger even more fear in us—*we get afraid of being afraid; our own body responses send us deeper into our feelings of fear*. This can send us into a vicious circle where the physiological changes we're experiencing make us more afraid, and our fear produces more physiological changes. As an attempt to protect ourselves or avoid these uncomfortable feelings, we may start to live small.

$\mathcal{H}$ow High States of Stress Contribute to Anxiety and Depression

> You can't necessarily trust your eyes
> if your mind is out of focus.
>
> —*Mark Twain*

*T*he other day Gillian came to my office upset from the previous evening. "My mother was supposed to join us for dinner," she said. "She was coming by on her way back upstate. She knows we eat early; I have to get the kids settled down and in bed. She said she'd be to us by six. At 6:20 I got a call from her saying she was twenty minutes away and asking me to wait. I was already starting to feed the kids. I hate it when she does this, and she does it all the time."

Gillian was a latchkey kid. At eight she was coming home from school and taking care of her four-year-old brother until her mother came back from her teaching job. It was scary and overwhelming to have so much responsibility so young, and she missed her mother and her father. She missed being a kid who didn't have adult responsibilities and worries piled on top of her. "And it wasn't like she came home at 3:30," recounted Gillian. "She'd show up whenever she got around to it. I just remember day after day of waiting for her, trying to take care of my brother, not ever knowing just when she would show up. She never let me know anything." Gillian was completely out of control of her mother's schedule. She was left in the dark as to her plans, and it produced a lot of stress in her.

Today, that same feeling comes back to haunt her when the situation repeats itself in grown-up form. It still sends Gillian into orbit when her mother is late. When she gets triggered by something like her mother's disregard for her schedule, her unconscious echoes with muffled voices from the past, her own and everyone else's. It makes her feel hurt all over again when her mother acts with indifference to her needs, just as it did when she was a child, and she can't keep her mind on what she's doing because she is so preoccupied with what's going on inside of her. Her stress just builds until she wants to explode, "Just don't come then."

One of the ways that Gillian parented herself and her brother was by trying to be a little adult. As a consequence she was very disciplined and responsible, but maybe a little too responsible for her own good. She overfunctioned in the home, to compensate for her mother's underfunctioning. She had taken on more than she could comfortably handle as a child, and it had left its mark. As we unpacked her feelings around this current trigger event, Gillian began to connect the dots, to understand her own overreaction. Understanding where all of this came from helped Gillian to come up with new coping strategies. For example, rather than make specific dinner plans with her mother, she'd say "Come by between this and this time for coffee." She decided to take a little less responsibility for everyone else's good time and give more of her energy to relaxing and enjoying her husband and children.

If dinner wasn't perfect and the clothes all folded, she gave it less importance, recognizing that being relaxed as a mother and enjoying her family might be better for all of them.

Feeling out of control within the families, relationships, or circumstances of our lives can be a source of stress. When the people we are meant to depend on act in ways that make them seem as if they aren't fully dependable, or don't care that much, it is confusing. And it hurts. We feel unimportant, forgotten, invisible. Gillian became much less anxious once she employed her new strategies; she felt less out of control. Part of the Serenity Prayer by Reinhold Neibuhr tells us to "accept the things we cannot change and change the things we can." It's excellent advice for managing stress.

One of the most basic forms of anxiety is referred to as "generalized anxiety," or anxiety that is experienced all of the time. For people suffering from panic attacks, anxiety may come out of the blue. Unlike generalized anxiety, panic is more episodic, more sudden. But in between, the fear of a reoccurring panic attack can be a nagging one.

Still another type of anxiety disorder is a phobia, in which people have problems in certain situations. Phobias can represent irrational fears of, say, spiders or enclosed spaces. Phobias come in all shapes and sizes. Social phobia, for example, can make one dread social gatherings, while agoraphobia, fear of the marketplace, represents a fear of going out in certain public places. Post-traumatic stress disorder is another form of severe anxiety that we have talked about much in this book, in which anxiety-related symptoms emerge weeks, months, or even years after the frightening events that caused them.

The psychological symptoms of anxiety include feelings of dread and irritability. The physiological symptoms may include heightened activity in the nervous system. This heightened activity leads to a variety of physical symptoms such as dry mouth, shortness of breath, muscle tension, dizziness, and trembling.

Anxiety and depression are two of the most common complaints of people who enter therapy. Throughout this book, we have been describing the kinds of chronic stressors that are a direct result of relationship trauma and can contribute to anxiety and depression. When clients come into therapy, often the simple act of doing something positive about their situation is relieving. As therapy progresses, small gains make big differences. With anxiety, for example, the kinds of fears and hypervigilance that surround it are greatly helped simply by talking about their anxious thoughts and feelings. As we share our fears, they tend to reduce in size, and fall into proportion. The parts of our fears that are irrational and therefore cause anxiety become clearer. We see which fears are reality-based and which are irrational, and we can come up with strategies to manage the fears that have more reality to them and recognize the irrational fears for what they are. Sometimes the strategy is simply to learn to see them differently, to reframe them.

ANXIETY: AN EQUAL OPPORTUNITY DISORDER

Human beings actually aren't the only ones who experience stress. All vertebrates—fish, birds, and reptiles—respond to stressful situations by secreting the same hormones that we humans do, such as adrenaline and glucocorticoids, which instantaneously increase the animal's heart rate and energy level. Our fear response, remember, is nature's way of keeping us safe. We all have it encoded into our DNA, whether fish or fowl, human or animal. But this first group's metabolism doesn't get derailed and deregulated the way it does in people and other primates. According to Stanford University's Dr. Robert Sapolsky (2006), "Primates are super smart and organized just enough to devote their free time to being miserable to each other and stressing each other out. . . . For example, having your worst rival taking a nap one hundred yards away gets you agitated." A professor of biological and neurological sciences, Sapolsky has spent more than three decades studying the physiological effects of stress on health. "If you're a gazelle, you don't have a very complex emotional life, despite being a social species," he says. "But primates are just smart enough that they can think their bodies into working differently. It's not until you get to primates that you get things that look like depression. . . . If you get chronically, psychosocially stressed, you're going to compromise your health. So, essentially, we've evolved to be smart enough to make ourselves sick." Sapolsky's team has found that baboons, especially "type A" baboons, often have chronically elevated levels of stress hormones that impact their health negatively. "Their reproductive system doesn't work as well, their wounds heal more slowly and they have elevated blood pressure. . . . So they're not in great shape." Interestingly, both low-ranking and type A baboons are among the most susceptible to stress.

Relationships and social connections can actually counter this stress response. Baboons who need baboons, it turns out, are the luckiest baboons in the world, just like people who need people. Among baboons, social isolation may play an even more important role than social rank as far as stress goes. "Up until fifteen years ago, the most striking thing we found," says Sapolsky, "was that, if you're a baboon, you don't want to be low-ranking, because your health is going to be lousy. But what has become far clearer, and probably took a decade's worth of data, is the recognition that protection from stress-related disease is most powerfully grounded in social connectedness, and that's far more important than rank."

Human beings can do something further that animals aren't equipped to even conceive of. We can think creatively. We can imagine ways of seeing a situation, for example, of reframing and understanding it that can turn what could be a stressor into something that we don't worry about or that we can manage differently. We can self-reflect and come up with imaginative and novel solutions. We can even work through historical pain and use it as fodder for personal growth and deepening the self, reframing past stressful events so that they no longer cause us as much pain. We can, as Marcel Proust says, "learn to see the same landscape though different eyes." Human beings can, in short, conceive of and create change; we can use our minds to reframe, to see things in a better light.

"We are capable of social supports that no other primate can even dream of," says Sapolsky:

> For example, I might say, "This job, where I'm a lowly mailroom clerk, really doesn't matter. What really matters is that I'm the captain of my softball team or deacon of my church"—that sort of thing. It's not just somebody sitting here, grooming you with their own hands [as in the primate world]. We can actually feel comfort from the discovery that somebody on the other side of the planet is going through the same experience we are and feel, I'm not alone. We can even take comfort reading about a fictional character, and there's no primate out there that can feel better in life just by listening to Beethoven. So the range of supports that we're capable of is extraordinary.

DEPRESSION

Paul goes through bouts of time when he doesn't feel like getting out of bed. Since he retired, it's become worse. Sometimes he overeats, sometimes food turns him off. He can't seem to get himself out the door to exercise, so he feels worse, and the worse he feels, the less he exercises. He knows exercising and getting out of the house help him; he just can't seem to do those things. The world looks like it's made up of various shades of gray. The thought of walking to the corner feels overwhelming. Paul's friends get confused when they don't hear from him for weeks on end. Some of his closer friends know what's going on, some of his other friends don't. They wonder what's up. They don't understand why he doesn't call them back; it feels rude, and they eventually give up. Paul has explained to his intimates that, in these states, he doesn't feel he can even compose a coherent sentence. He can't seem to string the words together so they make sense. The phone weighs five hundred pounds, and even e-mail feels like too much effort, so many clicks and possible connections. . . . Paul withdraws from his normal routines and most of his social world. And the more he withdraws, the harder it seems to get back in. He gets out of practice and his social skills get rusty.

STRESS AND DEPRESSION

Cortisol, which contributes to everything from thinning hair to locking in fat storage (Northrup 2001), has emerged as a major culprit in depression and anxiety. "One of the most consistent biological findings about depression is that the adrenal cortex secretes more of the stress-related hormone cortisol in depressed people. This simple fact, which can be determined from a cotton swab containing saliva, links depression to the biology of stress," says Antonio Damasio (1999). When we're stressed, the concentration of cortisol in our bloodstream goes up. "In the short run, stress responses are useful in mobilizing bodily resources to cope with danger. But if stress is severe and continuous, the consequences can be serious. Your cardiovascular system can be compromised, your muscles can weaken, and you can develop ulcers and become

more susceptible to developing certain kinds of infections"
(Damasio 1999). Too much cortisol contributes to problems
with short-term memory; it's elevated in elderly people, especially those with memory problems and depression.

TRANSFORMING STRESS

Stressful feelings aren't heart smart. Hostility, whether
directed toward the self or others, is one of several feelings
that trigger the release of stress hormones into our bloodstreams. These hormones cause our coronary arteries to con-
strict, and at the same time induce a more rapid and powerful
heartbeat. They also increase our blood pressure, the tendency for blood clotting, and the levels of sugar and fats in our
blood. The net result is an increase in demand on our hearts.

But other feelings can affect the heart, too. In a recent
study, Duke Medical School researchers asked fifty-eight
patients with myocardial ischemia, a painful condition of
insufficient blood flow to the heart, to wear heart monitors for
forty-eight hours (Razdan 2007).

The patients were instructed to keep a diary of their
emotions throughout the day, including tension, sadness, frustration, happiness, and feeling in control. The researchers
found that patients who had stressful feelings were twice as
likely to have a bout of ischemic pain an hour later as patients
who didn't have stressful feelings. Emotional stress reduces
blood flow to the heart.

Depression is also hard on the heart. In a long-term study of
twelve hundred male medical students, researchers at Johns
Hopkins School of Medicine found that those experiencing depression were, on average, twice as likely to develop coronary artery
disease or suffer a heart attack fifteen years later (Razdan 2007).

Other research studies examining the effects of depression in
people who already have heart disease found that these people

are up to eight times more likely to develop ventricular tachycardia (abnormal and dangerous heart rhythms) than their peers who are not depressed. If we want emotional sobriety, a healthy heart is a good motivator because the kinds of body/mind changes we need to make in order to maintain heart health are also those that will lead to better emotional balance.

The heart is turning out, through research, to be living up to its stereotype as a center for our emotions. In the last twenty years, the heart has been reclassified from just a pump to a hormonal gland that has its own "brain" of sorts that collects information from the entire body and then communicates it to the brain. "The heart sends more information to the brain than the brain sends back down to the heart. . . . When we're experiencing stress, the heart's pattern gets jerky and arrhythmic and signals a chaotic pattern to the brain. The heart tells the brain, *Go into survival mode. Shut down higher cortical functions.* Thus, when our heart registers stress, it signals our cortex to shut down and go into survival mode" (Rozman 2005).

Consciously focusing on the heart and shifting to thinking positive thoughts or pleasing memories for a few moments actually helps our "hearts" to calm down.

"When we perform simple relaxation or coherence exercises that encourage us to feel positive emotions—love, appreciation, tolerance—heart-rhythm patterns are smooth," continues Rozman. "The brain then tells the frontal lobes that all systems are go, and you are able to open up to your most creative, intuitive, clear thinking. It's safe to develop your potential and to transform stress into creative energy."

Working with stress in this positive manner can help us to transform a moment of stress into a moment of opening, relaxation, and resilience building. Stress can shut us down or signal us to open up, refocus, breathe deeply, and let go. It can be a moment of contraction or a moment of expansion depending on how we work with it.

Spheres of Control; Reframing Stress

Stress very often occurs at the intersection of a high perception of responsibility and a low perception of control. In other words, when we are or feel we are responsible for something, but we have or feel that we have little influence or control over what happens in a situation, stress inevitably follows.

What gets us locked into a stress cycle are our expectations and, most importantly, our sense of perceived lack of control. One way we can regain a sense of control over an event or circumstance is by reframing it in our minds so that it's no longer perceived as a source of unbearable stress. We can learn to perceive it differently so that it no longer feels so oppressive and overwhelming. The proverbial question, "How important will this be in twenty years?" is a quick way to reframe. Or we can go over the event and put it into perspective. We're not changing the circumstance, but the way we're perceiving it.

TAKING THE NEXT RIGHT ACTION

Another way to reduce stress is to clarify what we do and don't have real control over. We can then adjust our sense of responsibility accordingly. Sometimes merely understanding what we really do and don't have control over is enough to lift that burdensome sense of overresponsibility that causes us stress. In other situations, figuring out what actions we can actually take to change things for the better and which aspects we need to let go of can be very relieving. In both cases we are doing what we can do and letting go of what's outside our sphere of control.

When we just freeze and do nothing, our feelings of helplessness, hopelessness, and victimhood can expand. We need to reclaim control by actively doing something, whether reframing, taking action, or recognizing where we have no jurisdiction. We may not change the circumstance, but we can certainly change our perception of it and the manner in which we deal with it. If we're under continued stress, we need to understand that something in our life needs attention and perhaps changing. We need to see stress not only as a burden, but as an opportunity to make some changes for the better— to transform something that's not working into something that is working. If we ignore our stress and it becomes chronic, the quality of our lives, health, and relationships may well go down.

16

$\mathcal{A}$nger

What Is It All About?
What Do I Do with It?

It is easy to fly into a passion—anyone can do that.
But to be angry with the right person, to the right
extent, at the right time, and with the right object
and in the right way—that is not easy, and it is not
everyone who can do it.

—Aristotle

Resentment is like taking poison
and waiting for the other person to die.

—Malachy McCourt

U nresolved anger can be a secondary reaction to early
relationship wounds. We remain angry because,
beneath it, we still feel hurt. These early wounds occur
for everyone: they are part of growing up and developing a
separate sense of self that is no longer just an extension of our

parents. When we're young we're especially vulnerable to those we love and need because they have such power over our lives. Many of these early wounds resolve themselves naturally as we become secure in our sense of self and feel increasingly capable and self-reliant, or find other ways of getting our needs for love, attention, and security met. Some wounds, however, don't heal so easily, particularly those that are the result of relationship trauma, abuse, rupture, or neglect. These are the wounds that we need to consciously resolve in adulthood so that they don't burden our interactions in the present with large amounts of pent-up anger that slip out sideways.

DISPLACED OR TRANSFERRED ANGER

When anger from the past gets triggered and layered onto a circumstance in our present, we call it "transference." Old anger is being transferred or displaced onto a new situation. The problem with transference is that we may be entirely unaware that our intense reaction to a present-day circumstance is being fueled by pain we are still carrying from the past. When emotional pain remains unresolved, it lies in wait, often unconscious of its power and content, until some stimulus in the here-and-now triggers it and it rises to the surface. We might react to a perceived threat (as subtle as a change in vocal tone or the look in an eye) with a response that is far greater than the situation merits. Transference can be confusing to untangle as yesterday's pain gets incorporated into today's issues and they become hard to separate. This can be particularly gnarly when it comes to intimate relationships. If Bret's mother was a manic depressive, for example, he may read way too much into his wife's moods, and his hypervigilance may actually create tension and anger, contributing to his worst fears: that his wife is as problematic as his mother was.

HIDDEN OR SPLIT OFF ANGER

Anger can be split off (cast out of conscious awareness), repressed, denied, or turned inward. In these cases it may turn into depression or physical ailments (back pain, headaches, excessive muscle tension, for example), or lead to self-medication. Anger hurts. It's uncomfortable to feel. When our anger sits within us and never gets worked through, or when we don't have constructive ways of processing or dealing with it, we may try to get rid of it by projecting it at someone else, or we may try to drown out our frustration, resentment, and pain with alcohol, drugs, food, or compulsive behaviors.

Passive-Aggressive Anger

Those who are easily angered do not solely blow up, yell, and slam doors. People who go to an angry place quickly may also show it indirectly. When we don't want to openly own our angry feelings, we may act them out sideways. When anger is disowned but leaks out around the edges or is acted out in hidden, pathological, or even devious ways, we refer to it as passive-aggressive—that is, the behavior contains aggression, but the aggressive feelings are not owned or dealt with openly. Some examples of passive-aggressive anger are neglect, ignoring, the silent treatment, stonewalling, constant criticism, chronic grouchiness, constant lateness, constant negativity, or even constantly taking the "positive" or "high" road as a way of one-upping or feeling superior to the other person. This kind of anger is confusing to deal with because we don't always see it coming, and the person exhibiting these behaviors may quickly deny they're angry if we confront them. They are disowning the feeling inside themselves and are uncomfortable with the idea of their own anger, which is why it comes out through passive-aggressive channels.

RAGE: THE HIJACKED BRAIN

"During rage attacks . . . those parts of the brain that are central to feeling and expressing anger, such as the amygdala and the hypothalamus, commandeer the rest of the brain. In this wholesale takeover, the cerebral cortex is overwhelmed and restraint and reasoning are impossible. . . . Although rage—by which I mean anger that is extreme, immoderate or unrestrained—may be adaptive as a response to severe threat, in most situations it destroys much more than it accomplishes," says Dr. Norman Rosenthal (2002).

Chronic rage might also be an indicator of depression. It's been estimated that 40 percent of those suffering from rage attacks also suffer from clinical depression. Rage attacks can also be a part of PTSD. When we feel traumatized, we may be overcome with feelings of helplessness and rage.

Dr. Martin Teicher and colleagues at Harvard have found that adults who were abused as children, whether verbally, physically or sexually, show brain wave changes over the temporal lobe of the cerebral cortex. These changes resemble those seen in people with documented seizures in the temporal lobe, which surrounds the limbic structures. . . . Teicher suggests that early traumatic experiences might kindle seizure-type activity in this area, resulting in a storm of electrical activity in the emotional part of the cerebral cortex. . . . The end result could be a brain that is cocked and all too ready to fire off a limbic storm (Rosenthal 2002).

HOOKED ON ADRENALINE: THE BIOLOGY OF VIOLENT BEHAVIOR

Fear and anger are the emotions that lead us to choose more violent behaviors over more emotionally sober ones. Fear tends to create a sense of powerlessness and anger at feeling out of control, which increases feelings of powerlessness. Fear and anger release adrenaline into our bloodstreams, which pumps us up.

The more we rage or hit, the more deeply this behavior gets ingrained in our neural pathways. We become neurologically hooked on this type of release of our overwhelming emotions.

In his article, "Spanking Is an Addiction," Stan Dale writes:

> Adrenaline is probably the single most addictive substance known to humanity. Chemically, it is a near equivalent to the central nervous system as the stimulant known as amphetamine, or speed. Adrenaline keeps us feeling good. What's more, we do not have to leave the easy chair to get it—all we have to do is think! One solitary thought, and this powerful stimulant will pulse through our veins. So it is that we hit our children not only because we are programmed for violence, but also because we are addicted to the adrenaline it produces. We have become, in short, adrenaline junkies (Dale 2007).

Physically abusing children not only affects their hearts and minds, it has a long-term impact on their nervous systems as well:

> Research into the physiology of spanking, for example, reveals that swatting a child on the buttocks excites the sciatic nerve, which runs through the genitals. Many children who are spanked come to associate

sexual excitation with violence; as adults, they are
unable to experience orgasm without accompanying
feelings of physical or emotional abuse. The converse
is also true. Many children who are spanked shut down
their sexual responses out of fear, shame, or the sense
that they are somehow inappropriate; these children
enter adulthood with an inability to experience sexual
feelings (Dale 2007).

Though rage can feel gratifying and even integrating to
ragers because they are finally giving expression to split-off
feelings they may normally push out of consciousness, the irrational nature of rage keeps it from leading to any kind of true
or useful understanding. People can feel temporarily empowered by raging; they may have seen themselves as too weak,
humiliated, or beaten down to "let it fly" in the past, so it feels
gratifying to release pent-up emotions. They may experience
themselves as going from tiny to big, helpless to empowered if
the source of the pain getting triggered is from a past wound
inflicted or experienced when they felt unempowered. But
ultimately we need to make sense of our feelings in order to
use them to grow from; simply discharging them and walking
away doesn't do the job. Rage can be highly damaging to those
around the raging person and their relationships. "Letting it
rip" can escalate anger and aggression, and does not necessarily help us or the person with whom we're angry. In fact, "an
old myth is that it is best to let your anger out when you feel it.
New evidence, however, suggests that releasing it only makes it
worse. To your nervous system, the release may be more a
rehearsal, enhancing the neural pathways involved. It is far
better for your health to find ways to let the issue go, or to
channel the anger in a constructive way (Rosenthal 2002)." In
therapy, expressing anger in clinical safety through role-play is
relieving if it leads to resolution and a deeper understanding

of the self. However, if it doesn't lead to the kinds of resolutions that develop new neural pathways for managing anger, it may not be constructive in the long run.

CALMING THE LIMBIC STORM

Because the cortex is overridden in the rage state, sense is not likely to accompany rage, which is why a time-out is good. It gives the body a chance to reregulate. Another way to reregulate is through mobilizing the part of our brain that can make sense and meaning out of this limbic storm. Perhaps the rage state sets us up for the hope of solving an old pain-filled situation, a variation on what Freud called an attempt at mastery. Unconsciously we may feel that as long as we can stay invested in our anger, which over time fuels rage, there's still hope for ultimate resolution. But, in reality, not everything can get resolved. Sometimes—in fact, many times—resolution of past hurts is resolved within the self. That is, we don't necessarily change the problem; we learn instead to see it in a new light, to reframe it. We explore it, tease out the meaning we made of it and that we have been living by, and feel the feelings that we may have split off and out of our conscious awareness because they were too overwhelming for us to integrate at the time—the feelings that blew our available circuits. We understand the problem in the light of today, and reintegrate our memories with new understanding and insight. This is mostly an inside job. When this doesn't occur, our past tends to get layered onto our present in ways that make the present feel overwhelming, confusing, and disheartening.

STRATEGIES FOR MANAGING ANGER

Following are some realistic and genuinely helpful strategies for managing anger that stay away from quick fixes. Rosenthal (2002) outlines ten strategies, and I have added two others to the list.

1. *Recognize that your anger is a problem.* Nothing will change if we don't honestly admit to having a problem with anger. Even if we're not flying into rages, being angry on the inside keeps us in a fight-or-flight state and undermines our health and our relationships.

2. *Monitor your anger level.* Keep an informal chart that marks down times of the day when you're most likely to get angry: coming home from work, for example, or around the kids' bedtime.

3. *Look for a pattern.* Look for an identifiable pattern; if you find one, take steps to remain calm using some of the tips listed below, so that you can avoid getting angry at the same old things. Use a little prevention to head off a typical pitfall before it becomes a problem.

4. *Take a time-out.* The body physically responds to anger, so a time-out can allow the body, as well as emotions, to calm down. This keeps us from getting lost in a vicious cycle, where our upset bodies are feeding our upset emotions and thoughts, and our upset emotions and thoughts are feeding our upset bodies.

5. *Challenge perceptions and thoughts that fuel your anger.* We may be looking at the world in an "awfulizing" way, expecting the worst and helping to create it. If we have a constant negative read on things, we also have negative expectations, which can become a self-fulfilling prophecy.

6. *Dig deeper to understand the roots.* As we've discussed throughout this book, some anger can have historical roots. Maybe we came from families that were so angry, we were trained in it in both body and mind. Or maybe we're

expressing in our adult lives the anger we had to hold in as children. Our anger might also be acting as a defense against deeper feelings of pain and helplessness. We need to get to the root so that we can change the pattern.

7. *Change the messages you give to yourself.* Sometimes our "self messages" make situations much worse than they have to be. For example, if our boss is critical, we may say to ourselves, "She has no respect for me; she thinks I'm not very smart. Who does she think she is? I'm not at all appreciated." If we can change these messages to more useful ones like, "I'll listen to the criticism and see if I can use any of it to improve my work," or "I'm bright enough to figure out how to get this to work, and I'll use these ideas to help me," we will be empowering ourselves rather than running ourselves down, and we'll get a little distance from messages that feel hurtful.

8. *Use exposure and relaxation.* "Joseph Wolphe, a pioneer in behavioral therapy research, was the first to reason that it is impossible to feel highly aroused and relaxed at the same time. If you get a person to relax while exposing him to an unpleasant stimulus at the same time . . . you can recondition him. . . . The nervous system can be taught to greet that stimulus with relaxation, not the old, unpleasant emotions," says Rosenthal (2002). Next time you get triggered, you have an opportunity to recondition your response by actively changing the way you're thinking and using deep-breathing techniques to stay calm. You can recondition yourself.

9. *Use humor.* If there is a funny side to the situation, use it to create some new energy. This is different from using humor in a sarcastic or belittling way, or as a hiding place; it's using it to see things in a way that allows us to gain some emotional and psychological freedom and to maintain a healthy perspective.

10. *Listen to your limbic news and act appropriately.* This is where we can use our anger as information. What is my body telling me about how I'm feeling? Where am I tense, queasy, shaking, or tightened up? Do I need to breathe, take a break, or calm down so that my thinking mind can be more useful to me?

11. *Find out what triggers you and develop strategies to avoid getting triggered.* Many of us have hot spots. Often they have to do with our own insecurities getting touched, such as someone calling us out in an area in which we are already feeling bad about ourselves. Or we get triggered in an area in which we were hurt repeatedly so we're tender to the touch. Learn to recognize when that is happening so that you don't keep falling into your own trap.

12. *Do some cognitive restructuring or change the way you think.* When angry thoughts get exaggerated, overly dramatic, and "awfulized," try replacing them with more rational ones.

Some other strategies:

✦ Don't say, "It's awful, terrible, everything's ruined; it's always like this; it will never work out."

✦ Do say, "It's frustrating; it's undesirable that I'm upset but not the end of the world. I'm not pleased with the situation, but I can back up, regroup, and make changes to improve things."

✦ Avoid words like "never" and "always." They alienate and humiliate people and keep them from working with us. They also work us up into an unnecessary lather.

✦ Remind yourself that getting angry is not going to fix anything. It won't really make you feel better, and it may make you feel worse. Remember what you're doing to your body when you get angry.

Grief

Cleansing the Wound

If you suppress grief too much,
it can well redouble.

—Molière

 motional wounds, like wounds to the body, need to be
cleansed so that they can heal. People are often afraid to
enter grief because they fear they will never emerge.

Grief serves a number of important emotional, psychological and physiological functions. When we grieve, we naturally allow ourselves to feel the anger, hurt, disorientation, and sadness that are a part of processing pain. As we grieve, we let go of some of our hypervigilance. When we understand that feeling these feelings are part of the healing process, and that by feeling them we can allow them to dissipate, we begin to see light at the end of the tunnel.

Three decades ago, grief was seen primarily as death related. We weren't really talking about grief as a life issue, something that we needed to go through for any life-related loss. But it became increasingly obvious to me that what my own clients needed to do was to grieve the losses of self, childhood, stability, and those they loved to the disease of addiction or mental illness. The more I worked with clients' grief issues, the better they were getting. Additionally, trauma was not being talked about as a relational issue; it was talked about as if it happened just within a person. It was during this period that it also became clear to me that the trauma I was seeing in clients was the direct result of relationship pain, and that if it remained unresolved, it would continue to drive dysfunctional relationship patterns. During this time I wrote *Heartwounds: The Impact of Unresolved Trauma and Grief on Relationships* (1997) in order to address those concerns.

Anger, sadness, and depression are part of the grieving process and will inevitably surface during it. Grief, disruption to one's stable world, or fear of the future can also fuel anxiety. This is part of why grieving can be so healing. Spiritual renewal can also be part of the grieving process. Grief leads us back to emotional equilibrium and balance. We gain many gifts during the grief process: we learn more about the deeper sides of ourselves, develop empathy and understanding for ourselves and others, cleanse our souls, and renew our spirits. True grieving can bring us closer to life, which is why it can feel renewing.

WHEN TO LET NATURE TAKE ITS COURSE

In cases of loss to death, a growing body of research suggests that intervention is not necessarily beneficial in all situations. Feeling grief is a natural occurrence when we lose someone we care about; it is a testimony to our ability to become meaningfully attached and is not pathological or unnatural. A major new study entitled "Report on Bereavement and Grief Research" prepared by the Center for the Advancement of Health concluded:

A growing body of evidence indicates that interventions with adults who are not experiencing complicated grief cannot be regarded as beneficial in terms of diminishing grief-related symptoms. . . . In fact, the studies indicate, grief counseling may sometimes make matters worse for those who lost people they loved, regardless of whether the death was traumatic or occurred after a long illness, according to Dr. John Jordan, director of the Family Loss Project in the Boston area. Such people may include the only man in a group of women, a young person in a group of older people, or someone recently bereaved in a group that includes a person still suffering intensely a year or more after the loved one's death.

Further, the research suggests, bereavement counseling is least needed in the immediate aftermath of a loss. Yet it is then that most grieving people are invited to take part in the offered services. A more appropriate time is six to eighteen months later, if the person is still suffering intensely. The care and comfort offered by friends and relatives was found to be the most beneficial to the person suffering loss. Unless the loss is complicated, most people can work through their loss, even though it is painful and difficult. And men and women tend to grieve differently which can also influence how they experience grief counseling. For example, most bereavement groups focus on emotional issues, which seem to be most helpful to women. But men are more likely to benefit from an approach that focuses on their processes of thinking.

GRIEVING OLD LOSSES

Losses that have gone underground for years, that have remained open wounds deep within the self, may benefit greatly from grieving out in the open with the support and understanding of others. We experience a loss of self when we relegate emotional wounds into a sort of psychic silence. They are losses that become complicated over time, interwoven with other losses. In cases of addiction and divorce, family members often aren't able to acknowledge the depth of their pain around the loss of, for example, a sober parent or the family unit.

As with trauma, there is no one-size-fits-all approach to grief. Normal grief that occurs, for example, when someone we love dies, has a dignity that allows the griever the freedom to experience her emotions and feel accepted and understood by her surrounding communities. But grief over losses that are disenfranchised or out of the normal stream can be hidden or looked at askance, which tends to push the pain downward rather than allowing it to come up and out. This is why it so often comes out sideways in anger, for example, or in excessive hypervigilance and caretaking.

People in recovery from addiction, codependency, or PTSD may be at risk for becoming symptomatic around current life losses because of their earlier ungrieved losses. When we observe how current life issues may be triggering historical, unresolved pain, we can use today's overreactions or reenactment patterns as indicators pointing to the spot where our deeper wounds lie.

A surprisingly large number of life events go ungrieved, and thus they become disenfranchised. Some examples of these losses are:

+ The effects of divorce on spouses, children, and the family unit.

+ Dysfunction in the home; loss of family life.
+ Addiction; loss of periods of one's life to using and abusing.
+ Loss of an addictive substance or behavior.
+ Loss of a parent, spouse, or child to the diseases of addiction or mental illness.
+ Loss of job, health, youth, children in the home; retirement; life transitions.

If we cannot mourn these types of losses, we may:

+ Stay stuck in anger, pain, and resentment.
+ Lose access to important parts of our inner, feeling world.
+ Project unfelt, unresolved grief onto any situation, placing those feelings where they do not belong.
+ Lose personal history along with the unmourned person or situation; a part of us dies, too.
+ Carry deep fears of subsequent abandonment.

Unlike a loss to death, there is no funeral to acknowledge and honor disenfranchised losses, no grave to visit, no covered dishes dropped at the door, no sitting in the company of fellow mourners and supporting each other through the tears. These losses live in unmarked graves that sit within the unconscious of the family unit.

ADDICTION AND GRIEF

Many addicts have relied on a substance to manage emotional pain. In sobriety, they may have complicated issues of grief. They may need to grieve:

+ The life they have lost through addiction (lost time, lost years that they could have devoted to getting their lives in order).

✦ The painful issues that they were self-medicating with drugs, alcohol, food, sex, or gambling.

✦ The pain that they have caused those they love.

To make matters tougher still, recovering addicts will be grieving these issues with a weakened set of psychological and emotional tools, which is why it is often advisable to make sure sobriety is solid before dealing with early trauma, so that it doesn't lead to relapse. Ignoring these issues for years and years in sobriety is no answer either. They may then become the pain pump that fuels relapse because they are the pain we were medicating in the first place.

The ACOA or spouse of an addict also has mourning to do. But some of their losses can be complicated to mourn. For example, they may feel they have no right to mourn the loss of a problematic relationship, whether a parent, spouse, addict, or abusive person, because they are "better off without him." They may have conflicting feelings of love and hate, guilt and relief, that complicate their mourning process. But painful and complicated relationships can be very hard to let go of, exactly because there is so much unfinished business connected with them. Millions of dollars are often spent trying to locate the bodies of lost loved ones so that we can mourn them. This need to concretize the object of loss seems to be a deep psychic need, without which the mind and heart search and yearn without settling. This is why I find psychodrama so useful in helping clients to grieve. Through role-play we can concretize the lost person, object, or period of life and talk directly to it. We can create a ritual, in a sense, through which mourning can happen.

DIVORCE AND GRIEF

Divorce seems to occur between two people. This is an illusion. Divorce is a family affair. We lose not only one person, but we may even lose access to all of the relationships in the network that belong to that person. If we don't lose them, they certainly change.

For the child of divorce, losses are multiple and substantial. They lose easy access to one parent. Along with this, they may lose easy access to the network of that parent as well. They may also lose the comfort and security of knowing just where they belong; all of this is thrown into serious question during divorce. Children of divorce lose the security of coming from parents who are able to work out their differences and live comfortably together. And sometimes the anger and resentment that divorcing partners carry for one another is the stuff of novels and detective stories. All of these losses need to be acknowledged, understood, and grieved. The problem is that generally both parents are in so much pain themselves, the pain of their child overwhelms them.

Children may also experience divorce as fragmenting on a psychic level. The limbic bonds that have been woven into the fabric of their beings can become disrupted or even torn through divorce. The child feels fragmented inside. This needs to be recognized so that the pain, resentment, and sense of disconnection that is incumbent upon any divorce doesn't do long-lasting damage.

All this being said, a good divorce can be better than living in an unbearable circumstance. If handled well, it can show all concerned that life can be renewed and relationships can work. We all take a huge risk when we marry.

GRIEF AND SELF-MEDICATING

In sobriety, losses that went ungrieved and that were numbed through self-medication—rather than felt, understood, and integrated—will inevitably surface. Furthermore, the feelings they arouse will be confusing because they may reach back for years, even decades, in the life of the addict or recovering person. Without the coping strategy of self-medication, the sober addict will need to summon the strength to live through the pain that previously felt like too much to tolerate. The benefits of grieving are as follows:

✦ Grieving is necessary in order to release the anger and sadness that arise as part of the grieving process.

✦ Grieving allows us to integrate emotions and/or split off parts of self that may have been denied, repressed, or split out of consciousness, which helps us to become or remain more whole.

✦ Grieving allows the wound to heal. If we do not grieve, we build walls around the ungrieved wound in order to protect it. When a wound is not healed, it hurts. It is tender to the touch, so we push away any experience that might press on it.

✦ Grieving makes it easier not to retreat from deep connection when it presents itself again in our lives. We reduce the fear that we will not be able to handle the potential pain that could be associated with deep feeling and caring.

✦ Grieving can lead to a spiritual awakening.

Warning Signs of Unresolved Grief

Excessive guilt
Excessive anger/sudden angry outbursts
Recurring or long-lasting depression
Caretaking behavior
Self-mutilation
Emotional numbness or constriction

POSSIBLE GRIEF TRIGGERS

Following is a list of life situations that sometimes trigger grief that is unconscious.

Anniversary reactions. Anniversary reactions are common on or around the anniversary of a loss or death. One may feel a vague or even an overwhelming sense of pain related to a loss that feels as if it is coming out of nowhere. This reaction may also be experienced around previous significant dates such as hospitalization, sickness, sobriety, relapse, or divorce.

Holiday reactions. Holidays can stimulate pain from previous losses. Because they are traditional ritual gatherings, they heighten our awareness about what is missing or what has changed.

Age-correspondence reactions. This reaction occurs when, for example, a person reaches the age at which there was a loss by someone with whom he or she identified. A daughter whose mother divorced around age forty-five, for example, may find herself thinking about or even considering divorce when she reaches that approximate age.

Seasonal reactions. Change of seasons can stimulate grief; it's a transition that we would previously have shared.

Music-stimulated grief. Music can act as a doorway to the unconscious. It activates the right brain, drawing out associations and feelings that get stimulated by a particular song or piece of music.

Ritual-stimulated grief. Important, shared rituals can stimulate grief when there has been a loss. For example, family dinners or Sunday brunch can be a sad time for family members who have experienced divorce or death.

Smells or returning to a particular location. Smell is associated with the oldest part of the brain and can stimulate memories. Also, visiting a place that was previously shared with a loved one, now lost, can bring painful recollections—and eventually relief if feelings are confronted honestly and directly.

INADEQUATE ATTEMPTS
AT DEALING WITH GRIEF

Following are some attempts to deal with or manage grief that do not necessarily lead to satisfactory resolution and integration:

Premature resolution. Premature resolution occurs when people try to force themselves to resolve grief without allowing themselves to move through the full cycle of mourning. In these cases, the unresolved feelings tend to come out sideways in the form of projections, transferences, bursts of anger, simmering resentments, excessive criticism, bouts of depression, and so on.

Pseudoresolution. Pseudoresolution is a false resolution that occurs when a person fools himself or herself into feeling that grief has been resolved, when it actually has not run its course.

Replacement. Sometimes we replace the lost person or circumstance without mourning the previous loss first. For example, the divorced person who immediately marries again may feel he or she has solved the pain of loss when, in fact, the loss has not been learned from and processed. In the case of divorce, the same issues that led to one loss tend to reappear in the next relationship.

Displacement. Displacement occurs when mourners cannot connect their pain to what is actually causing it and instead displace their anger and sadness onto something or someone else where it does not belong. It becomes difficult to resolve pain in this case, because it is projected onto and experienced around the wrong object. The pain needs to be consciously linked back to what is actually causing it.

THE STAGES OF THE
NATURAL GRIEVING PROCESS

The stages that one can expect to pass through in the grieving process are laid out below. Loss here is defined as loss of a person, a part of the self, a period of life, or life circumstance. I have adapted John Bowlby's (1969) first four stages on loss of primary attachment figures and added a fifth stage that I have seen clients pass through when they can allow themselves to surrender to the process of grieving. Particularly when the grieving is of disenfranchised losses related to addiction, divorce, or dysfunction, we can feel a new lease on life when we move through the stages of loss. People's feelings do not necessarily follow an exact course, but the stages offer an overall map of the emotional terrain covered during the process of grieving loss. The stages are:

1. **Emotional numbness and shutdown.** In this stage, we may go through a period of feeling emotionally numb. We know something happened, but our feelings are shut down and out of reach.

2. **Yearning and searching.** There is deep yearning in this stage for what was lost, whether a stage of life, a part of the self, or a person, followed by searching for a way to replace the loss. Ghosting, or the sense of a continuing presence of a person, for example, or even feeling one is seeing that person, may be experienced. Drink signals, when an addict feels a strong psychic flash of drinking or wanting to drink, may be a form of ghosting.

3. **Disruption, anger, and despair.** In this stage, clients may experience anger, despair, sadness, and disappointment that comes and goes, and at times is overwhelming. Life feels disrupted. Many losses that have anger and resentment attached to them can get confusing at this point; for example, it may be easier for some ACOAs to feel the

anger rather than the sadness beneath it. Or there may be ambivalent feelings like longing and relief, or rage and yearning.

4. **Reorganization and integration.** In this stage we are able to articulate and experience either the natural, numbed, or split-off emotion connected with the loss and integrate it into the self system. This is a stage of acceptance and letting go.

5. **Reinvestment, spiritual growth, and renewed commitment to life.** In this stage, we come to believe in life's intrinsic ability to repair and rebuild itself. We experience firsthand that we can heal by reaching out and letting in love and caring from willing people. We have energy freed up that we can reinvest in life.

One of the most important functions a recovery support network can provide is a safe and supportive container that can help the recovering person to "hold" or experience feelings that may, at times, overwhelm them, rather than shut them down.

The beauty of grief is that it frees up our energy. We become unstuck, and we find that we have choices about how and where we want to invest our energy and time that may previously have been unavailable to us.

Grief Self-Test

Rate your answers to the following questions from 1–10.

1. How much do you feel unresolved emotions surrounding this loss?
2. How disruptive was this loss to your daily routines?
3. How much depression do you feel?
4. How much yearning do you feel?
5. How much emotional constriction do you experience?
6. How much sadness do you feel?
7. How much anger do you feel?
8. How much ghosting of the lost person, situation, substance, or part of self do you feel?
9. How much fear of the future do you feel?
10. How much trouble are you having organizing yourself?
11. How uninterested in your life do you feel?
12. How much old, unresolved grief is being activated and remembered as a result of this current issue?
13. How tired do you feel?
14. How much hope do you feel about your life and the future?
15. How much regret do you feel?
16. How much self-recrimination do you feel?
17. How much shame or embarrassment do you feel?

This self-assessment tool is designed to measure your level of grief. If the loss is current, high scores are considered a normal response. If the loss is historical areas in which you find yourself in the upper third (7, 8, 9, 10) they may be issues that you wish to address with the help of a trained professional.

$\mathcal{H}$ealthy Self-Soothing and Natural Highs

It takes courage to push yourself
to places that you have never been before . . .
to test your limits . . . to break through barriers. . . .
and the day comes when the risk . . .
to remain tight inside the bud is more
painful than the risk it takes to blossom.

—*Anïas Nin*

REPLACING THE "GOOD MOTHER FEELING"

W e never completely outgrow our need to seek emotional regulation from something outside ourselves. We are wired for clans, packs, herds, and groups. As we grow older, we turn to other regulating influences: family and friends, spiritual communities, the workplace, pets, even TV and the Internet. We are seeking a sense of connection so that we can feel good. We absorbed the sensation of self-regulation from our parents, and as we did this, we laid down a neural path back toward it. We are wired to want this good feeling as much as possible.

As adults, then, reaching for something that will make us feel good is natural. Addiction and self-medicating can be seen as attempts to replace what psychologists call "the good mother," to find a reliable way to feel that sense of oneness and equanimity we enjoyed as a child. Needless to say, addictions are a self-destructive way to achieve this sense of well-being. An important part of recovery is learning healthy ways to self-soothe and self-regulate, healthy ways to feel cozy and good inside.

THE FINE ART OF SELF-SOOTHING: LEARNING THE SKILLS OF SELF-REGULATION

Living in balance can challenge the most docile among us. Life happens. Work stress, family baggage, and the pressures of raising children can sometimes make living a balanced life seem like an impossible dream, but it's not. If we make living a sane and sensible life a priority, if we take being out of whack seriously and make it a life habit to restore our equilibrium as soon as we begin to fall out of it rather than allowing it to get out of hand, we'll find that a life lived in balance becomes its own reward. We'll come to value feeling in balance so much that we will naturally schedule ourselves with serenity in mind. We'll have a coterie of daily routines to maintain our equanimity, and we'll have a set of emergency tools for righting ourselves whenever we feel on tilt.

One of the first developmental tasks children need to learn is to self-soothe. We never outgrow our need for self-soothing activities; they are what allow us to calm down, to even out, to restore our equilibrium. Brain imaging shows, in living color, just how addictions of all kinds activate the brain's pleasure centers. Taking heroin, for example, causes dopamine, one of the brain's natural soothers, to flood into the brain. Sexual acting out, speeding, shopping, and gambling also light up pathways in the brain area associated with pain relief and feeling calm and soothed.

Brain imaging and other forms of tests provide a clear picture of the kinds of activities that soothe us and bring us into balance. There are many healthy ways of getting "natural highs." One of the developmental tasks of recovery is to learn new healthy skills of self-soothing and self-regulating and to make them part of our daily lives. We need to learn techniques that help us to live in balance and to pull us back into a state of equilibrium when we fall out of it. We need to develop user-friendly ways of activating our body/mind's natural feel-good chemicals and our brain's pleasure centers so we can gradually become less dependent on unhealthy ways of getting that high or calm feeling. Research is increasingly discovering that adult brains retain significant neural plasticity, meaning we can change our neural patterns throughout life. The "opiates of attachment" or "brain fertilizers" that are turned on through certain activities act as mood regulators.

Following are some healthy forms of self-soothing and self-regulating. As you read this list, you might find yourself surprised that a lot of the things you like doing most are on it. This is guilt-free self-care that can be a gift to you and to those who are close to you.

Exercise/Yoga

The soothing body chemicals that nature meant us to experience don't get a chance to work their daily magic if we don't stimulate them through exercise of some sort. Daily exercise evens out or elevates our moods, our motivation, and our pleasure in living. We need dopamine and serotonin to be released into our bodies in order to attain the feel-good state that helps us to self-regulate and balance our emotional states. This prescription, according to research, is as effective as any drug is for healing depression. In a recent study at Duke University, researchers Michael Babyak and James Blumenthal reported in the October 2000 issue of the journal *Psychosomatic Medicine,* that depressed patients who exercised had declines in depression equal to those who received antidepressants. In addition, those who continued to exercise after treatment were 50 percent less likely to become depressed again.

A ten-minute walk gives us more energy in the long run than a candy bar. Researchers find that exercising in whatever way is most convenient works best. If it's a brief walk during a lunch break, walking the dog, or biking to work, exercise seems to work well when combined with purposeful activity or when it's built easily into our lives. Research also reveals that exercising with other people helps us to make it a more regular part of our lives. Yoga is another very effective way to learn to self-soothe and calm the nervous system. It also has the added effects of creating a relaxed and supple body.

Breath Awareness

The breath is part of the unconscious brain process as well as part of the limbic system. Breathing is a bodily function that is regulated by the autonomic nervous system as well as the conscious voluntary nervous system. Breathing is the only body system that unites both this conscious and autonomic part of ourselves, acting as a bridge between the two systems. We can't always relieve anxiety by willpower alone, but we can slow our breathing down and gradually calm ourselves. If our breathing is uneven or labored, our mind is usually agitated. When we sleep or sit quietly reading, our breathing is slow and rhythmic. When our brains anticipate danger or we get scared, we tend to hold our breath or our breathing rate increases so that more oxygen can be sent to the blood cells and muscle fibers to prepare us to fight or run away to safety. The breath rate also increases to clean the blood of the kinds of toxins that are by-products of the body's chemical processes, which speed up in times of stress. We can try to consciously relax ourselves by slowing down and deepening our inhalations and exhalations, thereby stimulating our relaxation response. When the brain and body are calm and still, fewer toxins are introduced into the bloodstream, and respiration is able to slow down.

Thinking Positive Thoughts/Reading Uplifting Literature/Watching Uplifting Films or Videos

Researchers at Harvard conducted a study to determine whether or not our thoughts impact our bodies. They set up two control groups, the first group was asked to watch films of Nazi war crimes. The second watched films of Mother Teresa at work. After watching the films, each group had blood drawn. The group that had been watching films about Nazis had elevated levels of stress chemicals while the group watching the films about Mother Teresa had elevated levels of feel-good chemicals. Blood chemicals returned to normal after about twenty minutes. But here is the interesting part: in a second part of the study, subjects in each group were asked to continue to run the images they saw on the films in their mind's eye, throughout the day. Hours later, the results were the same. The group that had been thinking about the images they'd seen in the Nazi war films had continually high levels of stress chemicals in their blood, while the group that had been thinking of Mother Teresa had continued levels of feel-good body chemicals coursing through their bodies.

What we think about all day really does affect how we feel. When we think positive thoughts, our bodies actually respond by spurting out feel-good, self-soothing body chemicals that help us to stay calm and serene. When we read uplifting, spiritual, or motivating literature, we actively lift our own spirits.

Massage

In a 2005 review of research studies of patients with a broad range of physical and psychological conditions who used massage as part of their therapy, it was found that massage consistently lowered levels of cortisol while increasing activity of pleasure-related brain chemicals (Cochrane Database 2007). Massage also lowers blood pressure and heart rate, which may enhance immune function. One of the studies observed that women with breast cancer who participated in massage therapy three times a week for five weeks showed more immune system activity and reported less depression, anxiety, and fatigue than the women who didn't receive massages regularly. Massage also releases oxytocin, which is turned on by touch, into the bloodstream. Oxytocin regulates a variety of physical processes including emotion and is a natural and easily available mood stabilizer. It is also seen as one of the mood stabilizers that enhances feelings of trust and bonding and literally acts as fertilizer for neurons in the brain and body.

Proper Rest and Quiet Time

Researcher Thomas Wehr at the National Institute of Mental Health conducted studies during which he had people lie down in a quiet, darkened room for fourteen hours each night, conditions similar to those under which we evolved during the millions of years before the discovery of artificial light. Under these conditions, the subjects reported a state of pleasant relaxation coupled with a crystal-clear consciousness. Also, while they were in these states of relaxation and clarity, their pituitary glands were releasing prolactin into their bloodstreams. As the name implies, this chemical stimulates the breast tissue to release milk in nursing mothers. But even a slight, low level of anticipation during sleep was enough to keep prolactin from working its magic. In separate experiments, the researcher told subjects that at some point a nurse would enter the room to take blood. This semiconscious awareness during their sleep that they could be interrupted at any time was enough to stop the release of prolactin. (Men also release the hormone prolactin when they meditate or are in a state of deep relaxation.)

Warm Baths

One easy way to give yourself a little shot of prolactin is to take a warm bath. Research shows that heat causes prolactin to be released into the bloodstream.

Share with Others/Don't Isolate

Group therapy has repeatedly been studied for the effects of sharing emotions on the body. Over and over again, results reveal that talking over what's bothering us actually reduces stress chemicals in the body and elevates levels of the body's natural opioid system. Sharing feelings soothes the mind/body system, and crying does just the same. In fact tears shed in grief have a different chemical makeup from tears shed in joy. That's why we can feel so much better after a good cry. Pain and emotional trauma can make us want to isolate. Downtime and nourishing time alone is different from isolating. The kind of sharing of thoughts and feelings that can help to elevate our soothing body chemicals, along with being in the presence of other people who can help to regulate our body's vital rhythms, are both natural healers.

Thirty Minutes of Sunlight Daily

Thirty minutes of sunlight each day wards off depression, provides vitamins, and gives a much-needed boost to our immune systems. When we try to get our lives to work on a strictly psychological level, we ignore the fact that we live in a body, and that body has significant power over our moods. This is one of the easiest places to start to turn our lives around or to get out of an emotional slump. A daily, brisk, thirty-minute walk outdoors is free and is one of the best habits we can cultivate for our bodies, minds, and spirits. It can elevate our moods, keep us fit, control weight, relieve depression, and give us time with friends—to say nothing about connecting us with the great outdoors. There's just no downside to this one.

Journaling

Journaling also elevates the immune system and calms the autonomic system, smoothing out the heartbeat, breathing, and respiration, for example. James Pennebaker has documented this in his book *Opening Up* (1997), where he uses journaling to help people understand and work with the contents of their inner worlds. Pennebaker paints the picture of journaling as a very active, rather than passive, pursuit in which the body as well as the mind and emotions benefit. As we freely write our thoughts and feelings on paper, the associative process of our mind goes to work. Thoughts and feelings emerge onto the paper, finding their way from muteness into articulation. The more completely we can abandon our internal governors and trust the process of writing, the more penetrating our associations and glimpses into our inner world will be. Through journaling, we gain insight and perspective. We flush out concealed or veiled material and bring it out onto the page where we can see and reflect on it, creating new meaning to replace the old. We see a past problem through the eyes and maturity of today; what may have bewildered us once becomes clear, as we lay it out in front of ourselves.

The basic method is to simply put pen to paper and let your thoughts and feelings pour out freely. Give the editor who lives in your mind a vacation, and let go of worrying about saying things in a coherent or readable way. Simply trust the writing process. This is your private space for a full and unedited expression of self; no one needs to see what you write other than you. This is for your eyes alone, unless you choose to share it.

Recall a Pleasant Moment: Soothe the Heart and You Soothe the Self

You can calm and nourish your heart by regularly meditating or praying. These activities produce the relaxation response— a physiological state that is exactly the opposite of stress, a state that reduces blood pressure and increases blood flow to the heart. Many forms of meditation and prayer organically incorporate feelings of love, appreciation, and forgiveness. Some traditional Buddhist practices use lovingkindness meditation, during which they focus their attention on the heart and generate feelings of lovingkindness for others and themselves. Not only does this create the feelings in your mind, but it creates them in the body as well. A form of such intentional heart focus has been found by the HeartMath researchers to create greater coherence in heart rhythms in as little as one minute

To experience the benefits of this "intentional heart focus," try the following next time you're feeling stressed:

- Take a break and mentally disengage from the situation.
- Bring your attention to the area of your heart.
- Recall an experience with a loved one in which you felt happiness, love, or appreciation, or just meditate for a moment on those kinds of thoughts and feelings.
- Reexperience these feelings while keeping your attention on your heart. Let your breathing be relaxed and regular.

Creative Visualization and the Natural Trance State

Most people don't realize that self-hypnosis is a natural state; it is an altered state that we move in and out of many times a day.

Techniques like visualization can feel almost trancelike, but many people frequently go in and out of them all the time, like when we go into a trance driving along a highway or watching TV. "Self-hypnosis taps into a natural 'basal ganglia' soothing power source that most people do not even know exists," says Daniel G. Amen (1998). "It is found within you, within your ability to focus your concentration. The basal ganglia are involved with *integrating feelings and movement, shifting* and *smoothing motor behavior, setting the body's idle speed or anxiety level, modulating motivation,* and *driving feelings of pleasure and ecstasy.*" When you visualize, the idea is to imagine a situation, whether physical health, a successful job, or a relationship, as you wish it to be. We are constantly putting thoughts and feelings out into the world. Creative visualization allows us to do this intentionally, to trade negative images of self and life for positive ones. Consciously see your life as you wish it to be by visualizing yourself moving in and out of situations easily and successfully, seeing yourself not as hesitant and discouraged but as happy, confident, and comfortable. The thoughts and feelings we put out tend to come back to us. How we see ourselves becomes who we are, and how we interact with others sets the stage for how others interact with us.

Relaxation Technique

Deep relaxations are one way to slowly calm the nervous system. They have several advantages: they bring our nervous system into balance, they train us in how to find our own calm place when we do this regularly, and they help us develop a reservoir of internal calm that we can draw on throughout our day. I can talk you through a deep relaxation if you log on to tiandayton.com.

Meditation

Researchers at Harvard, Yale, and the Massachusetts Institute of Technology have found the first evidence that meditation can alter the physical structure of our brains. Brain scans reveal that experienced meditators have slightly increased thickness in parts of the brain that deal with attention and processing sensory input. "Our data suggests that meditation practice can provoke cortical plasticity in adults in areas important for cognitive and emotional processing and well-being," says Sara Lazar, leader of the study and a psychologist at Harvard Medical School (Lazar 2000).

The world is moving faster, and so are we. The more our human sides take a backseat to technology, the more we need to find alternative ways of nourishing them. Meditation has the following benefits:

✦ Because our pituitary gland is stimulated during meditation, our thinking becomes infused with a transcendent attitude, and we see the circumstances of our lives through calmer eyes.

✦ Meditation develops our ability to self-reflect by giving us practice identifying with the part of our mind that watches and witnesses our internal processes.

✦ Meditation calms the nervous system, bringing it into balance and soothes the basal ganglia, which allows us to enter and occupy our own bodies. This, of course, leads to greater emotional and psychological calm and balance.

✦ In these states of relaxation and clarity, our pituitary glands are releasing prolactin into our bloodstreams, which is associated with a state of calmness and serenity.

The Experience of Pleasure

Play, Laughter, and Creativity

The point is to develop the childlike inclination for
play and the childlike desire for
recognition and to guide the child
over to important fields for society.
Such a school demands from the teacher that he be
a kind of artist in his province.

—Albert Einstein

THE POWER OF PLAY

*P*lay, whether sports, engaging in the arts, socializing, leisure activities, or intimate recreation, is defined by researchers as an activity that encourages positive emotions and allows people to complete high-order relational goals, such as getting to know each other, learning about each other, or engaging in a mutual interest together. Play is accompanied by smiling and laughter, and should also allow participants to control both their joining into and their stepping away from the activity. In other words, play is not forced; it encourages autonomy, spontaneity, and creativity. Families, friends, and couples who play together report feeling greater intimacy and closeness, and this sense of closeness develops at a faster rate than normal. Adults spend too little time at play, according to research, and would benefit greatly from spending more time at it. In the workplace, for example, "Adult play helps to alleviate boredom, release tensions, prevent aggression, and create workgroup solidarity," says Norman C. H. Wong of the University of Hawaii. It also facilitates organizational learning, creativity, community building, and group cohesion, and overall enhances adaptability, attentiveness to quality, and performance (Dayton 2003).

PLAY GROWS BIGGER BRAINS

What gets accomplished in states of play is serious business. "Eighty percent of deaths among juvenile fur seals occur because playing pups fail to spot predators approaching. It is also extremely expensive in terms of energy. Playful young animals use around 2 or 3 percent of their energy cavorting, and in children that figure can be closer to 15 percent. For evolutionary biologists, even 2 or 3 percent is huge," says John Byers from the University of Idaho (1999).

"You just don't find animals wasting energy like that. There must be a reason for this dangerous and expensive activity." Researchers feel that play may have evolutionary advantages that go even beyond developing and learning social and survival skills. They feel that play may even have such an important place in both the animal and human kingdom because it helps to evolve bigger brains, making us more intelligent.

According to Byers, the timing of the playful stage in young animals provides an important clue to what's going on. If you record the amount of time a juvenile spends playing each day over the course of its development, you end up with an inverted U-shaped curve. This is the classic description of a "sensitive period" or a brief developmental window during which the brain can be modified in ways that are not easily replicated earlier or later in life. One of these periods is the child's "sensitive period" for learning a language, in which they pick up languages easily and without an accent.

Byers suspected that these sensitive periods may coincide with a particular phase of brain development referred to as terminal synaptogenesis. When it comes to brain development, the principle of "use it or lose it" gains new meaning. "In many parts of the brain, there is an overproduction of synapses or the connections between neighboring neurons, and then a specific culling," he says. "Synapses that are active are retained, while the ones that are less active end up being destroyed" (Byers 1999).

Byers teamed up with biologist Curt Walker from Dixie State College in St. George, Utah, to test the relationship between age and play and how it affected the development of a part of the brain called the cerebellum in cats, rats, and rodents (1995).

The team of researchers found that in all three species, play was at its most intense just as terminal synaptogenesis in the cerebellum was reaching its peak. "Since new brain cells are seldom produced after birth," says evolutionary anthropologist Kerrie Lewis from University College London, "synaptogenesis is the most likely way in which play could sculpt the developing brain. It might also include things that influence processing efficiency, like myelination" (Byers 1995). Myelin is a fatty sheath that insulates the tentacle-like axons of nerve cells, improving their ability to conduct electrical signals. Byers feels that animals at play, and we can infer children as well, are directing their own brain assembly through play at critical times throughout their development.

Marc Bekoff from the University of Colorado likens it to a behavioral kaleidoscope, with animals at play jumping rapidly from one activity to another. "They use behaviour from a lot of different contexts—predation, aggression, reproduction. . . . Their developing brain is getting all sorts of stimulation." So play not only stimulates feel-good body chemicals, but also teaches high orders of thinking and reasoning. "There's enormous cognitive involvement in play," says Bekoff. "Play often involves complex assessments of playmates, ideas of reciprocity and the use of specialized signals and rules." He believes that play creates a brain that has greater behavioral flexibility and improved potential for learning later in life (Byers 1999).

The idea that play grows more flexible brains has also been explored by neuropsychologist Stephen Siviy of Gettysburg College in Pennsylvania (2007). Siviy studied how play affects the brain's levels of a protein called c-FOS—a substance associated with the stimulation and growth of nerve cells. "Play just lights everything up," says Siviy, referring to brain scans. Play may be enhancing to creativity, Siviy speculates, by allowing connections between brain areas that might not normally be connected.

All these findings paint a picture of how play might have come about to begin with and suggests that there is a relationship between our increasing brain volume and the evolution of play.

Adding another piece to the puzzle of play, Kerrie Lewis's findings point to the possibility that different types of play may have evolved at different stages in evolutionary history, to allow the development of distinct regions of the brain. Lewis examined the size of the neocortex—a center for social reasoning— in primates, and found that the larger the neocortex in each species, the more social play they indulged in. But this finding didn't extend to playing with an object or being in motion. Lewis believes that social play may help wire up the social brain, while other forms of play do not. "I think it's reasonably safe to assume that different types of play did emerge at different points in time, but possibly with some overlap," she says (Lewis and Barton 2004).

MBA programs across the country are adding grown-up versions of "social play" to their curriculum because they recognize the importance of social skills in business success. Rat pups denied the opportunity to play grow smaller neocortices and lose the ability to apply social rules when they interact with their peers. "When play drops out, something is wrong," says Bekoff. "Children who suffer mental illnesses such as schizophrenia as adults, for example, engage in precious little social play early in life. Kids are discouraged from playing because they've got to go to school," says Bekoff. "They have all these things to do after school that adults think of as play—but Little League isn't play, in many ways." Play should be without pressure and driven by those involved so that their own creativity and spontaneity can drive the process.

According to Brian Sutton-Smith: "The opposite of play is not work. It's depression. . . . anyone who becomes a professional player such as a comedian, explorer, actor, narrator, athlete, collector, hostess, model, or artist of any kind inevitably plays with these mental and behavioural play frames at earlier ages, and probably maintains playful accompaniments during their artistic involvement even at the adult stage" (www.deepfun.com).

LAUGHTER

We love the people who make us laugh. Whether it's the class clown, the funny guy at the office, or a favorite, zany old aunt, we value humor so highly that we forgive the shortcomings of those who tickle our funny bone, perhaps more readily than we might otherwise. Being the one who can be funny generally elevates their status in any given group. The group just wants that person around; at a party to get it going, at a family gathering to ensure that it will be fun, and at the office to break tension, turn annoying situations on their head, or make a difficult boss more palatable. Humor keeps things in perspective, provides relief, gets us to see things in new lights, and yes, has tons of health benefits.

"Neural circuits for laughter exist in very ancient regions of the brain," according to Jan Panksepp, author of *Affective Neuroscience: The Foundations of Human and Animal Emotions,* "Ancestral forms of play and laughter existed in animals eons before we humans came along," she reports. Research in this area "is just the beginning wave of the future," says Gordon Burghardt, of the University of Tennessee, who studies the evolution of play. "It will allow us to bridge the gap with other species" (Bekoff & Byers, 1998). "Tickles are the key," Panksepp said. "They open up a previously hidden world." Panksepp had studied play vocalizations in animals for years before it occurred to him that they might be an ancestral form of laughter. Laughter establishes—or restores—a positive emotional climate and a sense of connection among people. Dr. Robert Provine found that speakers laugh even more than their listeners (2004).

Most of what makes people laugh is not thigh-slapper stuff but conversational comments. "Laughter is not primarily about humor," says Dr. Provine, "but about social relationships."

The Healing Power of Laughter

Because laughter is a high-order brain activity that uses many parts of the brain, including those shut down by trauma, laughter can have a profoundly healing effect. Many of the same parts of the brain that process pain also process laughter. The laughter that we share in therapeutic circles is healing, cathartic, and bonding. It is also very intimate and allows people to connect through humor as well as pain. I always encourage laughter in my groups. Psychodrama can be hilarious, which has always been one of the reasons that it appealed to me to begin with.

So often in psychodrama, I witness that after someone meets their tiger in the night, after the tears are shed, the anger and rage poured out, there is a kind of spontaneous moment when the client sees it all for what it was—paper tigers, their own fears, anxieties, and insecurities blocking them from feeling fully alive, blocking them from their own experience of life and passion. Or they realize that it's over, that they need not live in fear of themselves or anyone else anymore. And they laugh. They laugh at themselves, they laugh at the folly of it all, they laugh because there is nothing left to do but laugh, because it's all sort of funny.

YOUR BRAIN ON A JOKE

In looking at brain scans of people while enjoying a good laugh, researchers observed that while many emotional responses appear to be confined to specific areas of the brain, laughter seems to be produced via a circuit that runs through many regions of the brain. This means that damage to any of these regions can impair one's sense of humor and response to humor. Laughter is more than fun and more than something to just indulge in occasionally; it is central to our mind/body sense of health and well-being. Laughter, in other words, is something to take seriously in recovery. While laughing, the left side of the cortex analyzes the words and structure of the joke. The brain's large frontal lobe, which is involved in social-emotional responses, becomes very active. The right hemisphere of the cortex carries out the intellectual analysis required to "get" the joke or the humorous remark or situation, while all of this brainwave activity spreads to the sensory processing area of the occipital lobe (the area on the back of the head that contains the cells that process visual signals). It's the stimulation of the motor sections that evokes physical responses to the joke.

Physical Benefits of Laughter

Among the physical benefits of laughter are the following:

Muscle relaxation. Belly laughs result in muscle relaxation. While we laugh, the muscles that do not participate in the belly laugh relax. After we finish laughing, those muscles involved in the laughter start to relax. Thus, the releasing action takes place in two stages.

Reduction of stress hormones. Laughter reduces at least three of the neuroendocrine hormones associated with the stress response: epinephrine, cortisol, and dopac.

Pain reduction. Humor allows a person to "forget" about pains such as aches, arthritis, and so on.

Cardiac exercise. A belly laugh is equivalent to "internal jogging." Laughter can provide good cardiac conditioning, especially for those who are unable to perform physical exercises.

Blood pressure. Women seem to benefit from laughter more than men in the prevention of hypertension.

Respiration. Frequent belly laughter empties our lungs of more air than it takes in, resulting in a cleansing effect, similar to deep breathing. This is especially beneficial for patients who are suffering from emphysema and other respiratory ailments.

Elevates the immune system. Clinical studies have shown that humor strengthens the immune system because of the positive body chemicals that it engenders.

The Role of Humor

Humor plays many important roles in our interactions. Here are some theories as to what some of those might be.

The *incongruity theory* suggests that humor arises when logic and familiarity are replaced by things that don't normally go together. When a joke begins, our minds and bodies are already anticipating what's going to happen and how it's going to end. That anticipation takes the form of logical thought intertwined with emotion and is influenced by our past experiences and our thought processes. When the joke goes in an unexpected direction, our thoughts and emotions suddenly have to switch gears. In other words, we experience two sets of incompatible thoughts and emotions simultaneously. We experience this incongruity between the different parts of the joke as humorous. In this way humor teaches us to tolerate ambivalence.

The *superiority theory* comes into play when we laugh at jokes that focus on someone else's mistakes, stupidity, or misfortune. We feel superior to this person, experience a certain detachment from the situation, and so are able to laugh at it. Most of us like to laugh at someone sometimes; it's natural. A good laugh at someone else may provide momentary relief when something seems off or someone does something that just seems stupid or inept.

The *relief theory* is the basis for a device moviemakers have used effectively for a long time. In action films or thrillers where tension is high, the director uses comic relief at just the right times. He builds up the tension or suspense as much as possible and then breaks it down slightly with a side comment, enabling the viewer to relieve himself of pent-up emotion, just so the movie can build it up again. Similarly, an actual story or situation creates tension within us. As we try to cope with two sets of emotions and thoughts, we need a release, and laughter is the way of cleansing our system of the built-up tension and incongruity.

According to Dr. Lisa Rosenberg, humor, especially dark

humor, can help workers cope with stressful situations. Humor keeps us young and healthy. Find your laugh and add years to your life (http://people.howstuffworks.com/laughter5.htm). "The act of producing humor, of making a joke, gives us a mental break and increases our objectivity in the face of overwhelming stress," she says. The class clown, the mascot, or the child in the family who makes us laugh are highly prized by the group because we look to them to break a mounting tension with a joke so that we can laugh, relieve some stress, and begin to get our bodies back to normal.

CREATIVITY

The key question isn't "What fosters creativity?" But it is "Why in God's name isn't everyone creative?" Where was the human potential lost? How was it crippled? I think therefore a good question might be not why do people create, but why do people not create or innovate? We have got to abandon that sense of amazement in the face of creativity, as if it were a miracle if anybody created anything.

—*Abraham Maslow*

Creativity gives us the ability to envision what we want to happen in our lives and to imagine what steps we might take to actualize our vision. It allows us to combine and recombine our knowledge in order to come up with novel approaches to everything from what to do with an empty day to how to lay out a five-year plan.

Creativity is often seen as the province of artists and creatives, but this is a dangerously limited vision of what it actually is.

The part of the brain that can envision and play with mental constructs is the cortex. The prefrontal cortex might be seen as the brain's CEO as it oversees and manages complex brain interactions. Though creativity is often seen as the province of the right brain, we need the prefrontal cortex to play with, order, and reorder the visions and emotional impulses coming to us from deeper regions of the brain. We need it to synthesize experience and make high-level and symbolic meaning of our life activities.

The Right and Left Brain Theory

In the late 1960s American psychobiologist Roger W. Sperry observed that the human brain has two very different ways of thinking. The right brain, Sperry saw as the intuitive, visual, and spatial part of the brain that processes information simultaneously, looking first at the whole picture, then the details. The left brain he categorized as the verbal, logical side that processes information in an analytical and sequential way, looking first at the pieces, then putting them together to get the whole. Sperry was awarded a Nobel Prize in 1981, though subsequent research has shown that things aren't quite as polarized as was once thought—that the brain, in fact, is a complex and integrated system that is constantly interfacing with itself and the rest of our bodies.

Creativity: Thinking Outside the Box and Finding the Uniting Thread

Creative innovation is "the ability to understand and express novel orderly relationships," says Dr. Kenneth Heilman, professor of neurology and health psychology at University of Florida's College of Medicine. "In order to come up with these *novel* approaches, the trick is to get parts of the brain to interact that don't normally interact. Thus, creative innovation might require the coactivation and communication between regions of the brain that ordinarily are not strongly connected. To be creative, people need to break away from what they have been taught to believe, and thus divergent thinking is a critical element of creativity," he said (Heilman 2004). Divergent thinking is our ability to follow increasingly different or separate paths of reasoning and imagining. The ability to mingle thoughts, balancing one against the other—to order, reorder, throw them up in the air, and make still new sense of them as they fall—is crucial to the creative process.

> Patients who have their frontal lobe[s] removed or injured cannot perform divergent thinking. The major hypothesis . . . is that creativity is dependent upon the ability to diverge and then form innovative solutions. . . . The development of innovative solutions is dependent on the ability to co-activate anatomically distinct representational networks that store different forms of knowledge. This simultaneous distributed activation . . . may allow people to develop alternative innovative solutions, thereby finding the thread that unites the various parts. The CEO part of the brain, or the frontal lobes, appear to be the part of the cortex that are most important for creativity, in that they are critical for divergent thinking and might modulate the coactivation of diverse cognitive networks so important in innovation.

Two components indispensable to divergent thinking appear to be a certain detachment, so that we aren't overwhelmed by our own emotions, along with the ability to develop alternative solutions. To arrive at a creative solution to a persistently unsolvable problem, an individual must often change the method by which he or she has already attempted to solve the problem—in other words, to think outside the box.

Mind Templates: From Old to New Paradigms

Templates play a key role in creativity. Templates that are new paradigms develop out of a very good understanding of the old paradigms. Picasso is a perfect example of an artist who had complete mastery over line and form. If you look at his early work, he had all the skill of the great draftsmen of the nineteenth century; his ability to draw a human face was dazzling. This may be why, when he took all of these elements and distorted them, moved them about in order to reflect accurately an inner experience of self, he was so stunningly successful. Ease of learning and ability to create well depend partially on how well templated your mind is before the learning experience. Accepted structures and templates have always been important to creativity and are the basis for improvisation. Creative composers of music know the rules, and when they break them, they do so within acceptable boundaries as they combine and recombine known elements to produce a new piece.

Templates help keep people's attention and provide a secure base from which to move out. Even large departures from what is normally expected are often the juxtaposition of familiar elements brought together from different contexts. This allows the audience or anyone looking at, listening to, or participating in someone's "creation" to safely stay anchored in what they know as they follow the mind of the artist who is creating something new. The unexpected, novel, or even hidden symmetries and previously accepted templates that we discover as we view or listen to a work of art are our source of pleasure as we enjoy and participate in the artist's creative flight.

"I believe creativity can be 'encouraged,'" says Dr. Heilman. "We have known for decades that when young rodents are put in a stimulating environment, they have a much richer neural network than their sibs who were not raised in this environment. Thus, bringing up children in an enriched environment and making certain that they receive a good education is critical for their brain development" (Heilman 2004).

Creativity and Mood Disorders

Heilman observes from the literature on the brain and creativity that "many people who are very creative have a higher incidence of mood and addiction disorders, [and that while] many neurologic disorders can reduce creativity . . . there are some that might enhance it." Heilman referred to the work of Miller and colleagues at the University of California, San Francisco, who studied a series of patients with frontotemporal dementia, people whose frontal lobes were not working properly. These patients actually acquired new artistic abilities despite evidence of deterioration in the left anterior temporal lobe. Heilman said, "These are people who had no history of artistic production who actually became creative—perhaps because the deterioration on the left side 'disinhibited' their right side, and the right side got creative doing artistic things."

Addicts and others with mood disorders are often said to thrive on novelty seeking. High rates of alcoholism, drug abuse, bipolar depression, and monodepression are found among creative types such as writers, composers, musicians, and fine artists. Heilman feels that these associations raise as many questions as answers. "For example, does treatment of depression and bipolar disorder influence creativity, and what are the effects of different treatments?" Heilman explored the links among creativity and sleep, dreaming, rest, relaxation, depression, and addiction and observed that one thread uniting them all is changes in neurotransmitter systems.

Numerous scientists, for example, report solving a difficult scientific problem while asleep or when falling asleep or awakening from sleep. Based on the findings of anatomic studies, it appears that creative individuals such as Einstein may have alterations of specific regions of the brain's posterior neocortical region. At the same time, it has been observed that creative innovation frequently takes place during times of diminished arousal, when the thinking parts of our brain are toned down—for example, during sleep—and that many well-known creative people have experienced depression, suggesting that alterations of such neurotransmitters as norepinephrine might play a critical role in creativity. In the view of Heilman and his coauthors, highly creative individuals "may be endowed with brains that are capable of storing extensive specialized knowledge in their temporoparietal cortex, be capable of frontal mediated divergent thinking, and have a special ability to modulate the frontal lobe-locus coeruleus (norepinephrine) system, such that during creative innovation cerebral levels of norepinephrine diminish, leading to the discovery of novel orderly relationships" (Heilman et al 2003).

ENTERING A CREATIVE FLOW

If I had my life to live over again, I would
have made a rule to read some poetry
and listen to some music at least once a week.

—*Charles Darwin*

When we create, play, listen to music, write, read, or engage in something of great interest to us, we enter what Mihalyi Csikszentmihalyi of the University of Chicago calls the "flow state" (1990). Certain passions—say, for painting, writing, sports, or cooking, whatever activity we're truly absorbed by—can also allow us to enter what can quiet our conscious mind while allowing other parts of us to begin to get more involved in an activity. In his extensive research in this area, Csikszentmihalyi has found that people are most likely to enter this state when their skill level and the difficulty of the task itself are properly matched. Too little skill leads to frustration, and too little challenge leads to boredom. In the flow state, time tends to disappear; we engage in a deep, effortless involvement where ordinary cares are out of consciousness. We're receiving immediate feedback, and we're goal-oriented. While in this flow state, our concern for self disappears; however, when we emerge, our self feels strengthened.

*F*inding Forgiveness

I was doing a show on victims confronting their
criminals. A seventeen-year-old girl was on the air
speaking to the man who, four years earlier, had
beaten her beyond recognition and left her for dead.
She'd had seventeen surgeries and complete facial
reconstruction. She said to him, "I don't hate you.
I hate what you did to me. And I have had to learn to
forgive you so I could go on with my own life." To this
day it is the most powerful thing I've ever seen. In
that moment, she expressed why we're here—to learn
to love in spite of the human condition, to transcend
the human condition of being fearful. We get so
bogged down in worldly things we don't understand
that we're here for a spiritual quest. Understanding
that this is a journey is the most exciting part of being
human. It has revolutionized my life.

—*Oprah Winfrey*

*F*orgiveness is a process, not an event. Rather than an endgame, what's important and beneficial about forgiveness is that it motivates us to work through the powerful feeling and thought patterns that block it. Carl Jung, the famous Swiss psychiatrist, felt that we don't really solve a problem, rather we go to the mountaintop, figuratively speaking, and learn to "see it differently." Forgiveness involves both a willingness to work through the reverberating and often painful emotions that make forgiveness seem impossible, as well as a willingness to view an old situation in a new light, to give it a positive spin, perhaps as an opportunity for personal growth or a readiness to accept humanity with all its flaws and not get overly caught up with the disappointing side of life. It is a form of reframing.

Forgiveness is often a by-product of resolving painful issues. As we put more and more energy and work into our own personal growth, we may find that we come to value our own peace of mind more than holding on to resentments, and so we just, somewhere along the line, lay the sword down. It becomes too heavy in our hand; the weight of carrying it encumbers our own freedom.

Another freeing aspect of forgiveness is that it allows us to see our own or another person's bad behavior for what it is. Children who grow up with the kind of denial that accompanies addiction, for example, may have learned to rationalize and manipulate what was happening around them in order to make it less disturbing to their equilibrium, to twist reality or to bend what they are seeing into a shape that is more acceptable to them. But distorting reality doesn't help us to work through its negative impact. Calling it by its right name and making the conscious choice to forgive it does. Seeing the glass as half full isn't the same as bending the truth. Looking on the bright side doesn't mean that we deny what is right in front of us. In fact, it can actually strengthen our confidence and sense of self to look at a situation as it is and make conscious choices to forgive. It weakens the self to rely on deception and denial in order to make a situation livable. Forgiveness allows us to live with the truth and transcend our circumstances. It allows us to keep our values and self-esteem intact.

Dr. Frederic Luskin, director of the Stanford University Forgiveness Project, describes forgiveness as a proven recipe for health and happiness because it helps to reduce anger, suffering, depression, and stress (2002). While harbored anger causes observable physiological changes that can impact the body negatively, forgiveness promotes such positive states as hope, patience, and self-confidence that actually elevate the immune system. Luskin writes:

> The thing about long-term or unresolved anger is we've seen it reset the internal thermostat. When you get used to a low level of anger all the time, you don't recognize what's normal. It creates a kind of adrenaline rush that people get used to. It burns out the body and makes it difficult to think clearly—making the situation worse. . . . When the body releases certain enzymes during anger and stress, cholesterol and blood pressure levels go up—not a good long-term disposition to maintain the body in.

If we're holding on to anger and resentment, it makes it harder to live in, attain, and maintain emotional sobriety. We're continually re-creating something painful in our minds, reexperiencing intense emotions like anger and sadness over and over with no resolution. Forgiveness gets us to work through those emotions toward a goal of letting them go. When we can't forgive, we may leave ourselves emotionally "crippled." Following is a most powerful interview of a man who found himself in this sort of circumstance (from *The*

Meaning of Life, by Joel Kinagwi):

A middle-aged man came to place his child in one of my classes, but I realized I had no room at all. I looked at this man and immediately knew. This was the guard who had beaten me nine years before. A spirit caught me. I understood that I had to find space for his boy. I could not repeat the harm that had been done to me. I asked him, "Do you know me?" He said, "No." I asked him if he remembered a night in July of 1956. Just then, the man looked at my face and started crying. He began to walk away, but I stopped him, saying, "Wait, I'll take the child. I have carried scars for years, but I have forgiven you all those things." That man might have left me permanently disabled, but in allowing me to help his boy, he made me feel fulfilled in what I wanted to do for young people.

Forgiveness, both of self and others, is only beginning to be looked at in therapeutic journals and research. Perhaps because it has been seen as the province of religion or because it feels too prescriptive or forced, it is not often directly addressed. Resolving inner conflicts and eventually moving beyond them or letting them go is a part of most therapeutic paths, though it is seldom called forgiveness. Whatever we choose to call it, the act of doing something inside of ourselves to move beyond emotional pain implies a recognition that some things don't change on the outside, so we need to come up with a way to change them on the inside. Forgiveness is a way to reframe a painful circumstance in such a way that our faith in life and relationships can be restored and we can move forward. Forgiveness doesn't mean condoning another person's bad behavior, which is often, I find, a major stumbling block for those considering it. The reframing that allows us to forgive is self-referential and allows us to move on with our own lives rather than be caught in self-perpetuating, painful patterns of anger and resentment. We forgive, in other words, for our own good.

Forgiveness is generally motivated by some kind of recognition that what we're holding on to is causing us more damage than the other guy, and holding on to it just isn't worth it anymore. If it's ourselves we're forgiving, we may have come to the realization that no one is benefiting from our holding a grudge against ourselves. Instead we're keeping ourselves glued to pain from the past, and we recognize that we want to find some way of letting go of it. We may benefit from just considering forgiveness, even if we only entertain the idea. After all, there may be no magic moment when all is forgiven; we may always carry some residual feelings of hurt or resentment toward ourselves or another.

Consider forgiveness as simply a way to lighten the load a day at a time, to live toward a solution even if we never fully get there. Forgiveness gives us a positive goal, so that in working with anger and sadness we remember that the goal is to live not in anger and sadness, but eventually to get beyond them, to let them go and move on. It is an organizing principle or emotion. Just as anger mobilizes us and makes us feel more directed and consolidated at those moments when we feel we're falling apart, so does forgiveness. They simply organize and mobilize us toward different ends.

We may need to consider forgiveness toward ourselves so that we can have the motivation to stay with recovery, and toward others so that we can get free of a past that may be keeping us locked in a cycle of self-destructive behavior. Forgiving, in my experience, is not necessarily a one-time act but a way of looking at a circumstance with a greater sense of compassion.

MYTHS SURROUNDING FORGIVENESS

Following are some of the myths and misconceptions surrounding forgiveness that seem to give some people pause
when contemplating it. When those whom I work with begin
to consider forgiveness as an option, these are the sorts of
thoughts that generally snag them:

*If I forgive, my relationship with the person I'm forgiving will defi-
nitely improve.* Not necessarily. We may not even choose to continue to see this other person and they may not be able to
accept our forgiveness or even care about it.

*If I forgive, it means I'm condoning the behavior of the person I'm
forgiving.* Not at all. In fact, quite the opposite. Forgiveness
implies a clearheaded recognition that we don't condone the
behavior that we're forgiving. That's why we need to forgive it.

*If I forgive, I'll no longer feel angry at the person for what
happened.* In my experience, anger can still come up, but when
it does, we remind ourselves that we've decided it isn't worth it
to hold on to it any longer.

If I forgive, I forgo my right to hurt feelings. We may still have
some residue of hurt feelings. Forgiveness is a process, and the
hurt feelings should diminish over time, but they may not disappear all at once.

*If I forgive, it means I want to continue to have a relationship with the
person I'm forgiving.* Not necessarily; you're forgiving for your own
inner growth and freedom, which is virtually always a desirable
thing to do. However, reconnecting or staying connected may or
may not be desirable, depending on the situation.

If I haven't forgotten, I haven't really forgiven. We do and should
remember; after all, just because we're forgiving doesn't mean
we want to set ourselves up for further hurt. It's more like we forgive and get out of the way; we forgive and set boundaries; we
forgive and see more clearly where we need to protect ourselves.

I only need to forgive once. Forgiveness is a decision to head in a certain direction. We may need to forgive many times, as the Bible suggests, "not seven but seventy times seven."

I forgive for the sake of the other person. No, we forgive to free ourselves. We forgive so that we can stop defining our future actions based on our own or someone else's wrongful actions.

Forgiving myself is selfish or wrong. As long as we look squarely at ourselves and recognize what we may be doing to add to a problematic situation, forgiving ourselves is a way of releasing both parties from the kind of shame that keeps us locked in self-defeating and negative patterns of relating.

MAKING AMENDS: WORKING THE NINTH STEP

Twelve-step programs have understood, since their beginnings, that forgiveness is an issue that needs to be addressed at some point in recovery for both the addict and those affected by addiction. Forgiving others who have hurt us, whether we're an addict, codependent, or ACOA in recovery, can seem insurmountable. Emotions like anger, resentment, and unresolved hurt come to the surface and cloud our willingness or ability to see past them. But in addressing these feelings openly and honestly, as a part of our fearless moral inventory, we can move through them toward healing. Additionally, all too often we're carrying a piece of self-loathing or anger toward ourselves when we constantly hang on to intense negative emotions. Even if we say it's all about the other guy, secretly we probably feel bad about ourselves, too. So there is often a bonus to forgiving because we sort of let ourselves off the hook at the same time as we're doing that for the other guy.

People in recovery sometimes struggle the hardest with self-forgiveness. Self-recrimination and shame can make us retreat into rigid positions that make intimacy and connection feel fraught with discomfort. Becoming willing to forgive the self implies a recognition that hanging on to anger toward ourselves not only hurts us, but everyone around us. For addicts, self-forgiveness helps to lighten the emotional burdens that can fuel relapse. Shame, unresolved anger, and sadness can contribute to a dry drunk syndrome. White knuckling it takes the comfort and joy out of life and relationships and can contribute to staying welded to addictive and compulsive patterns. The 12 steps have long recognized the need for addicts to make amends to those they hurt, except when to do so could cause further harm. This is considered a part of the process of recovering from drug and alcohol abuse, a preventative from relapse—and a part of attempting to restore both inner peace and relationship equanimity.

Addictive behaviors are often attempts at running from our own inner turbulence, misguided attempts at quieting an inner storm. The storm is often about feeling hurt by others or hurting others through our own behavior. The two are intertwined, feeding off and fueling each other. Asking for or granting forgiveness offers a way out, a way to make an attempt at restitution, to restore peace and serenity. We've done our part to right a wrong or to release a wrong done to us.

Dr. Ken Hart of the Leeds Forgiveness for Addiction Treatment Study says, "Controversy often arises because people fail to understand that forgiveness is always desirable, but attempts at reconciliation may sometimes be ill-advised." Dr. Hart's study is testing two different approaches to forgiveness: secular and spiritual (2003).

The secular approach aims to speed up the growth of empathy and compassion so that addicts can better understand the imperfections and flaws of those who have hurt them. Usually, they come to realize that the sense of "badness" they carry around from having interpreted their abuse to mean "something must be wrong with me or I wouldn't be treated this way" isn't and probably never was accurate. They were in the wrong place at the wrong time; they got hurt because another person was projecting his own unhealed pain on them. This awareness can be a great burden lifted and allows the hurt person to see her hurt differently and to take it less personally. It can also develop some empathy, as the next question is, "Well, if it wasn't about me in the first place, then what was it about? What was inside the person who hurt me?" This is a step toward real understanding.

The second type of forgiveness tested is spiritually based, 12-step–oriented forgiveness. In this approach, addicts who have harmed others are encouraged to apologize for their wrongdoing, thereby making attempts at restitution. According to Hart, "Seeking forgiveness through the amends process requires incredible humility; the assistance of a Higher Power (God) helps people to transcend their ego, which normally balks when asked to admit mistakes." He goes on to say, "We think the two treatments can help people in addiction recovery drop the burden of carrying around pain from the past" (Hart 2003).

These two approaches to forgiveness—gaining empathy if we're the hurt party, and making amends if we're the offending party—are useful cornerstones in our own practical approach to forgiveness.

LETTER WRITING

Letter writing is an amazing little tool that can help us to process our emotions and gain relief. These letters are not meant to be sent to anyone. They are like journal entries; we write them to relieve our own feelings. We can share them with a therapist or trusted friend but they are not meant to be sent to the person to whom we are writing.

Try writing a letter:

✦ To yourself at some other time in your life, forgiving yourself for something around which you carry pain and shame.
✦ To someone else, forgiving them for hurting you.
✦ Asking for another person's forgiveness.

21

Growing Soul

Either we have hope within us or we don't. It is a dimension of the soul, and it is not essentially dependent on some particular observation of the heart. It transcends the world that is immediately experienced and is anchored somewhere beyond its horizons. Hope in this deep sense is not the same as joy that things are going well, or the willingness to invest in enterprises that are obviously headed for early success, but rather an ability to work for something because it is good, not just because it stands a chance to succeed. Hope is definitely not the same thing as optimism. It is not the conviction that something will turn out well, but the certainty that something makes sense, regardless of how it turns out. It is hope, above all, which gives us the strength to live and continually try new things.

—*Vaclav Havel*

I may not have the life I wanted,
but I am learning to live the life I have.

—*Lois W.*

Recovery is a process of growing soul. People with a spiritual framework often find their belief system, along with the sense of community that accompanies it, helpful in sustaining the deep inner and outer changes that they experience in recovery.

People who have been traumatized can fight positive change because it doesn't fit their mental map. Believing in something bigger than we are helps to restore that sense of trust and faith in an orderly universe that trauma undermines. It lets the *helplessness* of trauma shift to a more positive position of surrender or a chosen *powerlessness*. Our *hypervigilance* can lessen as we learn to lean on our faith, and our anxiety can abate as we accept that, there is a power greater than us that can restore us to sanity; we don't have to figure everything out on our own.

Additionally, community itself is both sustaining and healing. Weekly worship, 12-step meetings, prayer and social groups are nourishing throughout life. And community rituals such as marriages, funerals, and holidays guide us through life's joys, traumas, and transformations, allowing us to experience our deep feelings surrounding those events and mark their meaning and importance in our lives.

SCIENCE MEETS RELIGION

Researchers are seeing a possible biological underpinning for spiritual experiences. Our bodies, researchers speculate, may be hardwired for entering transcendent or spiritual states.

One of the same self-soothing mind/body chemicals, namely serotonin, that we have discussed throughout this book, scientists see as a possible biological underpinning for spiritual experience. This brain chemical, crucial to mood and motivation and the shaping of our personalities, also makes us susceptible to spiritual experiences. A team of Swedish researchers has found that the presence of a receptor that regulates serotonin activity in the brain correlates with people's capacity for transcendence or the ability to apprehend phenomena that cannot be explained objectively. Scientists have long suspected that serotonin influences spirituality, because drugs known to alter serotonin, such as LSD, also induce mystical experiences. Now there is concrete proof from brain scans linking the capacity for spirituality with a major biological element. The concentration of serotonin receptors normally varies markedly among individuals. Those whose brain scans showed the most receptor activity proved, on personality tests, to have the strongest proclivity for spiritual experiences.

In fact, it may be this experience that we seek when we take drugs or engage in self-medicating behaviors: this feeling of transcendence, of everything falling into perspective, of feeling at one. The kinds of spiritual experiences described by saints, yogis, and sadhus who sat in meditation for many hours a day have also been reported by addicts. Addicts and drug users often report a sense of overall calm, of connecting with a universal oneness, of feeling a high state of well-being due to their drug use or when engaged in self-medicating behaviors.

Developing a sense of the sacred and spiritual in the world can help the self-medicator to find an alternative pathway toward achieving a sense of transcendence, a pathway of daily action through which we can consciously build our ability to enter states where we experience a sense of deep well-being and oneness with God.

THE POWER OF PRAYER

Science has also been studying prayer and its rather stunning power to help people. Studies show that prayer has as profound a beneficial effect on depression as drugs do, reports Larry Dossey in his book *Healing Words* (1993). Praying to God actually elevates the immune system. The same kinds of body chemicals that are present in the mother/child connection are present when we pray. Spiritual connection, it seems, is something akin to an intimate experience of touching and being touched.

One of the more compelling findings reported by Dossey was a study in which cardiology patients who were in a prayed-for group proved to be five times less likely to require antibiotics and three times less likely to develop pulmonary edema (fluid in the lungs). Countless studies echoed similar findings in the efficacy of prayer in healing the body. Time devoted to contemplation and prayer is also a way of healing the self and relationships. Prayer is deeply calming and allows us to have a sense of control, because prayer is something we can do. It is an action of sorts that we can take, while at the same time helping us let go of a problem that we can't solve immediately, by turning it over to a power greater than ourselves. It allows us to feel we are communicating our cares and concerns to a power greater than ourselves, that we don't have to struggle in isolation. As we place our worries into the loving hands of a Higher Power, we can go about our day less anxious and alone. Prayer is the language of the soul; it is communication that reflects a relationship with a benevolent and loving presence.

FILLING THE GOD-SHAPED HOLE

My clients sometimes bemoan the fact that just when they feel they have "gotten it," life hands them another set of problems to solve.

According to Eastern philosophy, the process of becoming an enlightened person consists of cleansing and refining our inner world. We cleanse our inner worlds, according to Eastern thought, by making the unconscious conscious, by understanding what drives us, by clearing our paths of the kinds of emotional and psychological complexes and debris that keep us from being unblocked on the inside, that keep us from spending more time in our own God-centered natures. God, philosophies say, is always present. It is we who stray. Yogis describe the process of purifying the personality as "peeling back layers of an onion."

This gradual peeling back or refining ourselves is perhaps why people who make recovery a lifelong commitment so often wind up becoming spiritual people. Indeed, the founders of the 12-step programs felt that addiction, in any form, reflects a sort of sickness of the soul, and that when we self-medicate, we're feeding our own existential emptiness, often referred in the 12-step rooms as a "God-shaped hole." We are looking for chemical solutions to human problems.

It's when we try to fill this God-shaped hole with something other than natural or spiritual energy, grace, wisdom, or light that we get into trouble. We get into trouble because we cannot sustain the feeling of fullness that we're seeking. We always want more. It takes ever-increasing amounts of alcohol, drugs, sex, spending, food, and so on to get the same high that we used to get for less. This is why addiction of any kind eventually spirals out of control. We can never get enough, and what feels like enough is constantly escalating.

In recovery we learn a new level of self-awareness and self-acceptance. We deepen our capacity for experiencing strong emotions without acting out or self-medicating and in so doing, we deepen our capacity for joy and transcendence. We learn to look at life, to self-reflect, to see beyond the surface. We refine our natures, which often has the effect of allowing us to experience ever-increasing amounts of the kinds of experiences that are often associated with spirituality, such as inner peace, a sense of oneness, groundedness, and joy. The experience of transcendence and connection with our higher natures allows us to constantly expand into that feeling of bliss and well-being in a way that is life enhancing rather than life destructive. It is a different means to the same end, in a sense. Spirituality teaches us more reliable and healthy ways to self-sooth, to feel calm and good inside, and to experience the sacred in living—to grow soul.

Setting Up
Your Healing Network

Talk doesn't cook rice.

—Chinese proverb

*T*alk alone does not inscribe new hardwiring into our neural networks. Our emotions are in our bodies, as well as in our minds and hearts, and so is our balance. In order to restore emotional balance, we need to log the necessary hours in the presence of others who are experiencing balance and pleasure in their lives. Much healing takes place outside the clinic; we need to create a new design for living to create lasting change. Adding new relationships, as well as nourishing, creative, and physically enhancing activities such as hobbies, exercise, and relaxation, can help to reregulate a limbic system that talk alone cannot reach.

Because this is a journey, we need to prepare ourselves. We need to create what psychologists refer to as a "holding environment" in which we feel safe enough to heal. The feelings we are allowing to emerge within us may be scary, challenging, and beautiful. Our healing network will need to be strong enough to hold us through learning to tolerate not only painful emotions but beautiful ones as well, not only our feelings that arise around disconnection, but also those fears and anxieties that connection engenders.

Think of recovery as downloading new, more refined software, as creating and operating from new programs. We're cleaning out our self system, debugging and clearing out contaminated emotional, psychological, and physiological programs so that we can operate more smoothly. Once we have successfully accomplished all of this, which takes several years, we are operating from new, updated, and streamlined programming.

Some of the primary tasks of recovery are as follows:

- ✦ Learning the skills of mind, body, and emotional self-regulation.
- ✦ Resolving childhood wounds so they don't undermine self-regulation.
- ✦ Learning effective and healthy ways of self-soothing.
- ✦ Learning effective ways to manage stress.
- ✦ Developing emotional literacy so emotions can be talked out rather than acted out.
- ✦ Maintaining a healthy body; getting regular exercise, rest, and proper nutrition.
- ✦ Processing emotional ups and downs as they happen.
- ✦ Learning to consciously shift feeling and thinking states.
- ✦ Learning to use the thinking mind to regulate the feeling, limbic mind.
- ✦ Developing inner resources: quiet, meditation, spiritual pursuits.
- ✦ Developing outer resources: a strong relationship network, work, hobbies, social life, community.

THE BASICS: THE NUTS AND BOLTS OF YOUR RECOVERY NETWORK

Following are the elements that I have observed to be cornerstones of a recovery network. Don't panic; you needn't do all of this at once. Some aspects of your recovery plan will last longer than others, based on need and personal preference. But these are the basic elements that will be your resources. Think of this as an emotional diet. If you want to lose heavy, historical weight and keep it off, you need to change the way you live. You need a new design for living.

TWELVE-STEP PROGRAMS AND SUPPORT GROUPS

Twelve-step programs and support groups are the meat and potatoes of your recovery network. They provide a constantly available safety net so that you will have people to turn to whenever you need them. We all need friends on our journey of recovery, people who are going through what we're going through, who understand what we are experiencing, and what we're trying to accomplish. Additionally, our limbic system is soothed through the phenomenon of limbic resonance, which occurs naturally in these 12-step rooms and we feel less isolated as we listen to and identify with the stories of others.

Twelve-step programs and support groups generally have very clear ground rules that keep the environment feeling safe, which is part of why they allow us to heal at our own pace. Most areas have 12-step meetings each week to choose from; support groups vary from city to city. Information about all of these programs can be easily located on the Internet.

ONE-TO-ONE THERAPY

One-to-one therapy gives us the opportunity to build a consistent relationship in which we can develop a new sense of ourselves in relationship to another person. One-to-one therapy replicates the parent/child dyad and offers an opportunity to have a reparenting type of experience. One-to-one therapy works best when it is consistent. Sporadic sessions may not give you the opportunity to really develop a trusting bond; they swing the focus to "figuring out" the problem intellectually rather than allowing you to fully enter into and participate in a healing relationship. Through a consistent and trusting relationship we learn the skills of tolerating strong emotion in the presence of another, translating those emotions into words, communicating our thoughts, and listening to the thoughts of another.

GROUP THERAPY/PSYCHODRAMA

If one-to-one therapy replicates the parent/child dyad, then group therapy replicates the family. Both are very important in order to grow fully through recovery. Group mobilizes the sorts of intense feelings we experienced in our families and allows us to see ourselves in action, relationally speaking. We learn how to hang on to a sense of self while in the presence of others and be ourselves in the context of a group, to tolerate frustration, wait for our turn, and take our turn rather than give it away. For those who have grown up in troubled families, group, in my opinion, is essential. It should be accompanied with weekly one-to-one sessions so that the powerful feelings that do get aroused can be worked through with full attention from a therapist.

For early recovery from addiction, it may be wise to be part of a group that is centered around staying sober. Initially, going too deep and mobilizing too much pain can lead to relapse. Eventually, however, not addressing the early pain that may have led to self-medication can also lead to relapse, because our unresolved issues keep us stuck in the repetition of painful internal and relational dynamics. As your recovery progresses and sobriety is well established, you can look into groups that do deeper healing work, including family-of-origin issues. For those who are not addicted but have lived with relationship trauma of any kind, joining groups that address deeper family and relational issues is very helpful.

COMING TO TERMS WITH WHAT MAY NEVER BE

Recovering the self is coming to terms not only with what did happen but with what didn't happen for us. Constantly feeling disturbed about what went wrong hurts us in the present. It is highly stressful. It robs us of our peace of mind and loads up the relationships we're trying to create in the present with too much unresolved pain from the past.

Part of becoming emotionally mature is to realize that the time for getting certain things may be past. Even if we were to get them, it wouldn't feel right to us as adults anyway; it might even feel infantilizing. It's the wrong time and the wrong place. We may need, in a sense, to release our child mind from its unrequited yearning so that it can engage in what is available to us in the here and now. In that way, we don't block what we can have because it isn't what we used to want, but didn't get. Therapy helps us to do this.

Raising small children is enormously stressful. As the family matures and pressures lighten, connecting, even with those who may have hurt in the past, can become easier and more rewarding if we can let it. We live in a culture of planned obsolescence, of throwing away everything. But people don't take kindly to being thrown away. We can outgrow each other and still be civil. We can be hurt by each other and still remain connected in ways that don't leave us open to the kind of wounding we experienced as children. Not always, but frequently. Families have life cycles, just like any other living, breathing organism. They keep going and growing and changing. There are many points along the life cycle of a family at which we might be able to connect in satisfying ways, if we can take a long view rather than seeing families as something that end. The families we grew up in had so much effect on us because we were young and dependent, because we saw them as the whole world, and rejection by them felt like rejection by the world. But recovery can open another world to us, a new holding environment in which to consciously develop a solid and integrated sense of self.

Much of what I do in psychodrama is simply creating a safe enough situation so that the child self can emerge through role-play, say the things she needs to say, do the things she needs to do, and feel the things she needs to feel. As the child self reinhabits her own body, the adult self can witness. We unfreeze important parts of us, feel them, make sense of them, and integrate them back into our self system with new understanding. We become more refined, whole, and self-aware, and we come to understand and develop compassion for ourselves and those who surrounded us. We were all, after all, just people. As in the *Wizard of Oz,* our parents were merely the man behind the curtain who seemed big.

As we work through the emotional and psychological conflicts that were blocking our ability to take in caring and support from others, we can take in what we actually can have. We stop pushing away what is right around us because it isn't exactly what we think we want and start opening up to all that is available. The spiritual mystery is that, as we let go, we fill up on something else. We fill up on life itself, on spiritual energy, on the present moment and all the magic it contains. We can stand with clear vision and look around the world and make conscious choices about where and how we're going to meet our needs.

We have so much more control of our life experience than we may realize. Flexibility and adaptability aren't only traits that make survival of the fittest possible. Emotional and psychological flexibility and adaptability put survival of the wisest at our fingertips.

As we feel the pain, hurt, and anger that we have banished from consciousness as children—or as adults, for that matter—we have the curious experience of feeling it dissipate. When we don't feel our pain, we don't know what's driving us from within. Significant parts of us remain unconscious and immobilized. We're not claiming our feelings and experiencing them as our own. Instead we project them outward; it's the weather, that person and the way he acts, our spouse, our children, our bank accounts, or our job. But when we disown our own emotions by making them about everything outside of us, we don't mine them for personal meaning. And when we don't mine them, we can't use them to better understand ourselves, and we aren't in a position to make choices about how we live. Pain has to be conscious for us to think about it. While it remains denied and unconscious, it runs us from underneath.

But we also need to make our gratitude and good feelings conscious, too. We need to use our conscious mind to appreciate what we have, to value it and continue the kind of living that allows it to grow. Experiencing good feelings has the effect of expanding them. Seeing beauty in the life and relationships that surround us has the effect of creating more of it. Because beauty really is in the eye of the beholder, it does lie in our ability to see the beauty that is already around us, even if it's seeing the beauty in suffering. As we expand our ability

to feel, we make more room for *all* of our feelings; we develop
depth and breadth. We become deeper people when we
plumb the depths of one subject rather than dancing on the
surface of many. This happens as we go deeper and deeper
through the layers of self and life and as we make genuine self-
reflection a habit of mind.

SEPARATING THE PAST FROM THE PRESENT

My clients often feel guilty "outing" their parents; they want
me to know their parents have changed, they're nicer people
now, they aren't that bad anymore.

This is where I help them to gradually separate the past
from the present—where they learn that having young, inex-
perienced, stressed-out parents who were still working through
their own issues, combined with their own immature level of
development, may have contributed to their experiencing certain features of their childhood as traumatic. They don't need
to throw the baby out with the bathwater. They can still love
their parents and resolve relationship wounds that were an
inevitable part of growing up in any family, much less one with
additional problems, like self-medicating, that may have been
present. They can still love the parents they have today and be
angry at parts of their early experience. In fact, working
through past issues often relieves them of the hidden resentment, shame, or hurt that actually interferes with their close
relationships today, including with their parents.

Most of us want to let sleeping dogs lie. We want to leave the
past in the past and move on. The idea of working through
unresolved issues arises precisely so that we can leave them in
the past where they belong and stop re-creating them in our
present. As the child in us emerges and tells her story, the
adult in us looks on and makes sense of it through mature eyes

of today. This is healing and self-regulating. It's how we use our thinking minds to make sense of, draw meaning from, and regulate our emotions. It's how the past gets integrated into the present with new understanding and perspective rather than disowned or denied. It's how we incorporate our hidden parts and bring them up to date, integrate them into who we are today, and embrace the innocence, spontaneity, and willingness to love that are so much a part of feeling passionate and alive. This is the whole purpose of cleaning out emotional baggage from the past. We work through the emotional, psychological, and spiritual pain that keeps us from living freely and fully in the present and that drags at our inner world like a faint undertow. We bring more of us into consciousness, and in so doing, in making pain conscious, it resolves naturally as we view old hurt through new, more educated, and mature eyes. This is how we become more "balanced and mature," how we become emotionally sober.

OUR WOUNDS, PROCESSED AND INTEGRATED, BECOME OUR STRENGTH: VIGDOR'S VISIT

Vigdor, a longtime group member, came in for what he calls his annual review. Being a well-organized businessman, he has adopted this habit. Before Christmas he makes an appointment with me so that we can go over the last twelve months, acknowledge areas in which he feels he has grown, and set goals for the coming year. This is Vigdor's fifth year in group. Vigdor grew up in poverty in Brazil. He was cared for by his grandmother, as his mother worked all the time; when she wasn't working, she was out with friends. Vigdor's father was no part of his life. Vigdor was abused daily by his grandmother, beaten, burned, and isolated. He was tortured as a child, physically and emotionally. Today he is a successful businessman, a recovering addict who is a member of AA, and a man with love and friendship in his life. His passions are art, photography, and traveling. He has methodically and purposefully turned himself from an underdog into a winner.

When he reflects, he recalls his other grandmother with whom he spent some time as being a source of support and guidance as well as the people in his neighborhood who were kind to him. Other than this, his childhood was a place of great pain.

This morning he explained so beautifully where he was in his healing that it describes what living in the present is all about. "I feel I have worked through the tough stuff," he said. "I mean, I know it's still there, but I don't get trapped in it. I still get bruises, but my bruises don't become wounds." Here he is describing how, when we integrate wounds as we have talked about throughout this book, they don't disappear but we come to understand them. We no longer hide them from ourselves; we allow them space to breathe and dissipate so that their unconscious gravity ceases to have such a powerful pull.

"And I choose," he went on. "Lots of times I see something going on that seems bad to me, and I just choose not to go there. I don't get into it." This choice Vigdor is referring to is what happens when we resolve trauma. We can choose whether or not we want to think about our trauma or even other people's darker issues. The pull for us to go there is simply lessened, and when we do feel it, we have greater choice about how we want to see it. We recognize that getting into it with someone means that we have to go there, too. And once we get a taste for living with serenity, we come to value it and want to protect it. "The people in my life have changed. The ones where I was doing all the giving, well, when I stopped, the relationships sort of faded away. Now I like to give, but I know I should be getting something back, too. I used to feel needy, and I would manipulate to get my needs met. I would go in a circle. I used to be needier and take up more space. Now I am more direct. I think I am less confusing to other people and less confusing to myself, too. I've learned to set boundaries, to say no. And now, because I can say no, I can say yes. I can receive."

He referred to the spiritual idealogy which has been a guide throughout his life, and how, in his belief system, the idea is to always try to grow from life and what it brings. I commented to him on how hard he has worked, what a pleasure it is to work with someone who is so motivated. "I've learned how to reward myself," he said. "I mean, I've learned to give to myself. Whether it's a trip or a piece of art . . . these are my passions," he said as a smile dawned across his face. "I love these things."

Vigdor reflected as he was ending his session, "I feel proud of myself. I mean, I think what I went through could have put me under. But it didn't."

At this point he stood to his full height, and his face and body reflected the posture of a man who knows life for all it has to give and take away, and he loves it. And he is a man who loves himself, who feels proud of who he is. Though his slips into self-medicating behaviors haven't been completely eradicated as yet, they are few and far between. He recognizes what's going on when he goes overboard and takes clear and meaningful steps to continue his movement toward emotional sobriety. Today Vigdor's rewards are more refined; peace of mind, a pleasant dinner with a friend, a quiet evening of his own. Vigdor is now in a position to use the emotional sobriety he has worked so hard to achieve, to regulate his own thinking, feeling, and behavior, to bring his own life into balance.

One of the frequent outcomes of doing psychodrama with people seems to be that they develop a sense of perspective on and detachment from their own stories. As they role-play them and get the feelings out that they have been sitting on, as they express the pain and indignity of being rejected or wounded, something mysterious takes place. Through concretizing their story and role-playing it, they gain some separation and perspective. They see that their story is just their story. It's not all of who they are. And they begin to *stop living in the story and start living in the present*. They experience a powerful sense of "survivor's strength," which boosts their self-confidence and pride in themselves. It's not that pain disappears or they never feel anger again, but their knee-jerk attachment to it lessens and their story attains its proper proportion. Occasionally it can be reactivated, but the understanding, strength, and insight that have now been woven into it get reactivated as well.

Stick with the Winners

Habits of Emotionally Sober People

We do not receive wisdom, we must
discover it for ourselves, after a journey
through the wilderness which no one else can
make for us, which no one can spare us, for
our wisdom is the point of view from which
we come at last to regard the world.

—*Marcel Proust*

Our evolutionary mandate is to thrive. We are wired to heal. Just as a broken bone can knit itself back together, a broken heart can mend. We are designed to live with a degree of unpredictability and challenge; we've been equipped to roll with the punches. Nature knows life is tough; that's why she has built a medicine chest right into our DNA. All of our traits—this ability to care and be cared for, to get sick or hurt and to get better—have been selected throughout our evolution for their adaptability and resilience. That is the DNA that's in us. Thriving and healing in this sense is natural. If we can get ourselves onto a good and wholesome track, nature will help us do the rest. Nature wants us to heal, survive, and succeed.

Following are some of the key traits that people with good emotional sobriety seem to have in common.

THEY ARE ABLE TO SELF-REFLECT: THEY TAKE CHARGE OF THEIR OWN LIVES

Emotionally sober people tend to think about the direction of their own lives, and if needed, they take active steps toward self-improvement. The prefrontal cortex, that part of the brain that developed very late in human evolution, allows us to think in the abstract, to conceive of and consolidate the disparate, ephemeral pieces of our own personal experience and integrate them into the fluid but coherent whole that we call a self.

Our prefrontal cortex is the CEO of our brain (Goldberg 2001). It's where we process the feeling and sensorial messages from our world, make sense of them, and place them into an overall context. The prefrontal cortex allows us to imagine and shape the image of a separate sense of self within a world of other people. The ability to reflect upon the circumstances of our lives and balance them into a coherent picture of the self is what allows us to draw meaning from experience and to integrate it into a coherent, ever-growing, and changing picture of the self in relationship to others.

THEY TAKE RESPONSIBILITY FOR THEIR OWN ATTITUDES

Emotionally sober people understand that their own attitudes can get them into trouble and their own attitudes can get them out of trouble. As comedian George Burns said, when asked what his secret was for such a long and happy life, "Watch that attitude, kid. You gotta watch that attitude."

Research reveals that people seem to have a "happiness set point." Those whose set point is high, for example, will tend to return to that point within a reasonable time frame, even when they experience a serious loss, while those whose happiness set point is lower will tend to return to a lower point, interpreting even good turns of events from the point of view of a lowered set point. That is, people with a higher set point tend to put a more positive spin on the events of their lives, and people with a lower set point put a more negative spin on them.

Optimists, according to research, tend to do better in coping with life's stresses than pessimists. They are more likely to use problem-solving strategies to tackle difficulties as they arise, to put a positive spin on stressors, and to look for ways to make the best of a bad situation. Optimism has also been linked with longevity. In a thirty-year study published in Mayo Clinic Proceedings (2000), it was found that those classified as pessimists had a 19 percent higher risk of mortality than those who were optimists. Another ten-year study on aging from the Veterans Affairs Normative Aging Study found that a sense of optimism may protect older men against developing heart disease (Kubzansky et al 2001).

Seeing the glass as half full can be creating a glass that is half full. The thoughts that we dwell on, like the feelings we dwell on, create the path upon which we walk through our day-to-day lives.

THEY HAVE GOALS AND WORK TOWARD MEETING THEM

Emotionally sober people tend to have goals that they work toward pleasantly and methodically; they recognize that goals help them to live a happy life. One easy way of using the brain's neurotransmitter system in a way that helps us to remain in a positive frame of mind while dealing with the negative impact of stress is to have small, regular things to look forward to. "The expectation of something we are looking forward to causes the brain to release transmitters that allow us to experience pleasure. And because the feedback systems of pleasure and stress are connected, this expectation of pleasure can work in direct opposition to things that are upsetting us," says Stefan Klein in *The Science of Happiness* (2006).

We can get a little jump-start of positive thinking by using our minds to see our lives in an optimistic light. According to Peter Russell in *The Brain Book,* "The essential process behind positive thinking is first to set yourself goals and then to imagine them having been achieved. It is not just a question of setting goals, but of seeing in your mind's eye, the goals being fulfilled. The importance of this can be understood in terms of mental set. When we see our lives as working it sets us up positively for events and opportunities that will support our goals" (1979). People with a positive mental set tend to look over their lives for evidence to support that set, just as those with a negative mental set look for evidence to support that.

Low frustration tolerance and an inability to live in the present are hallmarks of addiction and self-medication. Part of recovery is to learn to delay gratification in the service of thriving in the bigger picture. To put off what we may want right now this minute, because we have a vision of something else that we want that is better, we learn to give up the small gain for the bigger, more important one. We learn to envision, set, and stay on a path toward the goals we wish to achieve.

THEY CONSCIOUSLY MAINTAIN GOOD HABITS

Emotionally sober people tend to lead orderly and well-regulated lives. Changing old patterns and maintaining new ones also requires a certain kind of gentle and loving discipline; there's no way around it. We may find ourselves at the point at which we have done all the right things, had all the liberating insights, and are familiar with recovery "aha's." But things aren't changing as fast as we might wish. We're feeling frustrated. This is a moment when we have to train our brains and bodies into new, rather unfamiliar patterns and repeat them until they become habit. It's helpful to make friends with our own way of disciplining ourselves. If we can learn to lead ourselves gently into better habits, to talk to ourselves about the short- and long-term benefits rather than approach them with dread, we'll get much further than if we're self-punishing. Self-punishing leads us to want to retaliate. Loving self-discipline allows us to self-actualize.

THEY HAVE GOOD BOUNDARIES

Emotionally sober people can tell where they leave off and someone else begins. Good boundaries grow naturally out of a well-individuated self. They develop slowly and over time. They indicate that we have a well-enough consolidated sense of self so that we can be with others without losing ourselves, so that we're able to hang on to our sense of self while in the presence of others. They are first and foremost an inside job.

Relationship trauma can lead to emotional fusion, which can contribute to identity fusion. Stress undermines our ability to think clearly and to form a well-consolidated self-image. Our ability to think through what we're feeling and reflect on how it fits or does not fit into our sense of self in relationship becomes confused.

Healthy boundaries are porous. They operate like computer

firewalls that allow us to modulate what we let in and what we don't. Rigid boundaries are unmodulated, as are weak boundaries. They let in too little or too much.

THEY KNOW THEIR OWN
SHORTCOMINGS AND INSECURITIES

Emotionally sober people tend to be aware of their shortcomings and insecurities; they don't feel a need to be problem free in order to feel okay about themselves. They know that their shortcomings and insecurities can get them into trouble if they aren't mindful about what they are and when they are being triggered.

If we try to deny to ourselves and others that our insecurities or sore spots are there, our uncomfortable feelings may get projected onto other people, or we'll read problems into situations where little or none may exist. We'll get caught in a web of our own making. And if we can't be honest about our own shortcomings, we'll never know what we're good at and what we're not so good at, which will get in the way of our own success.

THEY AVOID UNNECESSARY CONFLICT
BUT SPEAK UP WHEN NECESSARY

People with good emotional sobriety tend to avoid unnecessary conflict, but they do speak up where necessary. People with good emotional sobriety tend not to create unnecessary conflict in their lives; it is simply too costly to their own peace of mind. They understand that their inner peace is their responsibility, and that if they lose it, only they can get it back.

If we don't like the way someone is treating us, there may be subtle ways of getting the point across before we bring out the big guns. Changing the subject, removing ourselves, or a well-timed comment may do the job with a lot less wear and tear on ourselves. When speaking up, try to do it consciously, in such a way as not to rupture further but manage a situation skillfully.

THEY HAVE REALISTIC EXPECTATIONS OF LIFE

Emotionally sober people tend to have their feet on the ground; they live in real time and have realistic expectations of life and relationships. In studies done on animals, researchers studied the relationship between expectation and the body's release of dopamine, a mood-balancing body chemical. They found that dopamine levels went up when animals received a pleasant surprise. The more unexpected the pleasant stimulus, the higher the rise in dopamine. However, and herein lies the rub, when a stimulus was expected but did not come, the animals' disappointment could be measured by a drop in dopamine levels. So when we constantly want the situations of our lives to go a certain way, we may be setting ourselves up for disappointment. We get much further, in terms of pleasurable body chemicals and maintaining inner peace, when we take life as it comes and stay open to life's little pleasures and surprises and don't get fixated on things going just one way—that is, when we maintain our spontaneity.

When all is said and done, the simple things in life make or break us. Enjoying the simple pleasures of our day and managing the little stressors smoothly are central to emotional balance.

THEY TAKE RESPONSIBILITY FOR THEIR OWN MOODS

People with good emotional sobriety take responsibility for maintaining their own good mood. They don't blame other

people for the mood they are in and they don't wait for someone else to change before they let themselves feel better. They
know that like attracts like. As we become more adept at shifting our emotional states consciously, we'll be amazed that we
didn't start doing it earlier. Consciously shifting our moods is
the get-out-of-jail-free card in the Monopoly game. It is the
quickest solution to changing our lives. Each time we remember something, it is a reconstruction of data stored in our
memory banks. So if we're in a positive-feeling state, we'll tend
to remember even our own lives through a more pleasant lens.

THEY HAVE AND LIVE BY GOOD VALUES

Emotionally sober people gain some of their stability
through living by principles and values they respect. They
draw good feelings about themselves from the knowledge that
they are people who add dignity and stability to their families
and communities. They tend to attract and spend time with
other people who hold similar principles and standards; they
know what's right and wrong when they see it. Their values
tend not to be overly rigid and they allow for human foible.
But they have and hold themselves and those they love to
decent standards of behavior.

THEY ARE GRATEFUL AND
APPRECIATIVE OF WHAT LIFE GIVES THEM

Emotionally sober people have a look of self-possession on
their faces. They look like they know why they know what they
know. They get a kick out of the little things the day brings;
they tend to be easy to please. They also often tend to appreciate and value what they have rather than always imagining

that the grass is greener on the other side of the mountain. They understand that pouring your best into the life you have is its own reward, and that loving what you have builds a kind of self-assurance and sense of security that takes you through the hard times. They tend not to take relationships or blessings for granted; they value rather than devalue the people and opportunities of their lives. When we focus on what's missing, that's what we expand. When we focus on what is there, we expand what's there.

One of the attitudes that blocks gratitude is entitlement. If we feel we're entitled to receive all sorts of things automatically, we may take what we have for granted, seeing it as our due rather than a blessing. We'll essentially be unconscious of or negating the riches we already possess.

They Maintain Strong Relationship Networks

Emotionally sober people tend to value and maintain relationships. They recognize that a solid network of relationships is stabilizing for them, that they benefit from a sense of belonging with and to other people. Nearly twenty separate long-term studies attest to the benefits of a strong relationship network in such predictors as health, longevity, and an overall sense of well-being. For men particularly, relationships are linked with health. For women, relationships in which they are happy tend to be health enhancing, while unhappy intimate relationships can have a negative impact. But for both men and women, a network of stable relationships is sustaining. As we've talked about throughout the book, relationships balance our limbic systems. They also provide what Abraham Maslow highlighted in his famous hierarchy of needs as our basic human need for belonging (1987). Our relationship network doesn't have to look a certain way in order to do the job. It just needs to be stable and reasonably reliable.

THEY ARE ACTIVE: THEY GET INVOLVED IN LIFE

Emotionally sober people tend to be an active part of the world they live in. They have a sense of belonging to their communities and they are invested in them. Being active and involved may also have neurological wisdom behind it. Richard Davidson from the University of Wisconsin at Madison discovered through brain experiments that the more active the left or thinking side of the brain is, the less likely we are to get upset by negative stimuli that may be coming from the right or limbic brain. This accounts for why we often feel better when we just get going, whether on our day or on an engaging project: we're activating the thinking left brain, and that helps to offset emotional input that might be coming from our right brain. In other words, getting in motion can work to change our mood as it activates more parts of the brain/body circuitry.

THEY TEND TO HAVE A POSITIVE BELIEF SYSTEM OF SOME KIND

Emotionally sober people often have a positive worldview or belief system that gives life meaning and direction and sustains them through hard times. It also provides them with a framework or lens through which to view the world in a positive light. At the end of the day, our ability to see beauty, meaning, and purpose in our lives, in our world, and in our relationships is a fertilizer that grows rich fruit. Seeing life as a gift is what makes it a gift. Finding meaning and purpose in the life we lead is what gives it meaning and purpose. This ability to create meaning and transcendent purpose is a gift of the prefrontal cortex, a gift of being human.

A spiritual or transcendent belief system allows us to get out of our own way long enough to recognize the magic and mystery of life—to tap into the beauty that is always surrounding us. We need to come in touch with that stream of inner peace, that wellspring of security and bliss that is in us all the time. When we can daily visit that pool of quiet vibrating just beneath the surface of our own inner world, we see the same world with renewed vision. We transform our experience of life.

THEY LIVE IN THE PRESENT

Emotionally sober people tend not to be overly preoccupied with either the past or the future; they are present oriented. They do not ignore the past, but face it and do what's necessary to come to terms with it. They do not retreat from the future; they have goals, plans, and dreams that they are invested in and excited about. But beyond doing what's necessary on a daily basis to clean out the past or prepare for the future, they are present oriented. In fact, their willingness to deal with the past and plan for a future may be what actually frees them up to enjoy the present.

THEY HAVE A BALANCED AND MATURE OUTLOOK ON LIFE

Emotional sobriety describes a midrange of thinking, feeling, and behavior. Though at first blush the idea may seem as if we no longer experience highs and lows, this would be a limited idea of the scope of it. Emotional balance and maturity actually allow us tremendous freedom of inner movement because we're no longer living in reactive mode. We have a center from which we operate, and having a center gives us the freedom to measure our emotional, psychological, and behavioral responses to what is appropriate to any given situation. Our own hyperreactivity is in proportion, so it ceases to define how we experience the events of our days. We are living in the here and now, living in the present, living in balance and maturity.

There is no one-size-fits-all solution to getting our lives to work. If you want deep healing of your mind/body to happen this week or even by the end of this year, you will be disappointed. That's the bad news. But the good news is that once you get involved in living a healthier lifestyle, your new design for living, you won't care. You will draw self-esteem and satisfaction from doing the tough and challenging work that it takes to heal. If you are willing to make the sincere and solemn commitment to building or restoring your sense of inner safety and faith in life, you will be rewarded, and each step you take in that direction will carry with it a profound sense of accomplishment because each step you take will be your own.

Here is another piece of good news. You very likely will become fascinated with the experience of growing. You will become curious about why you do what you do. You will come to recognize that healing is a journey of the soul, stretching and expanding who you are on the inside, and your outward life will come to reflect that. You may come to want all of your life to be a journey of unfoldment. You will experience a new self-confidence that is the natural outgrowth of standing in your own shoes, of living a congruent life where thinking, feeling, and behavior have an integrity, a through line. You will find inner strength. It will be built a day at a time from the fortitude you will develop by learning to tolerate and manage the power of your own emotions, and from the insights that you will have into yourself and into other people as you do this. You will become a deep person, someone with very real value to give yourself and your world.

And you will have your joy, the joy that frozenness and relegating important parts of yourself into stony silence robbed from you. You will have yourself back, and in having yourself back you will be in a position to care and be cared for, to love and be loved.

When we learn to process and understand our emotions rather than run from them, our inner world becomes much less complicated, much more peaceful. We're no longer run by our early programming. We've downloaded new software, and we're working from a more sophisticated and streamlined program. Our mind becomes more refined. Life feels different; we feel different; relationships feel different. We have more energy to devote to things like life passions, relationships, having fun. We've stopped bouncing from one extreme to the other. We're living within a balanced range.

And then it's ours. We're no longer visiting a new body, we're living in it. We're in the present rather than the past. We have found and learned how to value and maintain our inner peace. We're comfortable living in our own skin. We're in our bodies rather than our heads. Our thinking, feeling, and behavior are congruent. This is emotional sobriety.

Bibliography

Ainsworth, M., M. Blehar, E. Waters, and S. Wall. 1978. *Patterns of Attachment*. Hillsdale, NJ: Erlbaum.

Alcoholics Anonymous. 1953. *Twelve Steps and Twelve Traditions*. New York: Alcoholics Anonymous World Services Inc.

———. 1967. *As Bill Sees It: The A.A. Way of Life . . . Selected Writings of A.A.'s Co-founder*. New York: Alcoholics Anonymous World Services Inc.

———. 1976. *Alcoholics Anonymous: The Story of How Many Thousands of Men and Women Have Recovered from Alcoholism*, 3rd ed. New York: Alcoholics Anonymous World Services Inc.

Amaral, Júlio Rocha do, and Jorge Martins de Oliveira. *Limbic System: The Center of Emotions*.

Amen, Daniel G. 1998. *Change Your Brain, Change Your Life*. New York: Three Rivers Press.

Babyak, Michael, and James Blumenthal. 2000. Exercise and Pharmacotherapy in the Treatment of Major Depressive Disorder *Journal of Psychosomatic Medicine*, October.

Begley, Sharon. 2001. "Your Brain on Religion: Mystic Visions or Brain Circuits at Work." *Newsweek*, May 7.

Bekoff, Marc. 2007. *The Emotional Lives of Animals: A Leading Scientist Explores Animal Joy, Sorrow, and Empathy—and Why They Matter*. Novato, CA: New World Library.

Bekoff, Marc, and John Byers, eds. 1998. *Animal Play: Evolutionary, Comparative, and Ecological Perspectives*. Cambridge and New York: Cambridge University Press.

Bittman, Barry. 2001. "The Glass That's Half Full: Optimism and Longevity." Psychosomatic Medicine.

Blume, S. B. 1985. "Psychodrama and the Treatment of Alcoholism." Pages 87–108 in *Practical Approaches to Alcoholism Psychotherapy*, 2nd ed., S. Zimberg, J. Wallace, and S. B. Blume, eds. New York: Plenum Press.

Boeree, C. George. *The Emotional Nervous System*.

Bowlby, John. 1969, 1982. Attachment. Vol. 1 of Attachment and Loss. London: Hogarth Press; New York: Basic Books.

————. 1973. *Separation: Anxiety and Anger.* Vol. 2 of *Attachment andLoss.* London: Hogarth Press; New York: Basic Books; Harmondsworth: Penguin.

————. 1980. *Loss: Sadness and Depression.* Vol. 3 of Attachment and Loss. London: Hogarth Press; New York: Basic Books; Harmondsworth: Penguin.

————. 1988. *A Secure Base: Parent-Child Attachment and Healthy Human Development.* London: Routledge; New York: Basic Books.

Brazelton, T. Berry, and Stanley Greenspan. 2000. *The Irreducible Needs of Children: What Every Child Must Have to Grow, Learn and Flourish.* New York: Perseus Books.

Brizendine, Louann. 2006. *The Female Brain.* Morgan Road Books.

Bulfinch, Thomas. 2000. *Bulfinch's Greek and Roman Mythology.* Mineola, NY: Dover Publications.

Burghardt, G. M. 1998. "The Evolutionary Origins of Play Revisited: Lessons from Turtles." Pages 1–26 in *Animal Play: Evolutionary, Comparative, and Ecological Perspectives,* M. Bekoff and J. A. Byers, eds. Cambridge and New York: Cambridge University Press.

Byers, J. A. 1999. "The Distribution of Play Behaviour among Australian Marsupials." *Journal of Zoology,* 247: 349–56.

Byers, J. A., and C. B. Walker. 1995. "Refining the Motor Training Hypothesis for the Evolution of Play." *American Naturalist,* 146: 25–40.

Canada NewsWire. 2003. "Research Breakthrough in Understanding Treatment-Resistant Depression: A Pioneering Research Study Using Brain Imaging Has Yielded New Clues to Help Sufferers from Severe Depression Who Do Not Respond to Conventional Treatment." October 3.

Carey, Benedict. 2005. "Watching New Love as It Sears the Brain." *New York Times,* May 31.

CBS Broadcasting Inc. 2006. "Study: Bad Relationships Bad for Heart: Hostility, Controlling Behavior Shown to Take Toll on Spouses' Hearts." March 3.

Childre, Doc. 2001. *Forgiveness—A Real Stress Buster.* Boulder, CO: HeartMath LLC.

Cochrane Database of Systematic Reviews. 2007. Issue 3. John Wiley and Sons, Ltd.

Corsini, Raymond J. 1994. *Encyclopedia of Psychology.* 2nd ed. New York: John Wiley and Sons.

Crosby Ouimette, P., P. J. Brown, L. M. Najavits. 1998. "Course and Treatment of Patients with Both Substance Use and Posttraumatic Stress Disorders." *Addictive Behaviors,* 23(6): 785–96.

Csikszentmihalyi, Mihaly. 1990. *Flow: The Psychology of Optimal Experience.* New York: Harper and Row.

————. 1996. *Creativity : Flow and the Psychology of Discovery and Invention.* New York: Harper Perennial.

————. 1997. *Finding Flow: The Psychology of Engagement with Everyday Life.* New York: Basic Books.

Dale, Stan. 2007. "Spanking Is an Addiction." 2007. *Mothering* (winter 1993): 31.

Damasio, Antonio. 1999. *The Feeling of What Happens.* New York: Harcourt.

Dayton, Tian. 1994. *The Drama Within.* Deerfield Beach, FL: Health Communications.

————. 1997. *Heartwounds: The Impact of Unresolved Trauma and Grief on Relationships.* Deerfield Beach, FL: Health Communications.

————. 2000. *Trauma and Addiction.* Deerfield Beach, FL: Health Communications.

————. 2003. *The Magic of Forgiveness.* Deerfield Beach, FL: Health Communications.

————. 1995. *The Soul's Companion.* Deerfield Beach, FL: Health Communications.

di Adam, Salimbene. 1972. From Saint Francis to Dante. University of Pennsylvania Press.

Dossey, Larry. 1993. *Healing Words.* San Francisco: Harper San Francisco.

————. 1997. *Be Careful What You Pray For . . . You Just Might Get It.* San Francisco: HarperSanFrancisco.

Elkind, David. 2001. *The Hurried Child: Growing Up Too Fast Too Soon.* New York: DeCapo Press.

Enright, Robert. 2000a. *Forgiveness Is a Choice.* Washington, DC: International Forgiveness Institute, APA Books.

————. 2000b. *Helping Clients Forgive.* Washington, DC: International Forgiveness Institute, APA Books.

Fisher, Helen. 2004. *Why We Love: The Nature and Chemistry of Romantic Love.* New York: Owl Books.

Frankl, Viktor. 1959. *Man's Search for Meaning.* Boston: Beacon Press.

Goldberg, Elkhonon. 2001. *The Executive Brain.* Oxford and New York: Oxford University Press.

Goleman, Daniel. 2006. "Friends for Life: An Emerging Biology of Emotional Healing." *New York Times,* October 10.

————. 2006. *Social Intelligence: The New Science of Social Relationships.* New York: Bantam Books.

Gottman, J. M., Levinson, R. W. 1979. *Marital Interaction.* San Francisco: Academic Press.

Grant, Linda. 2003. "Art of Therapy and Trauma." *Counselor Magazine.*

Greenspan, Stanley. 1999. *Building Healthy Minds*. New York: Perseus Books.

Gunner, Megan. 2007. *Social and Biological Aspects of Development*.

Hart, K.E. (1995). Recovery from Alcoholism: The 12 Steps of Alcoholics Anonymous and Easter Spirituality Pager presented at the International New Thought Alliance, Portland, Oregon, USA.

———. 2003. "Do Adult Offspring of Alcoholics Suffer from Poor Medical Health?" *Canadian Journal of Nursing*, 35: 52–72.

Heilman, Kenneth, Stephen E. Nadeau, and David O. Beversdorf. 2003. "Creative Innovation: Possible Brain Mechanisms." *Neurocase*, 9(5): 369–79.

Herman, Judith Lewis. 1997. *Trauma and Recovery*. New York: Guilford Press.

Howard, Pierce J. 2000. *The Owner's Manual for the Brain*. Atlanta: Bard Press.

Janov, Arthur. 2006. "The Biology of Love—Study: Happy Marriage Calms Nerves." *Psychological Science*. December.

Johnston, Victor S. 1999. *Why We Feel: The Science of Human Emotions*. New York: Perseus Books.

Joseph, R. 1999. "Environmental Influences on Neural Plasticity, the Limbic System, Emotional Development, and Attachment." *Child Psychiatry and Human Development*, 29: 187–203.

Klein, Stefan. 2006. *The Science of Happiness*. Marlowe & Company.

Korn, Martin L. 2001. "Trauma and PTSD: Aftermaths of the WTC Disaster: An interview with Bessel A. van der Kolk, MD." MedGenMed, 3(4): 2001, http://www.medscape.com/viewarticle/408691 (accessed September 15, 2007).

Kotulak, Ronald. 1996. *Inside the Brain*. Andrews McMeel Publishing.

Kubzansky L. D., D. Sparrow, P. Vokonas, and I. Kawachi. 2001. "Is the Glass Half Empty or Half Full? A Prospective Study of Optimism and Coronary Heart Disease in the Normative Aging Study." *Psychosomatic Medicine*, 63: 910–16.

Krystal, Henry, ed. 1968. *Massive Psychic Trauma*. New York: International Universities Press.

Lazar, S. W., G. Bush, R. L. Gollub, G. L. Fricchione, G. Khalsa, and H. Benson. 2000. "Functional Brain Mapping of the Relaxation Response and Meditation." *NeuroReport, 11:* 1581–85.

Lebow, J. L. 1999. "Building a Science of Couple Relationships: Comments on Two Articles by Gottman and Levenson." *Family Process*, 38(2): 167–74.

LeDoux, Joseph. 2002. *The Synaptic Self*. New York: Viking Penguin Group.

Lewis, K. P. 1997. *The Ambiguity of Play*. Cambridge, MA: Harvard University Press.

Lewis, K. P., and Barton, R. A. 2004. "Playing for Keeps: Evolutionary Relationships between the Cerebellum and Social Play Behaviour in Non-human Primates." *Human Nature,* 15(1): 5–21.

Lewis, Thomas, Fari Fmini, and Richard Lannon. 2000. *A General Theory of Love.* New York: Vintage Books.

Luskin, Frederic. 1999. "The Art and Science of Forgiveness." *Stanford Medicine,* 16(4): .

———. 1996. "Forgiveness." *Healing Currents Magazine,* September–October.

———. 1999–2001. "The Study of Forgiveness with Victims and Offenders." A Campaign for Forgiveness Research.

———. 2002. *Forgive for Good: A Proven Prescription for Health and Happiness.* San Francisco: HarperSanFrancisco.

Maslow, Abraham. 1987. *Motivation and Personality.* 3rd ed. New York: Addison-Wesley.

———. 1999. *Toward a Psychology of Being.* 3rd ed. New York: John Wiley and Sons.

McGeown, Kate. BBC News, July 13, 2005.

Miller, W. R. 1990. "*Spirituality: The Silent Dimension in Addiction Research.*" *Drug and Alcohol Review,* 9: 259–66.

———. 1998. "Researching the Spiritual Dimensions of Alcohol and Other Drug Problems." *Addiction, 93:* 979–90.

Moreno, J. L. 1934. *Who Shall Survive? A New Approach to the Problem of Human Interrelations.* Washington, DC: Nervous and Mental Disease Publishing.

———. 1946–1969. *Psychodrama.* Vols. 1, 2, and 3 (last two with Z. T. Moreno). Beacon, NY: Beacon House.

Moreno, Z. T., L. D. Blomkvist, and T. Rützel. 2000. *Psychodrama, Surplus Reality, and the Art of Healing.* London and Philadelphia: Routledge.

Northrup, Christiane. 2001. *The Wisdom of Menopause: Creating Physical and Emotional Health during the Change.* New York: Doubleday.

———. "The Mother of All Wake-Up Calls." 2002. *Today,* April 1.

Ornstein, Robert, and Charles Shencionis. 1999. *The Healing Brain: A Scientific Reader.* New York: Guilford Press.

Panksepp, Jan. 1998. *Affective Neuroscience: The Foundations of Human and Animal Emotions.* New York: Oxford University Press.

Pennebaker, James W. 1997. *Opening Up: The Healing Power of Expressing Emotions.* New York: Guilford Press.

Pert, Candace B. 1999. *Molecules of Emotion: Why You Feel the Way You Feel.* New York: Simon and Schuster.

Pfaus, J. G., and L. A. Scepkowski. 2005. The Biological Basis for Libido. *Current Sexual Health Reports,* 2: 95–100.

Provine, Robert R. 2004. "Laughing, Tickling, and the Evolution of Speech and Self." *Current Directions in Psychological Science,* 13(6): 215–18.

Razdan, Anjula. 2007. "Put Stress in Its Place." *Experience Life Magazine,* http://www.lifetimefitness.com/magazine/index.cfm?str WebAction=article_detail&intArticleId=660 (accessed September 15, 2007).

Rosenthal, Norman E. 2002. *The Emotional Revolution.* Secaucus, NJ: Citadel Press/Kensington Publishing.

Rozman, Deborah, with Doc Childre. 2005. *Transforming Stress: The HeartMath Solution for Relieving Worry, Fatigue and Tension.* Oakland, CA: New Harbinger Press,

Russell, Peter. 1979. *The Brain Book.* New York: Plume.

Sapolsky, Robert. 2006. *Monkeyluv: And Other Essays on Our Lives as Animals.* New York: Simon and Schuster.

Satir, Virginia. 1988. *The New Peoplemaking.* Science and Behavior Books.

Schore, A.N. 1999. *Affect Regulation and the Origin of the Self.* Mahwah, NJ: Lawrence Erlbaum.

———. 2000. "Attachment and the Regulation of the Right Brain." *Attachment and Human Development,* 2: 23-47.

———. 2001. "The Effects of Early Relational Trauma on Right Brain Development, Affect Regulation, and Infant Mental Health." *Infant Mental Health Journal,* 22: 201–69.

———. 2001. "The Effects of a Secure Attachment Relationship on Right Brain Development, Affect Regulation, and Infant Mental Health." *Infant Mental Health Journal,* 22: 7–66.

Siviy, Stephen. 2007. Conversation with author.

Smith, Deborah. 2002. "Major National Studies of Women's Health Are Providing New Insights." *Monitor on Psychology, 33.* May 5.

Solmes, Mark, and Oliver Turnbull. 2002. *The Brain and the Inner World.* New York: Other Press.

Stanton, Annette L. 1999. "Psychotherapy May Be as Useful as Drugs in Treating Depression, Study Suggests." *APA Monitor Online, 30.* September 8.

State University of New York at Buffalo.

Straussner, S. 1985. "Alcoholism in Women: Current Knowledge and Implications for Treatment." *Alcoholism Treatment Quarterly, 2:* 61–77.

Straussner, S. L. A. 1997. "Group Treatment with Substance Abusing Clients: A Model of Treatment during the Early Phases of Outpatient Group Therapy. *Journal of Chemical Dependency Treatment, 7:* 67–80.

Swanson, Naomi G. 2000. "Women Face Higher Risk at Work than Men." *Monitor on Psychology, 31.* September 8.

Thagard, Paul. 2005. *Mind: Introduction to Cognitive Science.* Cambridge: MA: MIT Press.

Thagard, Paul, and Allison Barnes. 1996. "Emotional Decisions." Pages 426–29 in *Proceedings of the Eighteenth Annual Conference of the Cognitive Science Society.* Erlbaum.

Thagard, P., and E. Millgram. 1995. Inference to the Best Plan: A Coherence Theory of Decision. Pages 439–54 in *Goal-Driven Learning,* A. Ram and D. B. Leake, eds. Cambridge, MA: MIT Press.

Tronick, Edward. 2007. *The Neurobehavioral and Social Emotional Development of Infants and Children.* New York: Norton Professional Books.

Uram, S. "Trauma and the Journey Home." *Addiction Today.* January/February 2006.

U.S. Department of Health and Human Services, Center for Substance Abuse Treatment. 1999. *Screening and Assessing Adolescents For Substance Use Disorders: Treatment Improvement Protocol (TIP) Series 31.* DHHS Publication No. (SMA) 993282.

Vaillant, George E. 2002. *Aging Well.* New York: Little, Brown and Company.

van der Kolk, Bessel. 1987. *Psychological Trauma.* Washington, DC: American Psychiatric Press.

———. 2007. "New Childhood Diagnosis for Trauma." *American Journal of Psychiatry, 164*(2): 309–17.

———. *The Body Keeps Score: Memory and the Evolving Psychobiology of Post Traumatic Stress.* David Baldwin's Trauma Information Pages, http://www.trauma-pages.com/a/vanderk4.php (accessed September 15, 2007).

van der Kolk, Bessel, and R. E. Fisler. 1994. "Childhood Abuse and Neglect and Loss of Self Regulation." *Bulletin of the Menninger Clinic, 58:* 145–68.

van der Kolk, et al. 2001. "Exploring the Nature of Traumatic Memory." The Haworth Press, Inc.

Vedamtam, Shankar. 2001. "Tracing the Synapses of Our Spirituality: Researchers Examine Relationship between Brain and Religion." *Washington Post,* June 17.

Werner, E. E. 1992. "The Children of Kauai: Resiliency and recovery in adolescence and adulthood." *Journal of Adolescent Health,* June 13: 262–68.

Woititz, J. 1983. *Adult Children of Alcoholics.* Hollywood, FL: Health Communications, Inc.

Wolin, S., and S. J. Wolin. 1993. *The Resilient Self: How Survivors of Troubled Families Rise Above Adversity.* New York: Villard Books.

————. 1995. "Morality in COAs: Revisiting the Syndrome of Over-Responsibility." In *Children of Alcoholics, Selected Readings,* ed. S. Abbott. Rockville, MD: NACoA.

Wylie, Mary Sykes. 2004 "The Limits of Talk: Bessel van der Kolk wants to transform the treatment of trauma." *Psychotherapy Networker.* http://www.traumacenter.org/products/pdf_files/ Networker.pdf (accessed September 15, 2007).

Index

About the Author

*T*ian Dayton, Ph.D., T.E.P., has a master's in educational psychology, a Ph.D. in clinical psychology, and is a board-certified trainer in psychodrama, sociometry, and group psychotherapy. She is also a certified Montessori teacher, having trained in both the United States and Europe. She is the Director of the New York Psychodrama Training Institute and the Director of Program Development and Staff Training for the Caron Center for Self Development in New York, where she runs training groups in psychodrama, sociometry, and experiential group therapy. Dr. Dayton is a nationally renowned speaker, expert, and consultant on trauma, addiction, ACOA and codependency issues and psychodrama, and is a fellow of the American Society of Psychodrama, Sociometry and Group Psychotherapy (ASGPP) and winner of their scholar's award. She is an executive editor of the *Journal of Group Psychotherapy, Psychodrama and Sociometry,* and sits on the society's professional standards committee. Dr. Dayton is on the board of the National Association for Children of Alcoholics (NACOA) and has been a guest expert on NBC, CNN, and MSNBC, and on Montel's, Rikki Lake's, John Walsh's, and Geraldo's shows. To contact Dr. Dayton about training in psychodrama or for speaking and workshop engagements, log on to www.tiandayton.com or e-mail her at tian@tiandayton.com. To sign up to receive Dr. Dayton's free newsletter on emotional sobriety and up-to-date research in the mental health field, go to www.tian-dayton.com/newsletter.

OTHER BOOKS BY TIAN DAYTON

*Modern Mothering: How to Teach Kids to Say What They Feel and
Feel What They Say*
*The Living Stage: A Step-by-Step Guide to Psychodrama, Sociometry
and Group Psychotherapy* (Tian Dayton and Zerka Moreno)
*The Magic of Forgiveness: Emotional Freedom and Transformation at
Midlife, A Book for Women*
Journey Through Womanhood: Meditations from Our Collective Soul
It's My Life! A Workout for Your Mind
*Trauma and Addiction: Ending the Cycle of Pain Through Emotional
Literacy*
*Heartwounds: The Impact of Unresolved Trauma and Grief on
Relationships*
The Soul's Companion
The Quiet Voice of Soul: How to Find Meaning in Ordinary Life
The Drama Within: Psychodrama and Experiential Therapy
Keeping Love Alive: Inspirations for Commitment
Daily Affirmations for Forgiving and Moving On
*Daily Affirmations for Parents: How to Nurture Your Children and
Renew Yourself During the Ups and Downs of Parenthood*
Drama Games: Techniques for Self-Development

Films and Videos
The Process